Imagined Communities

Imagined Communities

Reflections on the Origin and
Spread of Nationalism

◆

BENEDICT ANDERSON

Revised Edition

VERSO
London • New York

First published by Verso 1983
This edition published by Verso 2016, 2006
© Benedict Anderson, 1983, 1991, 2006, 2016

1 3 5 7 9 10 8 6 4 2

Verso
UK: 6 Meard Street, London W1F 0EG
US: 20 Jay Street, Suite 1010, Brooklyn, NY 11201
versobooks.com

Verso is the imprint of New Left Books

ISBN-13: 978-1-78478-675-5
ISBN-13: 978-1-84467-484-8 (US EBK)
ISBN-13: 978-1-78168-359-0 (UK EBK)

British Library Cataloguing in Publication Data
A catalogue record for this book is available from the British Library

Library of Congress Cataloging-in-Publication Data
A catalog record for this book is available from the Library of Congress

Typeset by Hewer Text UK Ltd, Edinburgh
Printed and bound by CPI Group (UK) Ltd, Croydon, CR0 4YY

For Mamma and Tantiette
in love and gratitude

Contents

Acknowledgments

As will be apparent to the reader, my thinking about nationalism has been deeply affected by the writings of Erich Auerbach, Walter Benjamin and Victor Turner. In preparing the book itself, I have benefitted enormously from the criticism and advice of my brother Perry Anderson, Anthony Barnett, and Steve Heder. J. A. Ballard, Mohamed Chambas, Peter Katzenstein, the late Rex Mortimer, Francis Mulhern, Tom Nairn, Shiraishi Takashi, Jim Siegel, Laura Summers, and Esta Ungar also gave me invaluable help in different ways. Naturally, none of these friendly critics should be held in any way accountable for the text's deficiencies, which are wholly my responsibility. I should perhaps add that I am by training and profession a specialist on Southeast Asia. This admission may help to explain some of the book's biases and choices of examples, as well as to deflate its would-be-global pretensions.

He regards it as his task to brush history against the grain.

Walter Benjamin, *Illuminations*

Thus from a Mixture of all kinds began,
That Het'rogeneous Thing, *An Englishman*:
In eager Rapes, and furious Lust begot,
Betwixt a Painted *Britton* and a *Scot*:
Whose gend'ring Offspring quickly learnt to bow,
And yoke their Heifers to the *Roman* Plough:
From whence a Mongrel half-bred Race there came,
With neither Name nor Nation, Speech or Fame.
In whose hot Veins now Mixtures quickly ran,
Infus'd betwixt a *Saxon* and a *Dane*.
While their Rank Daughters, to their Parents just,
Receiv'd all Nations with Promiscuous Lust.
This Nauseous Brood directly did contain
The well-extracted Blood of *Englishmen* . . .

From Daniel Defoe, *The True-Born Englishman*

Preface to the Second Edition

Who would have thought that the storm blows harder the farther it leaves Paradise behind?

The armed conflicts of 1978–79 in Indochina, which provided the immediate occasion for the original text of *Imagined Communities*, seem already, a mere twelve years later, to belong to another era. Then I was haunted by the prospect of further full-scale wars between the socialist states. Now half these states have joined the debris at the Angel's feet, and the rest are fearful of soon following them. The wars that the survivors face are civil wars. The likelihood is strong that by the opening of the new millennium little will remain of the Union of Soviet Socialist Republics except . . . republics.

Should all this have somehow been foreseen? In 1983 I wrote that the Soviet Union was 'as much the legatee of the prenational dynastic states of the nineteenth century as the precursor of a twenty-first century internationalist order.' But, having traced the nationalist explosions that destroyed the vast polyglot and polyethnic realms which were ruled from Vienna, London, Constantinople, Paris and Madrid, I could not see that the train was laid at least as far as Moscow. It is melancholy consolation to observe that history seems to be bearing out the 'logic' of *Imagined Communities* better than its author managed to do.

It is not only the world that has changed its face over the past twelve years. The study of nationalism too has been startlingly transformed – in method, scale, sophistication, and sheer quantity. In the English language alone, J.A. Armstrong's *Nations Before Nationalism* (1982), John Breuilly's *Nationalism and the State* (1982), Ernest Gellner's *Nations and Nationalism* (1983), Miroslav Hroch's *Social Preconditions of National Revival in Europe* (1985), Anthony Smith's *The Ethnic Origins of Nations* (1986), P. Chatterjee's *Nationalist Thought and the Colonial World* (1986), and Eric Hobsbawm's *Nations and Nationalism since 1788* (1990) – to name only a few of the key texts – have, by their historical reach and theoretical power, made largely obsolete the traditional literature on the subject. In part out of these works has developed an extraordinary proliferation of historical, literary, anthropological, sociological, feminist, and other studies linking the objects of these fields of enquiry to nationalism and nation.[1]

To adapt *Imagined Communities* to the demands of these vast changes in the world and in the text is a task beyond my present means. It seemed better, therefore, to leave it largely as an 'unrestored' period piece, with its own characteristic style, silhouette, and mood. Two things give me comfort. On the one hand, the full final outcome of developments in the old socialist world remain shrouded in the obscurity ahead. On the other hand, the idiosyncratic method and preoccupations of *Imagined Communities* seem to me still on the margins of the newer scholarship on nationalism – in that sense, at least, not fully superseded.

What I have tried to do, in the present edition, is simply to correct errors of fact, conception, and interpretation which I should have avoided in preparing the original version. These corrections – in the spirit of 1983, as it were – involve some alterations of the first edition, as well as two new chapters, which basically have the character of discrete appendices.

In the main text, I discovered two serious errors of translation, at least one unfulfilled promise, and one misleading emphasis. Unable to read Spanish in 1983, I thoughtlessly relied on Leon Ma. Guerrero's English translation of José Rizal's *Noli Me Tangere*, although earlier

---

1. Hobsbawm has had the courage to conclude from this scholarly explosion that the age of nationalism is near its end: Minerva's owl flies at dusk.

translations were available. It was only in 1990 that I discovered how fascinatingly corrupt Guerrero's version was. For a long, important quotation from Otto Bauer's *Die Nationalitätenfrage und die Sozialdemokratie* I lazily relied on Oscar Jászi's translation. More recent consultation of the German original has shown me how far Jászi's political predilections tinted his citations. In at least two passages I had faithlessly promised to explain why Brazilian nationalism developed so late and so idiosyncratically by comparison with those of other Latin American countries. The present text attempts to fulfil the broken pledge.

It had been part of my original plan to stress the New World origins of nationalism. My feeling had been that an unselfconscious provincialism had long skewed and distorted theorizing on the subject. European scholars, accustomed to the conceit that everything important in the modern world originated in Europe, too easily took 'second generation' ethnolinguistic nationalisms (Hungarian, Czech, Greek, Polish, etc.) as the starting point in their modelling, no matter whether they were 'for' or 'against' nationalism. I was startled to discover, in many of the notices of *Imagined Communities*, that this Eurocentric provincialism remained quite undisturbed, and that the crucial chapter on the originating Americas was largely ignored. Unfortunately, I have found no better 'instant' solution to this problem than to retitle Chapter 4 as 'Creole Pioneers.'

The two 'appendices' try to correct serious theoretical flaws in the first edition.[2] A number of friendly critics had suggested that Chapter 7 ('The Last Wave') oversimplified the process whereby early 'Third World' nationalisms were modelled. Furthermore the chapter did not seriously address the question of the role of the local colonial state, rather than the metropole, in styling these nationalisms. At the same time, I became uneasily aware that what I had believed to be a significantly new contribution to thinking about nationalism –

---

2. The first appendix originated in a paper prepared for a conference held in Karachi in January 1989, sponsored by the World Institute for Development Economics Research of the United Nations University. A sketch for the second appeared in *The Times Literary Supplement* of June 13, 1986, under the rubric 'Narrating the Nation.'

changing apprehensions of time – patently lacked its necessary coordinate: changing apprehensions of space. A brilliant doctoral thesis by Thongchai Winichakul, a young Thai historian, stimulated me to think about mapping's contribution to the nationalist imagination.

'Census, Map, Museum' therefore analyses the way in which, quite unconsciously, the nineteenth-century colonial state (and policies that its mindset encouraged) dialectically engendered the grammar of the nationalisms that eventually arose to combat it. Indeed, one might go so far as to say that the state imagined its local adversaries, as in an ominous prophetic dream, well before they came into historical existence. To the forming of this imagining, the census's abstract quantification/serialization of persons, the map's eventual logoization of political space, and the museum's 'ecumenical,' profane genealogizing made interlinked contributions.

The origin of the second 'appendix' was the humiliating recognition that in 1983 I had quoted Renan without the slightest understanding of what he had actually said: I had taken as something easily ironical what was in fact utterly bizarre. The humiliation also forced me to realize that I had offered no intelligible explanation of exactly how, and why, new-emerging nations imagined themselves antique. What appeared in most of the scholarly writings as Machiavellian hocus-pocus, or as bourgeois fantasy, or as disinterred historical truth, struck me now as deeper and more interesting. Supposing 'antiquity' were, at a certain historical juncture, the *necessary consequence* of 'novelty'? If nationalism was, as I supposed it, the expression of a radically changed form of consciousness, should not awareness of that break, and the necessary forgetting of the older consciousness, create its own narrative? Seen from this perspective, the atavistic fantasizing characteristic of most nationalist thought after the 1820s appears an epiphenomenon; what is really important is the structural alignment of post-1820s nationalist 'memory' with the inner premises and conventions of modern biography and autobiography.

Aside from any theoretical merits or demerits the two 'appendices' may prove to have, each has its own more everyday limitations. The data for 'Census, Map, Museum' are drawn wholly from Southeast Asia. In some ways this region offers splendid opportunities for comparative theorizing since it comprises areas formerly colonized by almost all the great imperial powers (England, France, Holland, Portugal, Spain and the United States) as well as uncolonized Siam. Nonetheless, it remains to be seen whether my analysis, even if plausible for this region, can be convincingly applied around the globe. In the second appendix, the sketchy empirical material relates almost exclusively to Western Europe and the New World, regions on which my knowledge is quite superficial. But the focus had to be there since it was in these zones that the amnesias of nationalism were first voiced over.

Benedict Anderson
February 1991

1

Introduction

Perhaps without being much noticed yet, a fundamental transformation in the history of Marxism and Marxist movements is upon us. Its most visible signs are the recent wars between Vietnam, Cambodia and China. These wars are of world-historical importance because they are the first to occur between regimes whose independence and revolutionary credentials are undeniable, and because none of the belligerents has made more than the most perfunctory attempts to justify the bloodshed in terms of a recognizable *Marxist* theoretical perspective. While it was still just possible to interpret the Sino-Soviet border clashes of 1969, and the Soviet military interventions in Germany (1953), Hungary (1956), Czechoslovakia (1968), and Afghanistan (1980) in terms of – according to taste – 'social imperialism,' 'defending socialism,' etc., no one, I imagine, seriously believes that such vocabularies have much bearing on what has occurred in Indochina.

If the Vietnamese invasion and occupation of Cambodia in December 1978 and January 1979 represented the first *large-scale conventional war* waged by one revolutionary Marxist regime against another,[1] China's assault on Vietnam in February rapidly confirmed

---

1. This formulation is chosen simply to emphasize the scale and the style of the fighting, not to assign blame. To avoid possible misunderstanding, it should be said that the December 1978 invasion grew out of armed clashes between partisans of the

the precedent. Only the most trusting would dare wager that in the declining years of this century any significant outbreak of inter-state hostilities will necessarily find the USSR and the PRC – let alone the smaller socialist states – supporting, or fighting on, the same side. Who can be confident that Yugoslavia and Albania will not one day come to blows? Those variegated groups who seek a withdrawal of the Red Army from its encampments in Eastern Europe should remind themselves of the degree to which its overwhelming presence has, since 1945, ruled out armed conflict between the region's Marxist regimes.

Such considerations serve to underline the fact that since World War II every successful revolution has defined itself in *national* terms – the People's Republic of China, the Socialist Republic of Vietnam, and so forth – and, in so doing, has grounded itself firmly in a territorial and social space inherited from the prerevolutionary past. Conversely, the fact that the Soviet Union shares with the United Kingdom of Great Britain and Northern Ireland the rare distinction of refusing nationality in its naming suggests that it is as much the legatee of the prenational dynastic states of the nineteenth century as the precursor of a twenty-first century internationalist order.[2]

Eric Hobsbawm is perfectly correct in stating that 'Marxist movements and states have tended to become national not only in form but in substance, i.e., nationalist. There is nothing to suggest

---

two revolutionary movements going back possibly as far as 1971. After April 1977, border raids, initiated by the Cambodians, but quickly followed by the Vietnamese, grew in size and scope, culminating in the major Vietnamese incursion of December 1977. None of these raids, however, aimed at overthrowing enemy regimes or occupying large territories, nor were the numbers of troops involved comparable to those deployed in December 1978. The controversy over the causes of the war is most thoughtfully pursued in: Stephen P. Heder, 'The Kampuchean–Vietnamese Conflict,' in David W. P. Elliott, ed., *The Third Indochina Conflict*, pp. 21–67; Anthony Barnett, 'Inter-Communist Conflicts and Vietnam,' *Bulletin of Concerned Asian Scholars*, 11: 4 (October–December 1979), pp. 2–9; and Laura Summers, 'In Matters of War and Socialism Anthony Barnett would Shame and Honour Kampuchea Too Much,' ibid., pp. 10–18.

2. Anyone who has doubts about the UK's claims to such parity with the USSR should ask himself what nationality its name denotes: Great Brito-Irish?

that this trend will not continue.'[3] Nor is the tendency confined to the socialist world. Almost every year the United Nations admits new members. And many 'old nations,' once thought fully consolidated, find themselves challenged by 'sub'-nationalisms within their borders – nationalisms which, naturally, dream of shedding this sub-ness one happy day. The reality is quite plain: the 'end of the era of nationalism,' so long prophesied, is not remotely in sight. Indeed, nation-ness is the most universally legitimate value in the political life of our time.

But if the facts are clear, their explanation remains a matter of long-standing dispute. Nation, nationality, nationalism – all have proved notoriously difficult to define, let alone to analyse. In contrast to the immense influence that nationalism has exerted on the modern world, plausible theory about it is conspicuously meagre. Hugh Seton-Watson, author of far the best and most comprehensive English-language text on nationalism, and heir to a vast tradition of liberal historiography and social science, sadly observes: 'Thus I am *driven* to the conclusion that no "scientific definition" of the nation can be devised; yet the phenomenon has existed and exists.'[4] Tom Nairn, author of the path-breaking *The Break-up of Britain*, and heir to the scarcely less vast tradition of Marxist historiography and social science, candidly remarks: 'The theory of nationalism represents Marxism's great historical failure.'[5] But even this confession is somewhat misleading, insofar as it can be taken to imply the regrettable outcome of a long, self-conscious search for theoretical clarity. It would be more exact to say that nationalism has proved an uncomfortable *anomaly* for Marxist theory and, precisely for that reason, has been largely elided, rather than confronted. How else to explain Marx's failure to explicate the crucial adjective in his memorable formulation of 1848: 'The proletariat of each country

---

3. Eric Hobsbawm, 'Some Reflections on "The Break-up of Britain"', *New Left Review*, 105 (September–October 1977), p. 13.

4. See his *Nations and States*, p. 5. Emphasis added.

5. See his 'The Modern Janus', *New Left Review*, 94 (November–December 1975), p. 3. This essay is included unchanged in *The Break-up of Britain* as chapter 9 (pp. 329–63).

must, of course, first of all settle matters with *its own* bourgeoisie'?[6] How else to account for the use, for over a century, of the concept 'national bourgeoisie' without any serious attempt to justify theoretically the relevance of the adjective? Why is *this* segmentation of the bourgeoisie – a world-class insofar as it is defined in terms of the relations of production – theoretically significant?

The aim of this book is to offer some tentative suggestions for a more satisfactory interpretation of the 'anomaly' of nationalism. My sense is that on this topic both Marxist and liberal theory have become etiolated in a late Ptolemaic effort to 'save the phenomena'; and that a reorientation of perspective in, as it were, a Copernican spirit is urgently required. My point of departure is that nationality, or, as one might prefer to put it in view of that word's multiple significations, nation-ness, as well as nationalism, are cultural artefacts of a particular kind. To understand them properly we need to consider carefully how they have come into historical being, in what ways their meanings have changed over time, and why, today, they command such profound emotional legitimacy. I will be trying to argue that the creation of these artefacts towards the end of the eighteenth century[7] was the spontaneous distillation of a complex 'crossing' of discrete historical forces; but that, once created, they became 'modular,' capable of being transplanted, with varying degrees of self-consciousness, to a great variety of social terrains, to merge and be merged with a correspondingly wide variety of political and ideological constellations. I will also attempt to show why these particular cultural artefacts have aroused such deep attachments.

---

6. Karl Marx and Friedrich Engels, *The Communist Manifesto*, in the *Selected Works*, I, p. 45. Emphasis added. In any theoretical exegesis, the words 'of course' should flash red lights before the transported reader.

7. As Aira Kemiläinen notes, the twin 'founding fathers' of academic scholarship on nationalism, Hans Kohn and Carleton Hayes, argued persuasively for this dating. Their conclusions have, I think, not been seriously disputed except by nationalist ideologues in particular countries. Kemiläinen also observes that the word 'nationalism' did not come into wide general use until the end of the nineteenth century. It did not occur, for example, in many standard nineteenth century lexicons. If Adam Smith conjured with the wealth of 'nations,' he meant by the term no more than 'societies' or 'states.' Aira Kemiläinen, *Nationalism*, pp. 10, 33, and 48–49.

CONCEPTS AND DEFINITIONS

Before addressing the questions raised above, it seems advisable to consider briefly the concept of 'nation' and offer a workable definition. Theorists of nationalism have often been perplexed, not to say irritated, by these three paradoxes: (1) The objective modernity of nations to the historian's eye vs. their subjective antiquity in the eyes of nationalists. (2) The formal universality of nationality as a socio-cultural concept – in the modern world everyone can, should, will 'have' a nationality, as he or she 'has' a gender – vs. the irremediable particularity of its concrete manifestations, such that, by definition, 'Greek' nationality is sui generis. (3) The 'political' power of nationalisms vs. their philosophical poverty and even incoherence. In other words, unlike most other isms, nationalism has never produced its own grand thinkers: no Hobbeses, Tocquevilles, Marxes, or Webers. This 'emptiness' easily gives rise, among cosmopolitan and polylingual intellectuals, to a certain condescension. Like Gertrude Stein in the face of Oakland, one can rather quickly conclude that there is 'no there there'. It is characteristic that even so sympathetic a student of nationalism as Tom Nairn can nonetheless write that: ' "Nationalism" is the pathology of modern developmental history, as inescapable as "neurosis" in the individual, with much the same essential ambiguity attaching to it, a similar built-in capacity for descent into dementia, rooted in the dilemmas of helplessness thrust upon most of the world (the equivalent of infantilism for societies) and largely incurable.'[8]

Part of the difficulty is that one tends unconsciously to hypostasize the existence of Nationalism-with-a-big-N (rather as one might Age-with-a-capital-A) and then to classify 'it' as *an* ideology. (Note that if everyone has an age, Age is merely an analytical expression.) It would, I think, make things easier if one treated it as if it belonged with 'kinship' and 'religion', rather than with 'liberalism' or 'fascism'.

In an anthropological spirit, then, I propose the following

---

8. *The Break-up of Britain*, p. 359.

definition of the nation: it is an imagined political community – and imagined as both inherently limited and sovereign.

It is *imagined* because the members of even the smallest nation will never know most of their fellow-members, meet them, or even hear of them, yet in the minds of each lives the image of their communion.[9] Renan referred to this imagining in his suavely back-handed way when he wrote that 'Or l'essence d'une nation est que tous les individus aient beaucoup de choses en commun, et aussi que tous aient oublié bien des choses.'[10] With a certain ferocity Gellner makes a comparable point when he rules that 'Nationalism is not the awakening of nations to self-consciousness: it *invents* nations where they do not exist.'[11] The drawback to this formulation, however, is that Gellner is so anxious to show that nationalism masquerades under false pretences that he assimilates 'invention' to 'fabrication' and 'falsity', rather than to 'imagining' and 'creation'. In this way he implies that 'true' communities exist which can be advantageously juxtaposed to nations. In fact, all communities larger than primordial villages of face-to-face contact (and perhaps even these) are imagined. Communities are to be distinguished, not by their falsity/genuineness, but by the style in which they are imagined. Javanese villagers have always known that they are connected to people they have never seen, but these ties were once imagined particularistically – as indefinitely stretchable nets of kinship and clientship. Until quite recently, the Javanese language had no word meaning the abstraction 'society.' We may today think of the French aristocracy of the *ancien régime* as a class; but surely it was

---

9. Cf. Seton-Watson, *Nations and States*, p. 5: 'All that I can find to say is that a nation exists when a significant number of people in a community consider themselves to form a nation, or behave as if they formed one.' We may translate 'consider themselves' as 'imagine themselves.'

10. Ernest Renan, 'Qu'est-ce qu'une nation?' in *OEuvres Complètes*, 1, p. 892. He adds: 'tout citoyen français doit avoir oublié la Saint-Barthélemy, les massacres du Midi an XIIIe siècle. Il n'y a pas en France dix familles qui puissent fournir la preuve d'une origine franque . . .'

11. Ernest Gellner, *Thought and Change*, p. 169. Emphasis added.

imagined this way only very late.[12] To the question 'Who is the Comte de X?' the normal answer would have been, not 'a member of the aristocracy,' but 'the lord of X,' 'the uncle of the Baronne de Y,' or 'a client of the Duc de Z.'

The nation is imagined as *limited* because even the largest of them, encompassing perhaps a billion living human beings, has finite, if elastic, boundaries, beyond which lie other nations. No nation imagines itself coterminous with mankind. The most messianic nationalists do not dream of a day when all the members of the human race will join their nation in the way that it was possible, in certain epochs, for, say, Christians to dream of a wholly Christian planet.

It is imagined as *sovereign* because the concept was born in an age in which Enlightenment and Revolution were destroying the legitimacy of the divinely-ordained, hierarchical dynastic realm. Coming to maturity at a stage of human history when even the most devout adherents of any universal religion were inescapably confronted with the living *pluralism* of such religions, and the allomorphism between each faith's ontological claims and territorial stretch, nations dream of being free, and, if under God, directly so. The gage and emblem of this freedom is the sovereign state.

Finally, it is imagined as a *community*, because, regardless of the actual inequality and exploitation that may prevail in each, the nation is always conceived as a deep, horizontal comradeship. Ultimately it is this fraternity that makes it possible, over the past two centuries, for so many millions of people, not so much to kill, as willingly to die for such limited imaginings.

These deaths bring us abruptly face to face with the central problem posed by nationalism: what makes the shrunken imaginings of recent history (scarcely more than two centuries) generate such colossal sacrifices? I believe that the beginnings of an answer lie in the cultural roots of nationalism.

---

12. Hobsbawm, for example, 'fixes' it by saying that in 1789 it numbered about 400,000 in a population of 23,000,000. (See his *The Age of Revolution*, p. 78). But would this statistical picture of the noblesse have been imaginable under the *ancien régime*?

2

Cultural Roots

No more arresting emblems of the modern culture of nationalism exist than cenotaphs and tombs of Unknown Soldiers. The public ceremonial reverence accorded these monuments precisely *because* they are either deliberately empty or no one knows who lies inside them, has no true precedents in earlier times.[1] To feel the force of this modernity one has only to imagine the general reaction to the busy-body who 'discovered' the Unknown Soldier's name or insisted on filling the cenotaph with some real bones. Sacrilege of a strange, contemporary kind! Yet void as these tombs are of identifiable mortal remains or immortal souls, they are nonetheless saturated with ghostly *national* imaginings.[2] (This is why so many different nations have such

---

1. The ancient Greeks had cenotaphs, but for specific, known individuals whose bodies, for one reason or another, could not be retrieved for regular burial. I owe this information to my Byzantinist colleague Judith Herrin.

2. Consider, for example, these remarkable tropes: 1. 'The long grey line has never failed us. Were you to do so, a million ghosts in olive drab, in brown khaki, in blue and grey, would rise from their white crosses, thundering those magic words: Duty, honour, country.' 2. 'My estimate of [the American man-at-arms] was formed on the battlefield many, many years ago, and has never changed. I regarded him then, as I regard him now, as one of the world's noblest figures; not only as one of the finest military characters, but also as one of the most stainless [sic]. . . . He belongs to history as furnishing one of the greatest examples of successful patriotism [sic]. He belongs to posterity as the instructor of future generations in the principles of liberty and freedom.

tombs without feeling any need to specify the nationality of their absent occupants. What else could they be *but* Germans, Americans, Argentinians . . .?)

The cultural significance of such monuments becomes even clearer if one tries to imagine, say, a Tomb of the Unknown Marxist or a cenotaph for fallen Liberals. Is a sense of absurdity avoidable? The reason is that neither Marxism nor Liberalism is much concerned with death and immortality. If the nationalist imagining is so concerned, this suggests a strong affinity with religious imaginings. As this affinity is by no means fortuitous, it may be useful to begin a consideration of the cultural roots of nationalism with death, as the last of a whole gamut of fatalities.

If the manner of a man's dying usually seems arbitrary, his mortality is inescapable. Human lives are full of such combinations of necessity and chance. We are all aware of the contingency and ineluctability of our particular genetic heritage, our gender, our life-era, our physical capabilities, our mother-tongue, and so forth. The great merit of traditional religious world-views (which naturally must be distinguished from their role in the legitimation of specific systems of domination and exploitation) has been their concern with man-in-the-cosmos, man as species being, and the contingency of life. The extraordinary survival over thousands of years of Buddhism, Christianity or Islam in dozens of different social formations attests to their imaginative response to the overwhelming burden of human suffering – disease, mutilation, grief, age, and death. Why was I born blind? Why is my best friend paralysed? Why is my daughter retarded? The religions attempt to explain. The great weakness of all evolutionary/progressive styles of thought, not excluding Marxism, is that such questions are answered with impatient silence.[3] At

---

He belongs to the present, to us, by his virtues and his achievements.' Douglas MacArthur, 'Duty, Honour, Country,' Address to the U.S. Military Academy, West Point, May 12, 1962, in his *A Soldier Speaks*, pp. 354 and 357.

3. Cf. Régis Debray, 'Marxism and the National Question,' *New Left Review*, 105 (September–October 1977), p. 29. In the course of doing fieldwork in Indonesia in the 1960s I was struck by the calm refusal of many Muslims to accept the ideas of Darwin. At first I interpreted this refusal as obscurantism. Subsequently I came to see it as an honourable attempt to be consistent: the doctrine of evolution was simply not compatible with the teachings of Islam. What are we to make of a scientific materialism

the same time, in different ways, religious thought also responds to obscure intimations of immortality, generally by transforming fatality into continuity (karma, original sin, etc.). In this way, it concerns itself with the links between the dead and the yet unborn, the mystery of re-generation. Who experiences *their* child's conception and birth without dimly apprehending a combined connectedness, fortuity, and fatality in a language of 'continuity'? (Again, the disadvantage of evolutionary/progressive thought is an almost Heraclitean hostility to any idea of continuity.)

I bring up these perhaps simpleminded observations primarily because in Western Europe the eighteenth century marks not only the dawn of the age of nationalism but the dusk of religious modes of thought. The century of the Enlightenment, of rationalist secularism, brought with it its own modern darkness. With the ebbing of religious belief, the suffering which belief in part composed did not disappear. Disintegration of paradise: nothing makes fatality more arbitrary. Absurdity of salvation: nothing makes another style of continuity more necessary. What then was required was a secular transformation of fatality into continuity, contingency into meaning. As we shall see, few things were (are) better suited to this end than an idea of nation. If nation-states are widely conceded to be 'new' and 'historical,' the nations to which they give political expression always loom out of an immemorial past,[4] and, still more important, glide

---

which formally accepts the findings of physics about matter, yet makes so little effort to link these findings with the class struggle, revolution, or whatever. Does not the abyss between protons and the proletariat conceal an unacknowledged metaphysical conception of man? But see the refreshing texts of Sebastiano Timpanaro, *On Materialism* and *The Freudian Slip*, and Raymond Williams' thoughtful response to them in 'Timpanaro's Materialist Challenge,' *New Left Review*, 109 (May–June 1978), pp. 3–17.

4. The late President Sukarno always spoke with complete sincerity of the 350 years of colonialism that his 'Indonesia' had endured, although the very concept 'Indonesia' is a twentieth-century invention, and most of today's Indonesia was only conquered by the Dutch between 1850 and 1910. Preeminent among contemporary Indonesia's national heroes is the early nineteenth-century Javanese Prince Diponegoro, although the Prince's own memoirs show that he intended to 'conquer [not liberate!] *Java*,' rather than expel 'the Dutch.' Indeed, he clearly had no concept of 'the Dutch' as a collectivity. See Harry J. Benda and John A. Larkin, eds., *The World of Southeast Asia*, p. 158; and Ann Kumar, 'Diponegoro (1778?–1855),' *Indonesia*, 13 (April 1972), p. 103.

into a limitless future. It is the magic of nationalism to turn chance into destiny. With Debray we might say, 'Yes, it is quite accidental that I am born French; but after all, France is eternal.'

Needless to say, I am not claiming that the appearance of nationalism towards the end of the eighteenth century was 'produced' by the erosion of religious certainties, or that this erosion does not itself require a complex explanation. Nor am I suggesting that somehow nationalism historically 'supersedes' religion. What I am proposing is that nationalism has to be understood by aligning it, not with self-consciously held political ideologies, but with the large cultural systems that preceded it, out of which – as well as against which – it came into being.

For present purposes, the two relevant cultural systems are the *religious community* and the *dynastic realm.* For both of these, in their heydays, were taken-for-granted frames of reference, very much as nationality is today. It is therefore essential to consider what gave these cultural systems their self-evident plausibility, and at the same time to underline certain key elements in their decomposition.

THE RELIGIOUS COMMUNITY

Few things are more impressive than the vast territorial stretch of the Ummah Islam from Morocco to the Sulu Archipelago, of Christendom from Paraguay to Japan, and of the Buddhist world from Sri Lanka to the Korean peninsula. The great sacral cultures (and for our purposes here it may be permissible to include 'Confucianism') incorporated conceptions of immense communities. But Christendom, the Islamic Ummah, and even the Middle Kingdom – which, though we think of it today as Chinese, imagined itself not as Chinese, but as

---

Emphasis added. Similarly, Kemal Atatürk named one of his state banks the Eti Banka (Hittite Bank) and another the Sumerian Bank. (Seton-Watson, *Nations and States*, p. 259). These banks flourish today, and there is no reason to doubt that many Turks, possibly not excluding Kemal himself, seriously saw, and see, in the Hittites and Sumerians their Turkish forebears. Before laughing too hard, we should remind ourselves of Arthur and Boadicea, and ponder the commercial success of Tolkien's mythographies.

central – were imaginable largely through the medium of a sacred language and written script. Take only the example of Islam: if Maguindanao met Berbers in Mecca, knowing nothing of each other's languages, incapable of communicating orally, they nonetheless understood each other's ideographs, *because* the sacred texts they shared existed only in classical Arabic. In this sense, written Arabic functioned like Chinese characters to create a community out of signs, not sounds. (So today mathematical language continues an old tradition. Of what the Thai call + Rumanians have no idea, and vice versa, but both comprehend the symbol.) All the great classical communities conceived of themselves as cosmically central, through the medium of a sacred language linked to a superterrestrial order of power. Accordingly, the stretch of written Latin, Pali, Arabic, or Chinese was, in theory, unlimited. (In fact, the deader the written language – the farther it was from speech – the better: in principle everyone has access to a pure world of signs.)

Yet such classical communities linked by sacred languages had a character distinct from the imagined communities of modern nations. One crucial difference was the older communities' confidence in the unique sacredness of their languages, and thus their ideas about admission to membership. Chinese mandarins looked with approval on barbarians who painfully learned to paint Middle Kingdom ideograms. These barbarians were already halfway to full absorption.[5] Half-civilized was vastly better than barbarian. Such an attitude was certainly not peculiar to the Chinese, nor confined to antiquity. Consider, for example, the following 'policy on barbarians' formulated by the early-nineteenth-century Colombian liberal Pedro Fermín de Vargas:

> To expand our agriculture it would be necessary to hispanicize our Indians. Their idleness, stupidity, and indifference towards normal endeavours causes one to think that they come from a degenerate race which deteriorates in proportion to the distance from its origin . . . *it would be very desirable that the Indians be extinguished, by miscegenation with*

---

5. Hence the equanimity with which Sinicized Mongols and Manchus were accepted as Sons of Heaven.

*the whites, declaring them free of tribute and other charges, and giving them
private property in land.*[6]

How striking it is that this liberal still proposes to 'extinguish' his
Indians in part by 'declaring them free of tribute' and 'giving them
private property in land', rather than exterminating them by gun and
microbe as his heirs in Brazil, Argentina, and the United States began to
do soon afterwards. Note also, alongside the condescending cruelty, a
cosmic optimism: the Indian is ultimately redeemable – by impreg-
nation with white, 'civilized' semen, and the acquisition of private
property, *like everyone else.* (How different Fermín's attitude is from the
later European imperialist's preference for 'genuine' Malays, Gurkhas,
and Hausas over 'half-breeds,' 'semi-educated natives,' 'wogs', and the
like.)

Yet if the sacred silent languages were the media through which the
great global communities of the past were imagined, the reality of
such apparitions depended on an idea largely foreign to the
contemporary Western mind: the non-arbitrariness of the sign. The
ideograms of Chinese, Latin, or Arabic were emanations of reality,
not randomly fabricated representations of it. We are familiar with
the long dispute over the appropriate language (Latin or vernacular)
for the mass. In the Islamic tradition, until quite recently, the Qur'an
was literally untranslatable (and therefore untranslated), because
Allah's truth was accessible only through the unsubstitutable true
signs of written Arabic. There is no idea here of a world so separated
from language that all languages are equidistant (and thus interchangeable) signs for it. In effect, ontological reality is apprehensible
only through a single, privileged system of re-presentation: the truth-
language of Church Latin, Qur'anic Arabic, or Examination Chinese.[7]
And, as truth-languages, imbued with an impulse largely foreign to

---

6. John Lynch, *The Spanish-American Revolutions, 1808–1826*, p. 260. Emphasis
added.

7. Church Greek seems not to have achieved the status of a truth-language. The
reasons for this 'failure' are various, but one key factor was certainly the fact that Greek
remained a *living* demotic speech (unlike Latin) in much of the Eastern Empire. This
insight I owe to Judith Herrin.

nationalism, the impulse towards conversion. By conversion, I mean
not so much the acceptance of particular religious tenets, but alchemic
absorption. The barbarian becomes 'Middle Kingdom', the Rif
Muslim, the Ilongo Christian. The whole nature of man's being is
sacrally malleable. (Contrast thus the prestige of these old world-
languages, towering high over all vernaculars, with Esperanto or
Volapük, which lie ignored between them.) It was, after all, this
possibility of conversion through the sacred language that made it
possible for an 'Englishman' to become Pope[8] and a 'Manchu' Son of
Heaven.

But even though the sacred languages made such communities as
Christendom imaginable, the actual scope and plausibility of these
communities can not be explained by sacred script alone: their readers
were, after all, tiny literate reefs on top of vast illiterate oceans.[9] A fuller
explanation requires a glance at the relationship between the literati and
their societies. It would be a mistake to view the former as a kind of
theological technocracy. The languages they sustained, if abstruse, had
none of the self-arranged abstruseness of lawyers' or economists'
jargons, on the margin of society's idea of reality. Rather, the literati
were adepts, strategic strata in a cosmological hierarchy of which the
apex was divine.[10] The fundamental conceptions about 'social groups'
were centripetal and hierarchical, rather than boundary-oriented and
horizontal. The astonishing power of the papacy in its noonday is only
comprehensible in terms of a trans-European Latin-writing clerisy, *and* a
conception of the world, shared by virtually everyone, that the bilingual
intelligentsia, by mediating between vernacular and Latin, mediated

---

8. Nicholas Brakespear held the office of pontiff between 1154 and 1159 under
the name Adrian IV.
9. Marc Bloch reminds us that 'the majority of lords and many great barons [in
mediaeval times] were administrators incapable of studying personally a report or an
account.' *Feudal Society*, I, p. 81.
10. This is not to say that the illiterate did not read. What they read, however, was
not words but the visible world. 'In the eyes of all who were capable of reflection the
material world was scarcely more than a sort of mask, behind which took place all the
really important things; it seemed to them also a language, intended to express by signs a
more profound reality.' Ibid. p. 83.

between earth and heaven. (The awesomeness of excommunication reflects this cosmology.)

Yet for all the grandeur and power of the great religiously imagined communities, their *unselfconscious coherence* waned steadily after the late Middle Ages. Among the reasons for this decline, I wish here to emphasize only the two which are directly related to these communities' unique sacredness.

First was the effect of the explorations of the non-European world, which mainly but by no means exclusively in Europe 'abruptly widened the cultural and geographic horizon and hence also men's conception of possible forms of human life.'[11] The process is already apparent in the greatest of all European travel-books. Consider the following awed description of Kublai Khan by the good Venetian Christian Marco Polo at the end of the thirteenth century:[12]

> The grand khan, having obtained this signal victory, returned with great pomp and triumph to the capital city of Kanbalu. This took place in the month of November, and he continued to reside there during the months of February and March, in which latter was *our* festival of Easter. Being aware that this was one of *our* principal solemnities, he commanded all the Christians to attend him, and to bring with them *their* Book, which contains the four Gospels of the Evangelists. After causing it to be repeatedly perfumed with incense, in a ceremonious manner, he devoutly kissed it, and directed that the same should be done by all his nobles who were present. This was his usual practice upon each of the principal Christian festivals, such as Easter and Christmas; and he observed the same at the festivals of the Saracens, Jews, and idolaters. Upon being asked his motive for this conduct, he said: 'There are four great Prophets who are reverenced and worshipped by the different classes of mankind. The Christians regard Jesus Christ as their divinity; the Saracens, Mahomet; the Jews, Moses; and the idolaters, Sogomombar-kan, the most eminent among their idols. I do honour and show respect to all the four,

---

11. Erich Auerbach, *Mimesis*, p. 282.

12. Marco Polo, *The Travels of Marco Polo*, pp. 158–59. Emphases added. Notice that, though kissed, the Evangel is not read.

and invoke to my aid *whichever amongst them is in truth supreme in heaven.*' But from the manner in which his majesty acted towards them, it is evident that he regarded the faith of the Christians as the truest and the best . . .

What is so remarkable about this passage is not so much the great Mongol dynast's calm religious relativism (it is still a *religious* relativism), as Marco Polo's attitude and language. It never occurs to him, even though he is writing for fellow-European Christians, to term Kublai a hypocrite or an idolater. (No doubt in part because 'in respect to number of subjects, extent of territory, and amount of revenue, he surpasses every sovereign that has heretofore been or that now is in the world.')[13] And in the unselfconscious use of 'our' (which becomes 'their'), and the description of the faith of the Christians as 'truest,' rather than 'true,' we can detect the seeds of a territorialization of faiths which foreshadows the language of many nationalists ('our' nation is 'the best' — in a competitive, *comparative field*).

What a revealing contrast is provided by the opening of the letter written by the Persian traveller 'Rica' to his friend 'Ibben' from Paris in '1712':[14]

The Pope is the chief of the Christians; he is an ancient idol, worshipped now from habit. Once he was formidable even to princes, for he would depose them as easily as our magnificent sultans depose the kings of Iremetia or Georgia. But nobody fears him any longer. He claims to be the successor of one of the earliest Christians, called Saint Peter, and it is certainly a rich succession, for his treasure is immense and he has a great country under his control.

The deliberate, sophisticated fabrications of the eighteenth century Catholic mirror the naive realism of his thirteenth-century predecessor, but by now the 'relativization' and 'territorialization' are utterly self-conscious, and political in intent. Is it unreasonable to see a paradoxical

---

13. *The Travels of Marco Polo*, p. 152.
14. Henri de Montesquieu, *Persian Letters*, p. 81. The *Lettres Persanes* first appeared in 1721.

17

elaboration of this evolving tradition in the Ayatollah Ruhollah Khomeini's identification of The Great Satan, not as a heresy, nor even as a demonic personage (dim little Carter scarcely fitted the bill), but as a *nation?*

Second was a gradual demotion of the sacred language itself. Writing of mediaeval Western Europe, Bloch noted that 'Latin was not only the language in which teaching was done, it was the *only language taught*.'[15] (This second 'only' shows quite clearly the sacredness of Latin – no other language was thought worth the teaching.) But by the sixteenth century all this was changing fast. The reasons for the change need not detain us here: the central importance of print-capitalism will be discussed below. It is sufficient to remind ourselves of its scale and pace. Febvre and Martin estimate that 77% of the books printed before 1500 were still in Latin (meaning nonetheless that 23% were already in vernaculars).[16] If of the 88 editions printed in Paris in 1501 all but 8 were in Latin, after 1575 a majority were always in French.[17] Despite a temporary come-back during the Counter-Reformation, Latin's hegemony was doomed. Nor are we speaking simply of a general popularity. Somewhat later, but at no less dizzying speed, Latin ceased to be the language of a pan-European high intelligentsia. In the seventeenth century Hobbes (1588–1678) was a figure of continental renown because he wrote in the truth-language. Shakespeare (1564–1616), on the other hand, composing in the vernacular, was virtually unknown across the Channel.[18] And had English not become, two hundred years later, the pre-eminent world-imperial language, might he not largely have retained his original insular obscurity? Meanwhile, these men's cross-Channel near-contemporaries, Descartes (1596–1650) and Pascal (1623–1662), conducted most of their correspondence in Latin; but virtually all of Voltaire's (1694–1778) was in the vernacular.[19] 'After 1640, with fewer and fewer books coming out in Latin, and more and more in the vernacular languages, publishing was ceasing to be an international [sic]

---

15. Bloch, *Feudal Society*, I, p. 77. Emphasis added.
16. Lucien Febvre and Henri-Jean Martin, *The Coming of the Book*, pp. 248–49.
17. Ibid., p. 321.
18. Ibid., p. 330.
19. Ibid., pp. 331–32.

enterprise.'[20] In a word, the fall of Latin exemplified a larger process in which the sacred communities integrated by old sacred languages were gradually fragmented, pluralized, and territorialized.

THE DYNASTIC REALM

These days it is perhaps difficult to put oneself empathetically into a world in which the dynastic realm appeared for most men as the only imaginable 'political' system. For in fundamental ways 'serious' monarchy lies transverse to all modern conceptions of political life. Kingship organizes everything around a high centre. Its legitimacy derives from divinity, not from populations, who, after all, are subjects, not citizens. In the modern conception, state sovereignty is fully, flatly, and evenly operative over each square centimetre of a legally demarcated territory. But in the older imagining, where states were defined by centres, borders were porous and indistinct, and sovereignties faded imperceptibly into one another.[21] Hence, paradoxically enough, the ease with which pre-modern empires and kingdoms were able to sustain their rule over immensely heterogeneous, and often not even contiguous, populations for long periods of time.[22]

One must also remember that these antique monarchical states

---

20. Ibid., pp. 232–33. The original French is more modest and historically exact: 'Tandis que l'on édite de moins en moins d'ouvrages en latin, et une proportion toujours plus grande de textes en langue nationale, le commerce du livre se morcelle en Europe.' *L'Apparition du Livre*, p. 356.

21. Notice the displacement in rulers' nomenclature that corresponds to this transformation. Schoolchildren remember monarchs by their first names (what *was* William the Conqueror's surname?), presidents by their last (what *was* Ebert's Christian name?). In a world of citizens, all of whom are theoretically eligible for the presidency, the limited pool of 'Christian' names makes them inadequate as specifying designators. In monarchies, however, where rule is reserved for a single surname, it is necessarily 'Christian' names, with numbers, or sobriquets, that supply the requisite distinctions.

22. We may here note in passing that Nairn is certainly correct in describing the 1707 Act of Union between England and Scotland as a 'patrician bargain,' in the sense that the union's architects were aristocratic politicians. (See his lucid discussion in *The Break-up of Britain*, pp. 136f.). Still, it is difficult to imagine such a bargain being

expanded not only by warfare but by sexual politics – of a kind very different from that practised today. Through the general principle of verticality, dynastic marriages brought together diverse populations under new apices. Paradigmatic in this respect was the House of Habsburg. As the tag went, *Bella gerant alii, tu felix Austria nube!* Here, in somewhat abbreviated form, is the later dynasts' titulature.[23]

Emperor of Austria; King of Hungary, of Bohemia, of Dalmatia, Croatia, Slavonia, Galicia, Lodomeria, and Illyria; King of Jerusalem, etc; Archduke of Austria [sic]; Grand Duke of Tuscany and Cracow; Duke of Loth[a]ringia, of Salzburg, Styria, Carinthia, Carniola, and Bukovina; Grand Duke of Transylvania, Margrave of Moravia; Duke of Upper and Lower Silesia, of Modena, Parma, Piacenza, and Guastella, of Ausschwitz and Sator, of Teschen, Friaul, Ragusa, and Zara; Princely Count of Habsburg and Tyrol, of Kyburg, Görz, and Gradiska; Duke of Trient and Brizen; Margrave of Upper and Lower Lausitz and in Istria; Count of Hohenembs, Feldkirch, Bregenz, Sonnenberg, etc.; Lord of Trieste, of Cattaro, and above the Windisch Mark; Great Voyvod of the Voyvodina, Servia . . . . etc.

This, Jászi justly observes, was, 'not without a certain comic aspect . . . the record of the innumerable marriages, hucksterings and captures of the Habsburgs.'

In realms where polygyny was religiously sanctioned, complex systems of tiered concubinage were essential to the integration of the realm. In fact, royal lineages often derived their prestige, aside from any aura of divinity, from, shall we say, miscegenation?[24] For such

---

struck between the aristocracies of two republics. The conception of a United *Kingdom* was surely the crucial mediating element that made the deal possible.

23. Oscar Jászi, *The Dissolution of the Habsburg Monarchy*, p. 34.

24. Most notably in pre-modern Asia. But the same principle was at work in monogamous Christian Europe. In 1910, one Otto Forst put out his *Ahnentafel Seiner Kaiserlichen und Königlichen Hoheit des durchlauchtigsten Hern Erzherzogs Franz Ferdinand*, listing 2,047 of the soon-to-be-assassinated Archduke's ancestors. They included 1,486 Germans, 124 French, 196 Italians, 89 Spaniards, 52 Poles, 47 Danes, 20 Englishmen/women, as well as four other nationalities. This 'curious document' is cited in ibid., p. 136, no. 1. I can not resist quoting here Franz Joseph's wonderful

mixtures were signs of a superordinate status. It is characteristic that there has not been an 'English' dynasty ruling in London since the eleventh century (if then); and what 'nationality' are we to assign to the Bourbons?[25]

During the seventeenth century, however – for reasons that need not detain us here – the automatic legitimacy of sacral monarchy began its slow decline in Western Europe. In 1649, Charles Stuart was beheaded in the first of the modern world's revolutions, and during the 1650s one of the more important European states was ruled by a plebeian Protector rather than a king. Yet even in the age of Pope and Addison, Anne Stuart was still healing the sick by the laying on of royal hands, cures committed also by the Bourbons, Louis XV and XVI, in Enlightened France till the end of the *ancien régime*.[26] But after 1789 the principle of Legitimacy had to be loudly and self-consciously defended, and, in the process, 'monarchy' became a semi-standardized model. Tennō and Son of Heaven became 'Emperors.' In far-off Siam Rama V (Chulalongkorn) sent his sons and nephews to the courts of St. Petersburg, London and Berlin to learn the intricacies of the world-model. In 1887, he instituted the requisite principle of succession-by-legal-primogeniture, thus bringing Siam 'into line with the "civilized" monarchies of Europe.'[27] The new system brought to the throne in 1910 an erratic homosexual who would certainly have been passed over in an earlier age. However, inter-monarchic approval of his ascension as Rama VI was sealed by the attendance at his coronation of princelings from Britain, Russia, Greece, Sweden, Denmark – and Japan![28]

---

reaction to the news of his erratic heir-apparent's murder: 'In this manner a superior power has restored that order which I unfortunately was unable to maintain' (ibid., p. 125).

25. Gellner stresses the typical foreignness of dynasties, but interprets the phenomenon too narrowly: local aristocrats prefer an alien monarch because he will not take sides in their internal rivalries. *Thought and Change*, p. 136.

26. Marc Bloch, *Les Rois Thaumaturges*, pp. 390 and 398–99.

27. Noel A. Battye, 'The Military, Government and Society in Siam, 1868–1910,' PhD thesis, Cornell 1974, p. 270.

28. Stephen Greene, 'Thai Government and Administration in the Reign of Rama VI (1910–1925),' PhD thesis, University of London 1971, p. 92.

As late as 1914, dynastic states made up the majority of the membership of the world political system, but, as we shall be noting in detail below, many dynasts had for some time been reaching for a 'national' cachet as the old principle of Legitimacy withered silently away. While the armies of Frederick the Great (r. 1740–1786) were heavily staffed by 'foreigners', those of his great-nephew Friedrich Wilhelm III (r. 1797–1840) were, as a result of Scharnhorst's, Gneisenau's and Clausewitz's spectacular reforms, exclusively 'national-Prussian.'[29]

APPREHENSIONS OF TIME

It would be short-sighted, however, to think of the imagined communities of nations as simply growing out of and replacing religious communities and dynastic realms. Beneath the decline of sacred communities, languages and lineages, a fundamental change was taking place in modes of apprehending the world, which, more than anything else, made it possible to 'think' the nation.

To get a feeling for this change, one can profitably turn to the visual representations of the sacred communities, such as the reliefs and stained-glass windows of mediaeval churches, or the paintings of early Italian and Flemish masters. A characteristic feature of such representations is something misleadingly analogous to 'modern dress'. The shepherds who have followed the star to the manger where Christ is born bear the features of Burgundian peasants. The Virgin Mary is figured as a Tuscan merchant's daughter. In many paintings the commissioning patron, in full burgher or noble costume, appears kneeling in adoration alongside the shepherds. What seems incongruous today obviously appeared wholly natural to the eyes of mediaeval worshippers. We are faced with a world in which

---

29. More than 1,000 of the 7,000–8,000 men on the Prussian Army's officer list in 1806 were foreigners. 'Middle-class Prussians were outnumbered by foreigners in their own army; this lent colour to the saying that Prussia was not a country that had an army, but an army that had a country.' In 1798, Prussian reformers had demanded a 'reduction by one half of the number of foreigners, who still amounted to about 50% of the privates. . . .' Alfred Vagts, *A History of Militarism*, pp. 64 and 85.

the figuring of imagined reality was overwhelmingly visual and aural. Christendom assumed its universal form through a myriad of specificities and particularities: this relief, that window, this sermon, that tale, this morality play, that relic. While the trans-European Latin-reading clerisy was one essential element in the structuring of the Christian imagination, the mediation of its conceptions to the illiterate masses, by visual and aural creations, always personal and particular, was no less vital. The humble parish priest, whose forebears and frailties everyone who heard his celebrations knew, was still the direct intermediary between his parishioners and the divine. This juxtaposition of the cosmic-universal and the mundane-particular meant that however vast Christendom might be, and was sensed to be, it manifested itself *variously* to particular Swabian or Andalusian communities as replications of themselves. Figuring the Virgin Mary with 'Semitic' features or 'first-century' costumes in the restoring spirit of the modern museum was unimaginable because the mediaeval Christian mind had no conception of history as an endless chain of cause and effect or of radical separations between past and present.[30] Bloch observes that people thought they must be near the end of time, in the sense that Christ's second coming could occur at any moment: St. Paul had said that 'the day of the Lord cometh like a thief in the night.' It was thus natural for the great twelfth-century chronicler Bishop Otto of Freising to refer repeatedly to 'we who have been placed at the end of time.' Bloch concludes that as soon as mediaeval men 'gave themselves up to meditation, nothing was farther from their thoughts than the prospect of a long future for a young and vigorous human race.'[31]

Auerbach gives an unforgettable sketch of this form of consciousness:[32]

---

30. For us, the idea of 'modern dress,' a metaphorical equivalencing of past with present, is a backhanded recognition of their fatal separation.

31. Bloch, *Feudal Society*, I, pp. 84–86.

32. Auerbach, *Mimesis*, p. 64. Emphasis added. Compare St. Augustine's description of the Old Testament as 'the shadow of [i.e. cast backwards by] the future.' Cited in Bloch, *Feudal Society*, I, p. 90.

If an occurrence like the sacrifice of Isaac is interpreted as prefiguring the sacrifice of Christ, so that in the former the latter is as it were announced and promised and the latter 'fulfills' . . . the former, then a connection is established between two events which are linked neither temporally nor causally – a connection which it is impossible to establish by reason in the horizontal dimension . . . It can be established only if both occurrences are vertically linked to Divine Providence, which alone is able to devise such a plan of history and supply the key to its understanding . . . the here and now is no longer a mere link in an earthly chain of events, it is *simultaneously* something which has always been, and will be fulfilled in the future; and strictly, in the eyes of God, it is something eternal, something omnitemporal, something already consummated in the realm of fragmentary earthly event.

He rightly stresses that such an idea of *simultaneity* is wholly alien to our own. It views time as something close to what Benjamin calls Messianic time, a simultaneity of past and future in an instantaneous present.[33] In such a view of things, the word 'meanwhile' cannot be of real significance.

Our own conception of simultaneity has been a long time in the making, and its emergence is certainly connected, in ways that have yet to be well studied, with the development of the secular sciences. But it is a conception of such fundamental importance that, without taking it fully into account, we will find it difficult to probe the obscure genesis of nationalism. What has come to take the place of the mediaeval conception of simultaneity-along-time is, to borrow again from Benjamin, an idea of 'homogeneous, empty time,' in which simultaneity is, as it were, transverse, cross-time, marked not by prefiguring and fulfilment, but by temporal coincidence, and measured by clock and calendar.[34]

Why this transformation should be so important for the birth of the imagined community of the nation can best be seen if we consider the basic structure of two forms of imagining which first flowered in

---

33. Walter Benjamin, *Illuminations*, p. 265.
34. Ibid., p. 263. So deep-lying is this new idea that one could argue that every essential modern conception is based on a conception of 'meanwhile'.

Europe in the eighteenth century: the novel and the newspaper.[35] For these forms provided the technical means for 're-presenting' the *kind* of imagined community that is the nation.

Consider first the structure of the old-fashioned novel, a structure typical not only of the masterpieces of Balzac but also of any contemporary dollar-dreadful. It is clearly a device for the presentation of simultaneity in 'homogeneous, empty time,' or a complex gloss upon the word 'meanwhile'. Take, for illustrative purposes, a segment of a simple novel-plot, in which a man (A) has a wife (B) and a mistress (C), who in turn has a lover (D). We might imagine a sort of time-chart for this segment as follows:

Time:	I	II	III
Events:	A quarrels with B	A telephones C	D gets drunk in a bar
	C and D make love	B shops	A dines at home with B
		D plays pool	C has an ominous dream

Notice that during this sequence A and D never meet, indeed may not even be aware of each other's existence if C has played her cards right.[36] What then actually links A to D? Two complementary conceptions: First, that they are embedded in 'societies' (Wessex, Lübeck, Los Angeles). These societies are sociological entities of such firm and stable reality that their members (A and D) can even be described as passing each other on the street, without ever becoming acquainted, and still be connected.[37] Second, that A and D are

---

35. While the *Princesse de Clèves* had already appeared in 1678, the era of Richardson, Defoe and Fielding is the early eighteenth century. The origins of the modern newspaper lie in the Dutch gazettes of the late seventeenth century; but the newspaper only became a general category of printed matter after 1700. Febvre and Martin, *The Coming of the Book*, p. 197.

36. Indeed, the plot's grip may *depend* at Times I, II, and III on A, B, C and D not knowing what the others are up to.

37. This polyphony decisively marks off the modern novel even from so brilliant a forerunner as Petronius's *Satyricon*. Its narrative proceeds single file. If Encolpius bewails his young lover's faithlessness, we are not simultaneously shown Gito in bed with Ascyltus.

25

embedded in the minds of the omniscient readers. Only they, like God, watch A telephoning C, B shopping, and D playing pool all *at once*. That all these acts are performed at the same clocked, calendrical time, but by actors who may be largely unaware of one another, shows the novelty of this imagined world conjured up by the author in his readers' minds.[38]

The idea of a sociological organism moving calendrically through homogeneous, empty time is a precise analogue of the idea of the nation, which also is conceived as a solid community moving steadily down (or up) history.[39] An American will never meet, or even know the names of more than a handful of his 240,000,000-odd fellow-Americans. He has no idea of what they are up to at any one time. But he has complete confidence in their steady, anonymous, simultaneous activity.

The perspective I am suggesting will perhaps seem less abstract if we turn to inspect briefly four fictions from different cultures and different epochs, all but one of which, nonetheless, are inextricably bound to nationalist movements. In 1887, the 'Father of Filipino Nationalism', José Rizal, wrote the novel *Noli Me Tangere*, which today is regarded as the greatest achievement of modern Filipino literature. It was also almost the first novel written by an 'Indio.'[40] Here is how it marvellously begins:[41]

Towards the end of October, Don Santiago de los Santos, popularly known as Capitan Tiago, was giving a dinner party. Although,

---

38. In this context it is rewarding to compare any historical novel with documents or narratives from the period fictionalized.

39. Nothing better shows the immersion of the novel in homogeneous, empty time than the absence of those prefatory genealogies, often ascending to the origin of man, which are so characteristic a feature of ancient chronicles, legends, and holy books.

40. Rizal wrote this novel in the colonial language (Spanish), which was then the lingua franca of the ethnically diverse Eurasian and native elites. Alongside the novel appeared also for the first time a 'nationalist' press, not only in Spanish but in such 'ethnic' languages as Tagalog and Ilocano. See Leopoldo Y. Yabes, 'The Modern Literature of the Philippines,' pp. 287–302, in Pierre-Bernard Lafont and Denys Lombard (eds), *Littératures Contemporaines de l'Asie du Sud-Est*.

41. José Rizal, *Noli Me Tangere* (Manila: Instituto Nacional de Historia, 1978), p. 1. My translation. At the time of the original publication of *Imagined Communities*, I

contrary to his usual practice, he had announced it only that after-
noon, it was already the subject of every conversation in Binondo, in
other quarters of the city, and even in [the walled inner city of]
Intramuros. In those days Capitan Tiago had the reputation of a lavish
host. It was known that his house, like his country, closed its doors to
nothing, except to commerce and to any new or daring idea.

So the news coursed like an electric shock through the community
of parasites, spongers, and gatecrashers whom God, in His infinite
goodness, created, and so tenderly multiplies in Manila. Some hunted
polish for their boots, others looked for collar-buttons and cravats.
But one and all were preoccupied with the problem of how to greet
their host with the familiarity required to create the appearance of
longstanding friendship, or, if need be, to excuse themselves for not
having arrived earlier.

The dinner was being given at a house on Anloague Street. Since
we do not recall the street number, we shall describe it in such a way
that it may still be recognized – that is, if earthquakes have not yet
destroyed it. We do not believe that its owner will have had it torn
down, since such work is usually left to God or to Nature, which,
besides, holds many contracts with our Government.

Extensive comment is surely unnecessary. It should suffice to note that
right from the start the image (wholly new to Filipino writing) of a dinner-
party being discussed by hundreds of unnamed people, who do not know
each other, in quite different parts of Manila, in a particular month of a
particular decade, immediately conjures up the imagined community. And
in the phrase 'a house on Anloague Street' which 'we shall describe in such a
way that it may still be recognized,' the would-be recognizers are we-
Filipino-readers. The casual progression of this house from the 'interior'
time of the novel to the 'exterior' time of the [Manila] reader's everyday life
gives a hypnotic confirmation of the solidity of a single community,
embracing characters, author and readers, moving onward through
calendrical time.[42] Notice too the tone. While Rizal has not the faintest

---

had no command of Spanish, and was thus unwittingly led to rely on the instructively
corrupt translation of Leon Maria Guerrero.

42. Notice, for example, Rizal's subtle shift, in the same sentence, from the past
tense of 'created' (*crió*) to the all-of-us-together present tense of 'multiplies' (*multiplica*).

idea of his readers' individual identities, he writes to them with an ironical intimacy, as though their relationships with each other are not in the smallest degree problematic.[43]

Nothing gives one a more Foucauldian sense of abrupt discontinuities of consciousness than to compare *Noli* with the most celebrated previous literary work by an 'Indio', Francisco Balagtas (Baltazar)'s *Pinagdaanang Buhay ni Florante at ni Laura sa Cahariang Albania* [The Story of Florante and Laura in the Kingdom of Albania], the first printed edition of which dates from 1861, though it may have been composed as early as 1838.[44] For although Balagtas was still alive when Rizal was born, the world of his masterpiece is in every basic respect foreign to that of *Noli*. Its setting – a fabulous mediaeval Albania – is utterly removed in time and space from the Binondo of the 1880s. Its heroes – Florante, a Christian Albanian nobleman, and his bosom-friend Aladin, a Muslim ('Moro') Persian aristocrat – remind us of the Philippines only by the Christian-Moro linkage. Where Rizal deliberately sprinkles his Spanish prose with Tagalog words for 'realistic', satirical, or nationalist effect, Balagtas unselfconsciously mixes Spanish phrases into his Tagalog quatrains simply to heighten the grandeur and sonority of his diction. *Noli* was meant to be read, while *Florante at Laura* was to be sung aloud. Most striking of all is Balagtas's handling of time. As Lumbera notes, 'the unravelling of the plot does not follow a chronological order. The story begins in *medias res*, so that the complete story comes to us through a series of speeches that serve as flashbacks.'[45] Almost half of the 399 quatrains are accounts of Florante's childhood, student years in Athens, and subsequent military exploits, given by the hero in conversation with

---

43. The obverse side of the readers' anonymous obscurity was/is the author's immediate celebrity. As we shall see, this obscurity/celebrity has everything to do with the spread of print-capitalism. As early as 1593 energetic Dominicans had published in Manila the *Doctrina Christiana*. But for centuries thereafter print remained under tight ecclesiastical control. Liberalization only began in the 1860s. See Bienvenido L. Lumbera, *Tagalog Poetry 1570–1898, Tradition and Influences in its Development*, pp. 35, 93.
44. Ibid., p. 115.
45. Ibid., p. 120.

Aladin.[46] The 'spoken flashback' was for Balagtas the only alternative
to a straightforward single-file narrative. If we learn of Florante's and
Aladin's 'simultaneous' pasts, they are connected by their conversing
voices, not by the structure of the epic. How distant this technique is
from that of the novel: 'In that same spring, while Florante was still
studying in Athens, Aladin was expelled from his sovereign's court
. . .' In effect, it never occurs to Balagtas to 'situate' his protagonists in
'society,' or to discuss them with his audience. Nor, aside from the
mellifluous flow of Tagalog polysyllables, is there much 'Filipino'
about his text.[47]

In 1816, seventy years before the writing of *Noli*, José Joaquín
Fernandez de Lizardi wrote a novel called *El Periquillo Sarniento* [The
Itching Parrot], evidently the first Latin American work in this genre. In
the words of one critic, this text is 'a ferocious indictment of Spanish
administration in Mexico: ignorance, superstition and corruption are
seen to be its most notable characteristics.'[48] The essential form of this
'nationalist' novel is indicated by the following description of its
content:[49]

From the first, [the hero, the Itching Parrot] is exposed to bad
influences – ignorant maids inculcate superstitions, his mother in-
dulges his whims, his teachers either have no vocation or no ability to

---

46. The technique is similar to that of Homer, so ably discussed by Auerbach,
Mimesis, ch. 1 ('Odysseus' Scar').
47. 'Paalam Albaniang pinamamayanan
ng casama, t, lupit, bangis caliluhan,
acong tangulan mo, i, cusa mang pinatay
sa iyo, i, malaqui ang panghihinayang.'
'Farewell, Albania, kingdom now
of evil, cruelty, brutishness and deceit!
I, your defender, whom you now murder
Nevertheless lament the fate that has befallen you.'
This famous stanza has sometimes been interpreted as a veiled statement of Filipino
patriotism, but Lumbera convincingly shows such an interpretation to be an
anachronistic gloss. *Tagalog Poetry*, p. 125. The translation is Lumbera's. I have
slightly altered his Tagalog text to conform to a 1973 edition of the poem based on
the 1861 imprint.
48. Jean Franco, *An Introduction to Spanish-American Literature*, p. 34.
49. Ibid., pp. 35–36. Emphasis added.

discipline him. And though his father is an intelligent man who wants his son to practise a useful trade rather than swell the ranks of lawyers and parasites, it is Periquillo's over-fond mother who wins the day, sends her son to university and thus ensures that he will learn only superstitious nonsense . . . Periquillo remains incorrigibly ignorant despite many encounters with good and wise people. He is unwilling to work or take anything seriously and becomes successively a priest, a gambler, a thief, apprentice to an apothecary, a doctor, clerk in a provincial town . . . These episodes *permit the author to describe hospitals, prisons, remote villages, monasteries*, while at the same time driving home one major point – that Spanish government and the education system encourage parasitism and laziness . . . Periquillo's adventures several times take him among Indians and Negroes . . .

Here again we see the 'national imagination' at work in the movement of a solitary hero through a sociological landscape of a fixity that fuses the world inside the novel with the world outside. This picaresque *tour d'horizon* – hospitals, prisons, remote villages, monasteries, Indians, Negroes – is nonetheless not a *tour du monde*. The horizon is clearly bounded: it is that of colonial Mexico. Nothing assures us of this sociological solidity more than the succession of plurals. For they conjure up a social space full of *comparable* prisons, none in itself of any unique importance, but all representative (in their simultaneous, separate existence) of the oppressiveness of *this* colony.[50] (Contrast prisons in the Bible. They are never imagined as *typical* of this or that society. Each, like the one where Salome was bewitched by John the Baptist, is magically alone.)

Finally, to remove the possibility that, since Rizal and Lizardi both wrote in Spanish, the frameworks we have been studying are somehow 'European', here is the opening of *Semarang Hitam* [Black Semarang], a tale by the ill-fated young Indonesian communist-nationalist Mas Marco Kartodikromo,[51] published serially in 1924:[52]

---

50. This movement of a solitary hero through an adamantine social landscape is typical of many early (anti-)colonial novels.

51. After a brief, meteoric career as a radical journalist, Marco was interned by the Dutch colonial authorities in Boven Digul, one of the world's earliest concentration camps, deep in the interior swamps of western New Guinea. There he died in 1932, after six years confinement. Henri Chambert-Loir, 'Mas Marco Kartodikromo (c.

It was 7 o'clock, Saturday evening; young people in Semarang never stayed at home on Saturday night. On this night however nobody was about. Because the heavy day-long rain had made the roads wet and very slippery, all had stayed at home.

For the workers in shops and offices Saturday morning was a time of anticipation – anticipating their leisure and the fun of walking around the city in the evening, but on this night they were to be disappointed – because of lethargy caused by the bad weather and the sticky roads in the kampungs. The main roads usually crammed with all sorts of traffic, the footpaths usually teeming with people, all were deserted. Now and then the crack of a horse-cab's whip could be heard spurring a horse on its way – or the clip-clop of horses' hooves pulling carriages along.

Semarang was deserted. The light from the rows of gas lamps shone straight down on the shining asphalt road. Occasionally the clear light from the gas lamps was dimmed as the wind blew from the east. . . .

A young man was seated on a long rattan lounge reading a newspaper. He was totally engrossed. His occasional anger and at other times smiles were a sure sign of his deep interest in the story. He turned the pages of the newspaper, thinking that perhaps he could find something that would stop him feeling so miserable. All of a sudden he came upon an article entitled:

PROSPERITY
A destitute vagrant became ill
and died on the side of the road from exposure.

The young man was moved by this brief report. He could just imagine the suffering of the poor soul as he lay dying on the side of the road . . . One moment he felt an explosive anger well up inside. Another moment he felt pity. Yet another moment his anger was

---

1890–1932) ou L'Education Politique,' p. 208, in *Littératures contemporaines de l'Asie du Sud-Est*. A brilliant recent full-length account of Marco's career can be found in Takashi Shiraishi, *An Age in Motion: Popular Radicalism in Java, 1912–1926*, chapters 2–5 and 8.

52. As translated by Paul Tickell in his *Three Early Indonesian Short Stories by Mas Marco Kartodikromo (c. 1890–1932)*, p. 7. Emphasis added.

directed at the social system which gave rise to such poverty, while making a small group of people wealthy.

Here, as in *El Periquillo Sarniento*, we are in a world of plurals: shops, offices, carriages, kampungs, and gas lamps. As in the case of *Noli*, we-the-Indonesian-readers are plunged immediately into calendrical time and a familiar landscape; some of us may well have walked those 'sticky' Semarang roads. Once again, a solitary hero is juxtaposed to a socioscape described in careful, *general* detail. But there is also something new: a hero who is never named, but who is frequently referred to as '*our* young man'. Precisely the clumsiness and literary naivety of the text confirm the unselfconscious 'sincerity' of this pronominal adjective. Neither Marco nor his readers have any doubts about the reference. If in the jocular-sophisticated fiction of eighteenth- and nineteenth-century Europe the trope 'our hero' merely underlines an authorial play with a(ny) reader, Marco's 'our young man,' not least in its novelty, *means* a young man who belongs to the collective body of readers of *Indonesian*, and thus, implicitly, an embryonic Indonesian 'imagined community.' Notice that Marco feels no need to specify this community by name: it is already there. (Even if polylingual Dutch colonial censors could join his readership, they are excluded from this 'ourness,' as can be seen from the fact that the young man's anger is directed at 'the,' not 'our,' social system.)

Finally, the imagined community is confirmed by the doubleness of our reading about our young man reading. He does not find the corpse of the destitute vagrant by the side of a sticky Semarang road, but imagines it from the print in a newspaper.[53] Nor does he care the slightest who the dead vagrant individually was: he thinks of the representative body, not the personal life.

It is fitting that in *Semarang Hitam* a newspaper appears embedded in

53. In 1924, a close friend and political ally of Marco published a novel titled *Rasa Merdika* [Feeling Free/The Feel of Freedom]. Of the hero of this novel (which he wrongly attributes to Marco) Chambert-Loir writes that 'he has no idea of the meaning of the word "socialism": nonetheless he feels a profound malaise in the face of the social organization that surrounds him and he feels the need to enlarge his horizons by two methods: *travel and reading*.' ('Mas Marco', p. 208. Emphasis added.) The Itching Parrot has moved to Java and the twentieth century.

fiction, for, if we now turn to the newspaper as cultural product, we will be struck by its profound fictiveness. What is the essential literary convention of the newspaper? If we were to look at a sample front page of, say, *The New York Times*, we might find there stories about Soviet dissidents, famine in Mali, a gruesome murder, a coup in Iraq, the discovery of a rare fossil in Zimbabwe, and a speech by Mitterrand. Why are these events so juxtaposed? What connects them to each other? Not sheer caprice. Yet obviously most of them happen independently, without the actors being aware of each other or of what the others are up to. The arbitrariness of their inclusion and juxtaposition (a later edition will substitute a baseball triumph for Mitterrand) shows that the linkage between them is imagined.

This imagined linkage derives from two obliquely related sources. The first is simply calendrical coincidence. The date at the top of the newspaper, the single most important emblem on it, provides the essential connection – the steady onward clocking of homogeneous, empty time.[54] Within that time, 'the world' ambles sturdily ahead. The sign for this: if Mali disappears from the pages of *The New York Times* after two days of famine reportage, for months on end, readers do not for a moment imagine that Mali has disappeared or that famine has wiped out all its citizens. The novelistic format of the newspaper assures them that somewhere out there the 'character' Mali moves along quietly, awaiting its next reappearance in the plot.

The second source of imagined linkage lies in the relationship between the newspaper, as a form of book, and the market. It has been estimated that in the 40-odd years between the publication of the Gutenberg Bible and the close of the fifteenth century, more than 20,000,000 printed volumes were produced in Europe.[55] Between 1500 and 1600, the number manufactured had reached between

---

54. Reading a newspaper is like reading a novel whose author has abandoned any thought of a coherent plot.

55. Febvre and Martin, *The Coming of the Book*, p. 186. This amounted to no less than 35,000 editions produced in no fewer than 236 towns. As early as 1480, presses existed in more than 110 towns, of which 50 were in today's Italy, 30 in Germany, 9 in France, 8 each in Holland and Spain, 5 each in Belgium and Switzerland, 4 in England, 2 in Bohemia, and 1 in Poland. 'From that date it may be said of Europe that the printed book was in universal use.' (p. 182).

150,000,000 and 200,000,000.[56] 'From early on . . . the printing shops looked more like modern workshops than the monastic workrooms of the Middle Ages. In 1455, Fust and Schoeffer were already running a business geared to standardised production, and twenty years later large printing concerns were operating everywhere in all [sic] Europe.'[57] In a rather special sense, the book was the first modern-style mass-produced industrial commodity.[58] The sense I have in mind can be shown if we compare the book to other early industrial products, such as textiles, bricks, or sugar. For these commodities are *measured* in mathematical amounts (pounds or loads or pieces). A pound of sugar is simply a quantity, a convenient load, not an object in itself. The book, however – and here it prefigures the durables of our time – is a distinct, self-contained object, exactly reproduced on a large scale.[59] One pound of sugar flows into the next; each book has its own eremitic self-sufficiency. (Small wonder that libraries, personal collections of mass-produced commodities, were already a familiar sight, in urban centres like Paris, by the sixteenth century.)[60]

In this perspective, the newspaper is merely an 'extreme form' of the book, a book sold on a colossal scale, but of ephemeral popularity.

---

56. Ibid., p. 262. The authors comment that by the sixteenth century books were readily available to anyone who could read.

57. The great Antwerp publishing house of Plantin controlled, early in the sixteenth century, 24 presses with more than 100 workers in each shop. Ibid., p. 125.

58. This is one point solidly made amidst the vagaries of Marshall McLuhan's *Gutenberg Galaxy* (p. 125). One might add that if the book market was dwarfed by the markets in other commodities, its strategic role in the dissemination of ideas nonetheless made it of central importance to the development of modern Europe.

59. The principle here is more important than the scale. Until the nineteenth century, editions were still relatively small. Even Luther's Bible, an extraordinary bestseller, had only a 4,000-copy first edition. The unusually large first edition of Diderot's *Encyclopédie* numbered no more than 4,250. The average eighteenth-century run was less than 2,000. Febvre and Martin, *The Coming of the Book*, pp. 218–20. At the same time, the book was always distinguishable from other durables by its inherently limited market. Anyone with money can buy Czech cars; only Czech-readers will buy Czech-language books. The importance of this distinction will be considered below.

60. Furthermore, as early as the late fifteenth century the Venetian publisher Aldus had pioneered the portable 'pocket edition.'

Might we say: one-day best-sellers?[61] The obsolescence of the
newspaper on the morrow of its printing – curious that one of
the earlier mass-produced commodities should so prefigure the
inbuilt obsolescence of modern durables – nonetheless, for just this
reason, creates this extraordinary mass ceremony: the almost precisely
simultaneous consumption ('imagining') of the newspaper-as-fiction.
We know that particular morning and evening editions will overwhelmingly be consumed between this hour and that, only on this
day, not that. (Contrast sugar, the use of which proceeds in an
unclocked, continuous flow; it may go bad, but it does not go out of
date.) The significance of this mass ceremony – Hegel observed that
newspapers serve modern man as a substitute for morning prayers –
is paradoxical. It is performed in silent privacy, in the lair of the
skull.[62] Yet each communicant is well aware that the ceremony he
performs is being replicated simultaneously by thousands (or millions) of others of whose existence he is confident, yet of whose
identity he has not the slightest notion. Furthermore, this ceremony
is incessantly repeated at daily or half-daily intervals throughout the
calendar. What more vivid figure for the secular, historically clocked,
imagined community can be envisioned?[63] At the same time, the
newspaper reader, observing exact replicas of his own paper being
consumed by his subway, barbershop, or residential neighbours, is
continually reassured that the imagined world is visibly rooted in

---

61. As the case of *Semarang Hitam* shows, the two kinds of best-sellers used to be
more closely linked than they are today. Dickens too serialized his popular novels in
popular newspapers.

62. 'Printed materials encouraged silent adherence to causes whose advocates
could not be located in any one parish and who addressed an invisible public from afar.'
Elizabeth L. Eisenstein, 'Some Conjectures about the Impact of Printing on Western
Society and Thought,' *Journal of Modern History*, 40: 1 (March 1968), p. 42.

63. Writing of the relationship between the material anarchy of middle-class
society and an abstract political state-order, Nairn observes that 'the representative
mechanism converted real class inequality into the abstract egalitarianism of citizens,
individual egotisms into an impersonal collective will, what would otherwise be chaos
into a new state legitimacy.' *The Break-up of Britain*, p. 24. No doubt. But the
representative mechanism (elections?) is a rare and moveable feast. The generation
of the impersonal will is, I think, better sought in the diurnal regularities of the
imagining life.

everyday life. As with *Noli Me Tangere*, fiction seeps quietly and continuously into reality, creating that remarkable confidence of community in anonymity which is the hallmark of modern nations.

Before proceeding to a discussion of the specific origins of nationalism, it may be useful to recapitulate the main propositions put forward thus far. Essentially, I have been arguing that the very possibility of imagining the nation only arose historically when, and where, three fundamental cultural conceptions, all of great antiquity, lost their axiomatic grip on men's minds. The first of these was the idea that a particular script-language offered privileged access to ontological truth, precisely because it was an inseparable part of that truth. It was this idea that called into being the great transcontinental sodalities of Christendom, the Islamic Ummah, and the rest. Second was the belief that society was naturally organized around and under high centres – monarchs who were persons apart from other human beings and who ruled by some form of cosmological (divine) dispensation. Human loyalties were necessarily hierarchical and centripetal because the ruler, like the sacred script, was a node of access to being and inherent in it. Third was a conception of temporality in which cosmology and history were indistinguishable, the origins of the world and of men essentially identical. Combined, these ideas rooted human lives firmly in the very nature of things, giving certain meaning to the everyday fatalities of existence (above all death, loss, and servitude) and offering, in various ways, redemption from them.

The slow, uneven decline of these interlinked certainties, first in Western Europe, later elsewhere, under the impact of economic change, 'discoveries' (social and scientific), and the development of increasingly rapid communications, drove a harsh wedge between cosmology and history. No surprise then that the search was on, so to speak, for a new way of linking fraternity, power and time meaningfully together. Nothing perhaps more precipitated this search, nor made it more fruitful, than print-capitalism, which made it possible for rapidly growing numbers of people to think about themselves, and to relate themselves to others, in profoundly new ways.

3

The Origins of
National Consciousness

If the development of print-as-commodity is the key to the generation of wholly new ideas of simultaneity, still, we are simply at the point where communities of the type 'horizontal-secular, transverse-time' become possible. Why, within that type, did the nation become so popular? The factors involved are obviously complex and various. But a strong case can be made for the primacy of capitalism.

As already noted, at least 20,000,000 books had already been printed by 1500,[1] signalling the onset of Benjamin's 'age of mechanical reproduction.' If manuscript knowledge was scarce and arcane lore, print knowledge lived by reproducibility and dissemination.[2] If, as Febvre and Martin believe, possibly as many as 200,000,000 volumes had been manufactured by 1600, it is no wonder that Francis Bacon believed that print had changed 'the appearance and state of the world.'[3]

One of the earlier forms of capitalist enterprise, book-publishing

.

---

1. The population of that Europe where print was then known was about 100,000,000. Febvre and Martin, *The Coming of the Book*, pp. 248–49.

2. Emblematic is Marco Polo's *Travels*, which remained largely unknown till its first printing in 1559. Polo, *Travels*, p. xiii.

3. Quoted in Eisenstein, 'Some Conjectures,' p. 56.

felt all of capitalism's restless search for markets. The early printers established branches all over Europe: 'in this way a veritable "international" of publishing houses, which ignored national [sic] frontiers, was created.'[4] And since the years 1500–1550 were a period of exceptional European prosperity, publishing shared in the general boom. 'More than at any other time' it was 'a great industry under the control of wealthy capitalists.'[5] Naturally, 'booksellers were primarily concerned to make a profit and to sell their products, and consequently they sought out first and foremost those works which were of interest to the largest possible number of their contemporaries.'[6]

The initial market was literate Europe, a wide but thin stratum of Latin-readers. Saturation of this market took about a hundred and fifty years. The determinative fact about Latin – aside from its sacrality – was that it was a language of bilinguals. Relatively few were born to speak it and even fewer, one imagines, dreamed in it. In the sixteenth century the proportion of bilinguals within the total population of Europe was quite small; very likely no larger than the proportion in the world's population today, and – proletarian internationalism notwithstanding – in the centuries to come. Then and now the bulk of mankind is monoglot. The logic of capitalism thus meant that once the elite Latin market was saturated, the potentially huge markets represented by the monoglot masses would beckon. To be sure, the Counter-Reformation encouraged a temporary resurgence of Latin-publishing, but by the mid-seventeenth century the movement was in decay, and fervently Catholic libraries replete. Meantime, a Europe-wide shortage of money made printers think more and more of peddling cheap editions in the vernaculars.[7]

---

4. Febvre and Martin, *The Coming of the Book*, p. 122. (The original text, however, speaks simply of 'par-dessus les frontières.' *L'Apparition*, p. 184.)

5. Ibid., p. 187. The original text speaks of 'puissants' (powerful) rather than 'wealthy' capitalists. *L'Apparition*, p. 281.

6. 'Hence the introduction of printing was in this respect a stage on the road to our present society of mass consumption and standardisation.' Ibid., pp. 259–60. (The original text has 'une civilisation de masse et de standardisation,' which may be better rendered 'standardised, mass civilization.' *L'Apparition*, p. 394).

7. Ibid., p. 195.

The revolutionary vernacularizing thrust of capitalism was given further impetus by three extraneous factors, two of which contributed directly to the rise of national consciousness. The first, and ultimately the least important, was a change in the character of Latin itself. Thanks to the labours of the Humanists in reviving the broad literature of pre-Christian antiquity and spreading it through the print-market, a new appreciation of the sophisticated stylistic achievements of the ancients was apparent among the trans-European intelligentsia. The Latin they now aspired to write became more and more Ciceronian, and, by the same token, increasingly removed from ecclesiastical and everyday life. In this way it acquired an esoteric quality quite different from that of Church Latin in mediaeval times. For the older Latin was not arcane because of its subject matter or style, but simply because it was written at all, i.e. because of its status as *text*. Now it became arcane because of what was written, because of the language-in-itself.

Second was the impact of the Reformation, which, at the same time, owed much of its success to print-capitalism. Before the age of print, Rome easily won every war against heresy in Western Europe because it always had better internal lines of communication than its challengers. But when in 1517 Martin Luther nailed his theses to the chapel-door in Wittenberg, they were printed up in German translation, and 'within 15 days [had been] seen in every part of the country.'[8] In the two decades 1520–1540 three times as many books were published in German as in the period 1500–1520, an astonishing transformation to which Luther was absolutely central. His works represented no less than one third of *all* German-language books sold between 1518 and 1525. Between 1522 and 1546, a total of 430 editions (whole or partial) of his Biblical translations appeared. 'We have here for the first time a truly mass readership and a popular literature within everybody's reach.'[9] In effect, Luther became the first best-selling author *so known*. Or, to put it another way, the first writer who could 'sell' his *new* books on the basis of his name.[10]

---

8. Ibid., pp. 289–90.
9. Ibid., pp. 291–95.
10. From this point it was only a step to the situation in seventeenth-century

Where Luther led, others quickly followed, opening the colossal religious propaganda war that raged across Europe for the next century. In this titanic 'battle for men's minds', Protestantism was always fundamentally on the offensive, precisely because it knew how to make use of the expanding vernacular print-market being created by capitalism, while the Counter-Reformation defended the citadel of Latin. The emblem for this is the Vatican's *Index Librorum Prohibitorum* – to which there was no Protestant counterpart – a novel catalogue made necessary by the sheer volume of printed subversion. Nothing gives a better sense of this siege mentality than François I's panicked 1535 ban on the printing of *any* books in his realm – on pain of death by hanging! The reason for both the ban and its unenforceability was that by then his realm's eastern borders were ringed with Protestant states and cities producing a massive stream of smugglable print. To take Calvin's Geneva alone: between 1533 and 1540 only 42 editions were published there, but the numbers swelled to 527 between 1550 and 1564, by which latter date no less than 40 separate printing-presses were working overtime.[11]

The coalition between Protestantism and print-capitalism, exploiting cheap popular editions, quickly created large new reading publics – not least among merchants and women, who typically knew little or no Latin – and simultaneously mobilized them for politico-religious purposes. Inevitably, it was not merely the Church that was shaken to its core. The same earthquake produced Europe's first important non-dynastic, non-city states in the Dutch Republic and the Commonwealth of the Puritans. (François I's panic was as much political as religious.)

Third was the slow, geographically uneven, spread of particular vernaculars as instruments of administrative centralization by certain well-positioned would-be absolutist monarchs. Here it is useful to remember that the universality of Latin in mediaeval Western Europe never corresponded to a universal political system. The

---

France where Corneille, Molière, and La Fontaine could sell their manuscript tragedies and comedies directly to publishers, who bought them as excellent investments in view of their authors' market reputations. Ibid., p. 161.

11. Ibid., pp. 310–15.

contrast with Imperial China, where the reach of the mandarinal bureaucracy and of painted characters largely coincided, is instructive. In effect, the political fragmentation of Western Europe after the collapse of the Western Empire meant that no sovereign could monopolize Latin and make it his-and-only-his language-of-state, and thus Latin's religious authority never had a true political analogue.

The birth of administrative vernaculars predated both print and the religious upheaval of the sixteenth century, and must therefore be regarded (at least initially) as an independent factor in the erosion of the sacred imagined community. At the same time, nothing suggests that any deep-seated ideological, let alone proto-national, impulses underlay this vernacularization where it occurred. The case of 'England' – on the northwestern periphery of Latin Europe – is here especially enlightening. Prior to the Norman Conquest, the language of the court, literary and administrative, was Anglo-Saxon. For the next century and a half virtually all royal documents were composed in Latin. Between about 1200 and 1350 this state-Latin was superseded by Norman French. In the meantime, a slow fusion between this language of a foreign ruling class and the Anglo-Saxon of the subject population produced Early English. The fusion made it possible for the new language to take its turn, after 1362, as the language of the courts – and for the opening of Parliament. Wycliffe's vernacular *manuscript* Bible followed in 1382.[12] It is essential to bear in mind that this sequence was a series of 'state,' not 'national,' languages; and that the state concerned covered at various times not only today's England and Wales, but also portions of Ireland, Scotland *and France*. Obviously, huge elements of the subject populations knew little or nothing of Latin, Norman French, or Early English.[13] Not till almost a century *after* Early English's political enthronement was London's power swept out of 'France'.

On the Seine, a similar movement took place, if at a slower pace.

---

12. Seton-Watson, *Nations and States*, pp. 28–29; Bloch, *Feudal Society*, I, p. 75.

13. We should not assume that administrative vernacular unification was immediately or fully achieved. It is unlikely that the Guyenne ruled from London was ever primarily administered in Early English.

As Bloch wryly puts it, 'French, that is to say a language which, since it was regarded as merely a corrupt form of Latin, took several centuries to raise itself to literary dignity',[14] only became the official language of the courts of justice in 1539, when François I issued the Edict of Villers-Cotterêts.[15] In other dynastic realms Latin survived much longer – under the Habsburgs well into the nineteenth century. In still others, 'foreign' vernaculars took over: in the eighteenth century the languages of the Romanov court were French and German.[16]

In every instance, the 'choice' of language appears as a gradual, unselfconscious, pragmatic, not to say haphazard development. As such, it was utterly different from the selfconscious language policies pursued by nineteenth-century dynasts confronted with the rise of hostile popular linguistic-nationalisms. (See below, Chapter 6). One clear sign of the difference is that the old administrative languages were *just that*: languages used by and for officialdoms for their own inner convenience. There was no idea of systematically imposing the language on the dynasts' various subject populations.[17] Nonetheless, the elevation of these vernaculars to the status of languages-of-power, where, in one sense, they were competitors with Latin (French in Paris, [Early] English in London), made its own contribution to the decline of the imagined community of Christendom.

At bottom, it is likely that the esotericization of Latin, the Reformation, and the haphazard development of administrative vernaculars are significant, in the present context, primarily in a negative sense – in their contributions to the dethronement of Latin. It is quite possible to conceive of the emergence of the new imagined national communities without any one, perhaps all, of them being present. What, in a positive sense, made the new communities imaginable was a half-fortuitous, but explosive, interaction between

---

14. Bloch, *Feudal Society*, I, p. 98.
15. Seton-Watson, *Nations and States*, p. 48.
16. Ibid., p. 83.
17. An agreeable confirmation of this point is provided by François I, who, as we have seen, banned all printing of books in 1535 and made French the language of his courts four years later!

a system of production and productive relations (capitalism), a technology of communications (print), and the fatality of human linguistic diversity.[18]

The element of fatality is essential. For whatever superhuman feats capitalism was capable of, it found in death and languages two tenacious adversaries.[19] Particular languages can die or be wiped out, but there was and is no possibility of humankind's general linguistic unification. Yet this mutual incomprehensibility was historically of only slight importance until capitalism and print created monoglot mass reading publics.

While it is essential to keep in mind an idea of fatality, in the sense of a *general* condition of irremediable linguistic diversity, it would be a mistake to equate this fatality with that common element in nationalist ideologies which stresses the primordial fatality of *particular* languages and their association with *particular* territorial units. The essential thing is the *interplay* between fatality, technology, and capitalism. In pre-print Europe, and, of course, elsewhere in the world, the diversity of spoken languages, those languages that for their speakers were (and are) the warp and woof of their lives, was immense; so immense, indeed, that had print-capitalism sought to exploit each potential oral vernacular market, it would have remained a capitalism of petty proportions. But these varied idiolects were capable of being assembled, within definite limits, into print-languages far fewer in number. The very arbitrariness of any system of signs for sounds facilitated the assembling process.[20] (At the same time, the more ideographic the signs, the vaster the potential

---

18. It was not the first 'accident' of its kind. Febvre and Martin note that while a visible bourgeoisie already existed in Europe by the late thirteenth century, paper did not come into general use until the end of the fourteenth. Only paper's smooth plane surface made the mass reproduction of texts and pictures possible – and this did not occur for still another seventy-five years. But paper was not a European invention. It floated in from another history – China's – through the Islamic world. *The Coming of the Book*, pp. 22, 30, and 45.

19. We still have no giant multinationals in the world of publishing.

20. For a useful discussion of this point, see S. H. Steinberg, *Five Hundred Years of Printing*, chapter 5. That the sign *ough* is pronounced differently in the words although, bough, lough, rough, cough, and hiccough, shows both the idiolectic variety out of which the now-standard spelling of English emerged, and the ideographic quality of the final product.

assembling zone. One can detect a sort of descending hierarchy here from algebra through Chinese and English, to the regular syllabaries of French or Indonesian.) Nothing served to 'assemble' related vernaculars more than capitalism, which, within the limits imposed by grammars and syntaxes, created mechanically reproduced print-languages capable of dissemination through the market.[21]

These print-languages laid the bases for national consciousnesses in three distinct ways. First and foremost, they created unified fields of exchange and communication below Latin and above the spoken vernaculars. Speakers of the huge variety of Frenches, Englishes, or Spanishes, who might find it difficult or even impossible to understand one another in conversation, became capable of comprehending one another via print and paper. In the process, they gradually became aware of the hundreds of thousands, even millions, of people in their particular language-field, and at the same time that *only those* hundreds of thousands, or millions, so belonged. These fellow-readers, to whom they were connected through print, formed, in their secular, parti-cular, visible invisibility, the embryo of the nationally imagined community.

Second, print-capitalism gave a new fixity to language, which in the long run helped to build that image of antiquity so central to the subjective idea of the nation. As Febvre and Martin remind us, the printed book kept a permanent form, capable of virtually infinite reproduction, temporally and spatially. It was no longer subject to the individualizing and 'unconsciously modernizing' habits of monastic scribes. Thus, while twelfth-century French differed markedly from that written by Villon in the fifteenth, the rate of change slowed decisively in the sixteenth. 'By the 17th century languages in Europe had generally assumed their modern forms.'[22]

---

21. I say 'nothing served . . . more than capitalism' advisedly. Both Steinberg and Eisenstein come close to theomorphizing 'print' *qua* print as the genius of modern history. Febvre and Martin never forget that behind print stand printers and publishing firms. It is worth remembering in this context that although printing was invented first in China, possibly 500 years before its appearance in Europe, it had no major, let alone revolutionary impact – precisely because of the absence of capitalism there.

22. *The Coming of the Book*, p. 319. Cf. *L'Apparition*, p. 477: 'Au XVIIe siècle, les langues nationales apparaissent un peu partout cristallisées.'

To put it another way, for three centuries now these stabilized print-languages have been gathering a darkening varnish; the words of our seventeenth-century forebears are accessible to us in a way that to Villon his twelfth-century ancestors were not.

Third, print-capitalism created languages-of-power of a kind different from the older administrative vernaculars. Certain dialects inevitably were 'closer' to each print-language and dominated their final forms. Their disadvantaged cousins, still assimilable to the emerging print-language, lost caste, above all because they were unsuccessful (or only relatively successful) in insisting on their own print-form. 'Northwestern German' became Platt Deutsch, a largely spoken, thus sub-standard, German, because it was assimilable to print-German in a way that Bohemian spoken-Czech was not. High German, the King's English, and, later, Central Thai, were correspondingly elevated to a new politico-cultural eminence. (Hence the struggles in late-twentieth-century Europe by certain 'sub-' nationalities to change their subordinate status by breaking firmly into print – and radio.)

It remains only to emphasize that in their origins, the fixing of print-languages and the differentiation of status between them were largely unselfconscious processes resulting from the explosive interaction between capitalism, technology and human linguistic diversity. But as with so much else in the history of nationalism, once 'there,' they could become formal models to be imitated, and, where expedient, consciously exploited in a Machiavellian spirit. Today, the Thai government actively discourages attempts by foreign missionaries to provide its hill-tribe minorities with their own transcription-systems and to develop publications in their own languages: the same government is largely indifferent to what these minorities *speak*. The fate of the Turkic-speaking peoples in the zones incorporated into today's Turkey, Iran, Iraq, and the USSR is especially exemplary. A family of spoken languages, once everywhere assemblable, thus comprehensible, within an Arabic orthography, has lost that unity as a result of conscious manipulations. To heighten Turkish–Turkey's national consciousness at the expense of any wider Islamic identification, Atatürk imposed compulsory romanization.[23] The Soviet authorities followed suit, first with an anti-Islamic, anti-Persian compulsory romanization, then, in Stalin's 1930s, with a Russifying compulsory Cyrillicization.[24]

We can summarize the conclusions to be drawn from the argument thus far by saying that the convergence of capitalism and print technology on the fatal diversity of human language created the possibility of a new form of imagined community, which in its basic morphology set the stage for the modern nation. The potential stretch of these communities was inherently limited, and, at the same time, bore none but the most fortuitous relationship to existing political boundaries (which were, on the whole, the highwater marks of dynastic expansionisms).

Yet it is obvious that while today almost all modern self-conceived nations – and also nation-states – have 'national print-languages', many of them have these languages in common, and in others only a tiny fraction of the population 'uses' the national language in conversation or on paper. The nation-states of Spanish America or those of the 'Anglo-Saxon family' are conspicuous examples of the first outcome; many ex-colonial states, particularly in Africa, of the second. In other words, the concrete formation of contemporary nation-states is by no means isomorphic with the determinate reach of particular print-languages. To account for the discontinuity-in-connectedness between print-languages, national consciousness, and nation-states, it is necessary to turn to the large cluster of new political entities that sprang up in the Western hemisphere between 1776 and 1838, all of which self-consciously defined themselves as nations, and, with the interesting exception of Brazil, as (non–dynastic) republics. For not only were they historically the first such states to emerge on the world stage, and therefore inevitably provided the first real models of what such states should 'look like,' but their numbers and contemporary births offer fruitful ground for comparative enquiry.

23. Hans Kohn, *The Age of Nationalism*, p. 108. It is probably only fair to add that Kemal also hoped thereby to align Turkish nationalism with the modern, romanized civilization of Western Europe.
24. Seton-Watson, *Nations and States*, p. 317.

4

Creole Pioneers

The new American states of the late eighteenth and early nineteenth centuries are of unusual interest because it seems almost impossible to explain them in terms of two factors which, probably because they are readily derivable from the mid-century nationalisms of Europe, have dominated much provincial European thinking about the rise of nationalism.

In the first place, whether we think of Brazil, the USA, or the former colonies of Spain, language was not an element that differentiated them from their respective imperial metropoles. All, including the USA, were creole states, formed and led by people who shared a common language and common descent with those against whom they fought.[1] Indeed, it is fair to say that language was never even an issue in these early struggles for national liberation.

In the second place, there are serious reasons to doubt the applicability in much of the Western hemisphere of Nairn's otherwise persuasive thesis that:

> The arrival of nationalism in a distinctively modern sense was tied to
> the political baptism of the lower classes . . . Although sometimes

---

1. Creole (*Criollo*) – person of (at least theoretically) pure European descent but born in the Americas (and, by later extension, anywhere outside Europe).

hostile to democracy, nationalist movements have been invariably populist in outlook and sought to induct lower classes into political life. In its most typical version, this assumed the shape of a restless middle-class and intellectual leadership trying to sit up and channel popular class energies into support for the new states.[2]

At least in South and Central America, European-style 'middle classes' were still insignificant at the end of the eighteenth century. Nor was there much in the way of an intelligentsia. For 'in those quiet colonial days little reading interrupted the stately and snobbish rhythm of men's lives.'[3] As we have seen, the first Spanish-American novel was published only in 1816, well after the wars for independence had broken out. The evidence clearly suggests that leadership was held by substantial landowners, allied with a somewhat smaller number of merchants, and various types of professional (lawyers, military men, local and provincial functionaries).[4]

Far from seeking to 'induct the lower classes into political life,' one key factor initially spurring the drive for independence from Madrid, in such important cases as Venezuela, Mexico and Peru, was the *fear* of 'lower-class' political mobilizations: to wit, Indian or Negro-slave uprisings.[5] (This fear only increased when Hegel's 'secretary of the World-Spirit' conquered Spain in 1808, thereby depriving the creoles of peninsular military backup in case of emergency.) In Peru, memories of the great *jacquerie* led by Tupac Amarú (1740–1781) were still fresh.[6] In 1791, Toussaint L'Ouverture led an insurrection of black slaves that produced in 1804 the second independent republic in the Western hemisphere – and terrified the great slave-owning

---

2. *The Break-up of Britain*, p. 41.
3. Gerhard Masur, *Simón Bolívar*, p. 17.
4. Lynch, *The Spanish-American Revolutions*, pp. 14–17 and passim. These proportions arose from the fact that the more important commercial and administrative functions were largely monopolized by Spain-born Spaniards, while land-owning was fully open to creoles.
5. In this respect there are clear analogies with Boer nationalism a century later.
6. It is perhaps notable that Tupac Amarú did not entirely repudiate allegiance to the Spanish king. He and his followers (largely Indians, but also some whites and mestizos) rose in fury against the regime in Lima. Masur, *Bolívar*, p. 24.

planters of Venezuela.[7] When, in 1789, Madrid issued a new, more humane, slave law specifying in detail the rights and duties of masters and slaves, 'the creoles rejected state intervention on the grounds that slaves were prone to vice and independence [!], and were essential to the economy. In Venezuela – indeed all over the Spanish Caribbean – planters resisted the law and procured its suspension in 1794.'[8] The Liberator Bolívar himself once opined that a Negro revolt was 'a thousand times worse than a Spanish invasion.'[9] Nor should we forget that many leaders of the independence movement in the Thirteen Colonies were slave-owning agrarian magnates. Thomas Jefferson himself was among the Virginian planters who in the 1770s were enraged by the loyalist governor's proclamation freeing those slaves who broke with their seditious masters.[10] It is instructive that one reason why Madrid made a successful come-back in Venezuela from 1814–1816 and held remote Quito until 1820 was that she won the support of slaves in the former, and of Indians in the latter, in the struggle against insurgent creoles.[11] Moreover, the long duration of the continental struggle against Spain, by then a second-rate European power and one itself recently conquered, suggests a certain 'social thinness' to these Latin American independence movements.

Yet they *were* national independence movements. Bolívar came to change his mind about slaves,[12] and his fellow-liberator San Martín decreed in 1821 that 'in the future the aborigines shall not be called

---

7. Seton-Watson, *Nations and States*, p. 201.
8. Lynch, *The Spanish-American Revolutions*, p. 192.
9. Ibid., p. 224.
10. Edward S. Morgan, 'The Heart of Jefferson,' *The New York Review of Books*, August 17, 1978, p. 2.
11. Masur, *Bolívar*, p. 207; Lynch, *The Spanish-American Revolutions*, p. 237.
12. Not without some twists and turns. He freed his own slaves shortly after Venezuela's declaration of independence in 1810. When he fled to Haiti in 1816, he obtained military assistance from President Alexandre Pétion in return for a promise to end slavery in all territories liberated. The promise was redeemed in Caracas in 1818 – but it should be remembered that Madrid's successes in Venezuela between 1814 and 1816 were in part due to *her* emancipation of loyal slaves. When Bolívar became president of Gran Colombia (Venezuela, New Granada and Ecuador) in 1821, he asked for and obtained from Congress a law freeing the *sons* of slaves. He 'had not asked Congress to wipe out slavery because he did not want to incur the resentment of the big landowners.' Masur, *Bolívar*, pp. 125, 206–207, 329, and 388.

Indians or natives; they are children *and citizens* of Peru and they shall be known as Peruvians.'[13] (We might add: in spite of the fact that as yet print-capitalism had not reached these illiterates.)

Here then is the riddle: why was it precisely *creole* communities that developed so early conceptions of their nation-ness – *well before most of Europe?* Why did such colonial provinces, usually containing large, oppressed, non-Spanish-speaking populations, produce creoles who consciously redefined these populations as fellow-nationals? And Spain,[14] to whom they were, in so many ways, attached, as an enemy alien? Why did the Spanish-American Empire, which had existed calmly for almost three centuries, quite suddenly fragment into eighteen separate states?

The two factors most commonly adduced in explanation are the tightening of Madrid's control and the spread of the liberalizing ideas of the Enlightenment in the latter half of the eighteenth century. It is undoubtedly true that the policies pursued by the capable 'enlightened despot' Carlos III (r. 1759–1788) increasingly frustrated, angered, and alarmed the upper creole classes. In what has sometimes sardonically been called the second conquest of the Americas, Madrid imposed new taxes, made their collection more efficient, enforced metropolitan commercial monopolies, restricted intra-hemispheric trade to its own advantage, centralized administrative hierarchies, and promoted a heavy immigration of *peninsulares*.[15] Mexico, for example, in the early eighteenth century provided the Crown with an annual revenue of about 3,000,000 pesos. By the century's end, however, the sum had almost quintupled to 14,000,000, of which only 4,000,000 were used to defray the costs of local administration.[16] Parallel to this, the level of peninsular migration by the decade

---

13. Lynch, *The Spanish-American Revolutions*, p. 276. Emphasis added.

14. An anachronism. In the eighteenth century the usual term was still Las Españas [the Spains], not España [Spain]. Seton Watson, *Nations and States*, p. 53.

15. This new metropolitan aggressiveness was partly the product of Enlightenment doctrines, partly of chronic fiscal problems, and partly, after 1779, of war with England. Lynch, *The Spanish-American Revolutions*, pp. 4–17.

16. Ibid., p. 301. Four millions went to subsidize administration of other parts of Spanish America, while six millions were pure profit.

1780–1790 was five times as high as it had been between 1710–
1730.[17]

There is also no doubt that improving trans-Atlantic communications, and the fact that the various Americas shared languages and
cultures with their respective metropoles, meant a relatively rapid and
easy transmission of the new economic and political doctrines being
produced in Western Europe. The success of the Thirteen Colonies'
revolt at the end of the 1770s, and the onset of the French Revolution at the end of the 1780s, did not fail to exert a powerful influence.
Nothing confirms this 'cultural revolution' more than the pervasive
republicanism of the newly independent communities.[18] Nowhere was
any serious attempt made to recreate the dynastic principle in the
Americas, except in Brazil; even there, it would probably not have
been possible without the immigration in 1808 of the Portuguese
dynast himself, in flight from Napoléon. (He stayed there for 13 years,
and, on returning home, had his son crowned locally as Pedro I of
Brazil.)[19]

Yet the aggressiveness of Madrid and the spirit of liberalism, while
central to any understanding of the impulse of resistance in the Spanish
Americas, do not in themselves explain why entities like Chile,
Venezuela, and Mexico turned out to be emotionally plausible and

---

17. Ibid., p. 17.
18. The Constitution of the First Venezuelan Republic (1811) was in many places
borrowed verbatim from that of the United States. Masur, *Bolívar*, p. 131.
19. A superb, intricate analysis of the structural reasons for Brazilian exceptionalism can be found in José Murilo de Carvalho, 'Political Elites and State Building:
The Case of Nineteenth-Century Brazil', *Comparative Studies in Society and History*,
24:3 (1982), pp. 378–99. Two of the more important factors were: (1) Educational
differences. While 'twenty-three universities were scattered in what eventually would
become thirteen different countries' in the Spanish Americas, 'Portugal refused
systematically to allow the organization of any institution of higher learning in her
colonies, not considering as such the theological seminaries.' Higher education was
only to be had in Coimbra University, and thither, in the motherland, went the creole
elite's children, the great majority studying in the faculty of law. (2) Different career
possibilities for creoles. De Carvalho notes 'the much greater exclusion of American-
born Spaniards from the higher posts in the Spanish side [*sic*].' See also Stuart B.
Schwartz, 'The Formation of a Colonial Identity in Brazil,' chapter 2 in Nicholas
Canny and Anthony Pagden, eds, *Colonial Identity in the Atlantic World, 1500–1800*,
who notes in passing (p. 38) that 'no printing press operated in Brazil during the first
three centuries of the colonial era.'

politically viable,[20] nor why San Martín should decree that certain aborigines be identified by the neological 'Peruvians.' Nor, ultimately, do they account for the real sacrifices made. For while it is certain that the upper creole classes, *conceived as historical social formations*, did nicely out of independence over the long haul, many actual members of those classes *living* between 1808 and 1828 were financially ruined. (To take only one example: during Madrid's counter-offensive of 1814–16 'more than two-thirds of Venezuela's landowning families suffered heavy confiscations.'[21]) And just as many willingly gave up their lives for the cause. This willingness to sacrifice on the part of comfortable classes is food for thought.

What then? The beginnings of an answer lie in the striking fact that 'each of the new South American republics had been an administrative unit from the sixteenth to the eighteenth century.'[22] In this respect they foreshadowed the new states of Africa and parts of Asia in the mid twentieth century, and form a sharp contrast to the new European states of the late nineteenth and early twentieth centuries. The original shaping of the American administrative units was to some extent arbitrary and fortuitous, marking the spatial limits of particular military conquests. But, over time, they developed a firmer reality under the influence of geographic, political and economic factors. The very vastness of the Spanish American empire, the enormous variety of its soils and climates, and, above all, the immense difficulty of communications in a pre-industrial age, tended to give these units a self-contained character. (In the colonial era the sea journey from Buenos Aires to Acapulco took four months, and the return trip even longer; the overland trek from Buenos Aires to Santiago normally lasted two months, and that to Cartagena nine.[23]) In addition, Madrid's commercial policies had the effect of turning administrative units into separate economic zones. 'All competition

---

20. Much the same could be said of London's stance vis-à-vis the Thirteen Colonies, and of the ideology of the 1776 Revolution.
21. Lynch, *The Spanish-American Revolutions*, p. 208; cf. Masur, *Bolívar*, pp. 98–99 and 231.
22. Masur, *Bolívar*, p. 678.
23. Lynch, *The Spanish-American Revolutions*, pp. 25–26.

with the mother country was forbidden the Americans, and even the individual parts of the continent could not trade with each other. American goods en route from one side of America to the other had to travel circuitously through Spanish ports, and Spanish navigation had a monopoly on trade with the colonies.'[24] These experiences help to explain why 'one of the basic principles of the American revolution' was that of '*uti possidetis* by which each nation was to preserve the territorial status quo of 1810, the year when the movement for independence had been inaugurated.'[25] Their influence also doubtless contributed to the break-up of Bolívar's short-lived Gran Colombía and of the United Provinces of the Rio de la Plata into their older constituents (which today are known as Venezuela-Colombia-Ecuador and Argentina-Uruguay-Paraguay-Bolivia). None-theless, *in themselves*, market-zones, 'natural'-geographic or politico-administrative, do not create attachments. Who will willingly die for Comecon or the EEC?

To see how administrative units could, over time, come to be con-ceived as fatherlands, not merely in the Americas but in other parts of the world, one has to look at the ways in which administrative organizations create meaning. The anthropologist Victor Turner has written illuminatingly about the 'journey', between times, statuses and places, as a meaning-creating experience.[26] All such journeys require interpretation (for example, the journey from birth to death has given rise to various religious conceptions.) For our purposes here, the modal journey is the pilgrimage. It is not simply that in the minds of Christians, Muslims or Hindus the cities of Rome, Mecca, or Benares were the centres of sacred geographies, but that their centrality was experienced

---

24. Masur, *Bolívar*, p. 19. Naturally these measures were only partially enforceable, and a good deal of smuggling always went on.
    25. Ibid., p. 546.
    26. See his *The Forest of Symbols, Aspects of Ndembu Ritual*, especially the chapter 'Betwixt and Between: The Liminal Period in *Rites de Passage*.' For a later, more complex elaboration, see his *Dramas, Fields, and Metaphors, Symbolic Action in Human Society*, chapter 5 ('Pilgrimages as Social Processes') and 6 ('Passages, Margins, and Poverty: Religious Symbols of Communitas').

and 'realized' (in the stagecraft sense) by the constant flow of pilgrims moving towards them from remote and *otherwise unrelated* localities. Indeed, in some sense the outer limits of the old religious communities of the imagination were determined by which pilgrimages people made.[27] As noted earlier, the strange physical juxtaposition of Malays, Persians, Indians, Berbers and Turks in Mecca is something incomprehensible without an idea of their community in some form. The Berber encountering the Malay before the Kaaba must, as it were, ask himself: 'Why is this man doing what I am doing, uttering the same words that I am uttering, even though we can not talk to one another?' There is only one answer, once one has learnt it: 'Because *we . . . are Muslims*.' There was, to be sure, always a double aspect to the choreography of the great religious pilgrimages: a vast horde of illiterate vernacular-speakers provided the dense, physical reality of the ceremonial passage; while a small segment of literate bilingual adepts drawn from each vernacular community performed the unifying rites, interpreting to their respective followings the meaning of their collective motion.[28] In a pre-print age, the reality of the imagined religious community depended profoundly on countless, ceaseless travels. Nothing more impresses one about Western Christendom in its heyday than the uncoerced flow of faithful seekers from all over Europe, through the celebrated 'regional centres' of monastic learning, to Rome. These great Latin-speaking institutions drew together what today we would perhaps regard as Irishmen, Danes, Portuguese, Germans, and so forth, in communities whose sacred meaning was every day deciphered from their members' otherwise inexplicable juxtaposition in the refectory.

Though the religious pilgrimages are probably the most touching and

---

27. See Bloch, *Feudal Society*, I, p. 64.

28. There are obvious analogies here with the respective roles of bilingual intelligentsias and largely illiterate workers and peasants in the genesis of certain nationalist movements – prior to the coming of radio. Invented only in 1895, radio made it possible to bypass print and summon into being an aural representation of the imagined community where the printed page scarcely penetrated. Its role in the Vietnamese and Indonesian revolutions, and generally in mid-twentieth-century nationalisms, has been much underestimated and understudied.

grandiose journeys of the imagination, they had, and have, more modest and limited secular counterparts.[29] For our present purposes, the most important were the differing passages created by the rise of absolutizing monarchies, and, eventually, Europe-centred world-imperial states. The inner thrust of absolutism was to create a unified apparatus of power, controlled directly by, and loyal to, the ruler *over against* a decentralized, particularistic feudal nobility. Unification meant internal interchangeability of men and documents. Human interchangeability was fostered by the recruitment – naturally to varying extents – of *homines novi*, who, just for that reason, had no independent power of their own, and so could serve as emanations of their masters' wills.[30] Absolutist functionaries thus undertook journeys which were basically different from those of feudal nobles.[31] The difference can be represented schematically as follows: In the modal feudal journey, the heir of Noble A, on his father's death, moves up one step to take that father's place. This ascension requires a round-trip, to the centre for investiture, and then back home to the ancestral demesne. For the new functionary, however, things are more complex. Talent, not death, charts his course. He sees before him a summit rather than a centre. He travels up its corniches in a series of looping arcs which, he hopes, will become smaller and tighter as he nears the top. Sent out to township A at rank V, he may return to the capital at rank W; proceed to province B at rank X; continue to vice-royalty C at rank Y; and end his pilgrimage in the capital at rank Z. On this journey there is no assured resting-place; every pause is provisional. The last thing the functionary wants is to return home; for he *has* no home with any intrinsic value. And this: on his upward-spiralling road he encounters as eager fellow-pilgrims his functionary colleagues, from places and families he has scarcely heard

---

29. The 'secular pilgrimage' should not be taken merely as a fanciful trope. Conrad was being ironical, but also precise, when he described as 'pilgrims' the spectral agents of Léopold II in the heart of darkness.

30. Especially where: (a) monogamy was religiously and legally enforced; (b) primogeniture was the rule; (c) non-dynastic titles were both inheritable and conceptually and legally distinct from office-rank: i.e. where provincial aristocracies had significant independent power – England, as opposed to Siam.

31. See Bloch, *Feudal Society*, II, pp. 422ff.

of and surely hopes never to have to see. But in experiencing them as travelling-companions, a consciousness of connectedness ('Why are *we* . . . *here* . . . *together?*') emerges, above all when all share a single language-of-state. Then, if official A from province B administers province C, while official D from province C administers province B – a situation that absolutism begins to make likely – that experience of interchangeability requires its own explanation: the ideology of absolutism, which the new men themselves, as much as the sovereign, elaborate.

Documentary interchangeability, which reinforced human interchangeability, was fostered by the development of a standardized language-of-state. As the stately succession of Anglo-Saxon, Latin, Norman, and Early English in London from the eleventh through the fourteenth centuries demonstrates, *any* written language could, in principle, serve this function – provided it was given monopoly rights. (One could, however, argue that where vernaculars, rather than Latin, happened to hold the monopoly, a further centralizing function was achieved, by restricting the drift of one sovereign's officials to his rivals' machines: so to speak ensuring that Madrid's pilgrim-functionaries were not interchangeable with those of Paris.)

In principle, the extra-European expansion of the great kingdoms of early modern Europe should have simply extended the above model in the development of grand, transcontinental bureaucracies. But, in fact, this did not happen. The instrumental rationality of the absolutist apparatus – above all its tendency to recruit and promote on the basis of talent rather than of birth – operated only fitfully beyond the eastern shores of the Atlantic.[32]

The pattern is plain in the Americas. For example, of the 170 viceroys in Spanish America prior to 1813, only 4 were creoles. These figures are all the more startling if we note that in 1800 less than 5% of the 3,200,000 creole 'whites' in the Western Empire (imposed on about 13,700,000 indigenes) were Spain-born Spaniards. On the eve of

---

32. Obviously this rationality should not be exaggerated. The case of the United Kingdom, where Catholics were barred from office until 1829, is not unique. Can one doubt that this long exclusion played an important role in fostering Irish nationalism?

the revolution in Mexico, there was only one creole bishop, although creoles in the viceroyalty outnumbered *peninsulares* by 70 to 1.[33] And, needless to say, it was nearly unheard-of for a creole to rise to a position of official importance in Spain.[34] Moreover, the pilgrimages of creole functionaries were not merely vertically barred. If peninsular officials could travel the road from Zaragoza to Cartagena, Madrid, Lima, and again Madrid, the 'Mexican' or 'Chilean' creole typically served only in the territories of colonial Mexico or Chile: his lateral movement was as cramped as his vertical ascent. In this way, the apex of his looping climb, the highest administrative centre to which he could be assigned, was the capital of the imperial administrative unit in which he found himself.[35] Yet on this cramped pilgrimage he found travelling-companions, who came to sense that their fellowship was based not only on that pilgrimage's particular stretch, but on the shared fatality of trans-Atlantic birth. Even if he was born within one week of his father's

---

33. Lynch, *The Spanish-American Revolutions*, pp. 18–19, 298. Of the roughly 15,000 *peninsulares*, half were soldiers.

34. In the first decade of the nineteenth century there seem to have been about 400 South Americans resident in Spain at any one time. These included the 'Argentinian' San Martín, who was taken to Spain as a small boy, and spent the next 27 years there, entering the Royal Academy for noble youth, and playing a distinguished part in the armed struggle against Napoléon before returning to his homeland on hearing of its declaration of independence; and Bolívar, who for a time boarded in Madrid with Manuel Mello, 'American' lover of Queen Marie Louise. Masur describes him as belonging (*c.* 1805) to 'a group of young South Americans' who, like him, 'were rich, idle and in disfavour with the Court. The hatred and sense of inferiority felt by many Creoles for the mother country was in them developing into revolutionary impulses.' *Bolívar*, pp. 41–47, and 469–70 (San Martín).

35. Over time, military pilgrimages became as important as civilian. 'Spain had neither the money nor the manpower to maintain large garrisons of regular troops in America, and she relied chiefly on colonial militias, which from the mid-eighteenth century were expanded and reorganized.' (Ibid., p. 10). These militias were quite local, not interchangeable parts of a continental security apparatus. They played an increasingly critical role from the 1760s on, as British incursions multiplied. Bolívar's father had been a prominent militia commander, defending Venezuelan ports against the intruders. Bolívar himself served in his father's old unit as a teenager. (Masur, *Bolívar*, pp. 30 and 38). In this respect he was typical of many of the first-generation nationalist leaders of Argentina, Venezuela, and Chile. See Robert L. Gilmore, *Caudillism and Militarism in Venezuela, 1810–1910*, chapter 6 ['The Militia'] and 7 ['The Military'].

migration, the accident of birth in the Americas consigned him to subordination – even though in terms of language, religion, ancestry, or manners he was largely indistinguishable from the Spain-born Spaniard. There was nothing to be done about it: he was *irremediably* a creole. Yet how irrational his exclusion must have seemed! Nonetheless, hidden inside the irrationality was this logic: born in the Americas, he could not be a true Spaniard; *ergo*, born in Spain, the *peninsular* could not be a true American.[36]

What made the exclusion appear rational in the metropole? Doubtless the confluence of a time-honoured Machiavellism with the growth of conceptions of biological and ecological contamination that accompanied the planetary spread of Europeans and European power from the sixteenth century onwards. From the sovereign's angle of vision, the American creoles, with their ever-growing numbers and increasing local rootedness with each succeeding generation, presented a historically unique political problem. For the first time the metropoles had to deal with – for that era – vast numbers of 'fellow-Europeans' (over three million in the Spanish Americas by 1800) far outside Europe. If the indigenes were conquerable by arms and disease, and controllable by the mysteries of Christianity and a completely alien culture (as well as, for those days, an advanced political organization), the same was not true of the creoles, who had virtually the same relationship to arms, disease, Christianity and European culture as the metropolitans. In other words, in principle, they had readily at hand the political, cultural and military means for successfully asserting themselves. They constituted simultaneously a colonial community and an upper class. They were to be economically subjected and exploited, but they were also essential to the stability of the empire. One can see, in this light, a certain parallelism between the position of the creole

---

36. Notice the transformations that independence brought the Americans: first-generation immigrants now became 'lowest' rather than 'highest', i.e. the ones most contaminated by a fatal place of birth. Similar inversions occur in response to racism. 'Black blood' – *taint* of the tar-brush – came, under imperialism, to be seen as hopelessly contaminating for any 'white.' Today, in the United States at least, the 'mulatto' has entered the museum. The tiniest trace of 'black blood' makes one beautifully Black. Contrast Fermín's optimistic programme for miscegenation, and his absence of concern for the colour of the expected progeny.

magnates and of feudal barons, crucial to the sovereign's power, but also a menace to it. Thus the *peninsulares* dispatched as viceroys and bishops served the same functions as did the *homines novi* of the proto-absolutist bureaucracies.[37] Even if the viceroy was a grandee in his Andalusian home, here, 5,000 miles away, juxtaposed to the creoles, he was effectively a *homo novus* fully dependent on his metropolitan master. The tense balance between peninsular official and creole magnate was in this way an expression of the old policy of *divide et impera* in a new setting.

In addition, the growth of creole communities, mainly in the Americas, but also in parts of Asia and Africa, led inevitably to the appearance of Eurasians, Eurafricans, as well as Euramericans, not as occasional curiosities but as visible social groups. Their emergence permitted a style of thinking to flourish which foreshadows modern racism. Portugal, earliest of Europe's planetary conquerors, provides an apt illustration of this point. In the last decade of the fifteenth century Dom Manuel I could still 'solve' his 'Jewish question' by mass, forcible *conversion* – possibly the last European ruler to find this solution both satisfactory and 'natural'.[38] Less than a century later, however, one finds Alexandre Valignano, the great reorganizer of the Jesuit mission in Asia between 1574 and 1606, vehemently opposing the admission of Indians and Eurindians to the priesthood in these terms:[39]

> All these dusky races are very stupid and vicious, and of the basest spirits . . . As for the *mestiços* and *castiços*, we should receive either very few or none at all; especially with regard to the *mestiços*, since the more native blood they have, the more they resemble the Indians and the less they are esteemed by the Portuguese.

(Yet Valignano actively encouraged the admission of Japanese, Koreans, Chinese, and 'Indochinese' to the priestly function – perhaps

37. Given Madrid's deep concern that the management of the colonies be in trustworthy hands, 'it was axiomatic that the high posts be filled exclusively with native-born Spaniards'. Masur, *Bolívar*, p. 10.

38. Charles R. Boxer, *The Portuguese Seaborne Empire, 1415–1825*, p. 266.

39. Ibid., p. 252.

because in those zones mestizos had yet to appear in any numbers?) Similarly, the Portuguese Franciscans in Goa violently opposed admission of creoles to the order, alleging that 'even if born of pure white parents [they] have been suckled by Indian ayahs in their infancy and thus had their blood contaminated for life.'[40] Boxer shows that 'racial' bars and exclusions increased markedly during the seventeenth and eighteenth centuries by comparison with earlier practice. To this malignant tendency the revival of large-scale slavery (for the first time in Europe since antiquity), which was pioneered by Portugal after 1510, made its own massive contribution. Already in the 1550s, 10% of Lisbon's population were slaves; by 1800 there were close to a million slaves among the 2,500,000 or so inhabitants of Portugal's Brazil.[41]

Indirectly, the Enlightenment also influenced the crystallization of a fatal distinction between metropolitans and creoles. In the course of his twenty-two years in power (1755–1777), the enlightened autocrat Pombal not only expelled the Jesuits from Portuguese domains, but made it a criminal offence to call 'coloured' subjects by offensive names, such as 'nigger' or 'mestiço' [sic]. But he justified this decree by citing ancient Roman conceptions of imperial citizenship, not the doctrines of the *philosophes*.[42] More typically, the writings of Rousseau and Herder, which argued that climate and 'ecology' had a constitutive impact on culture and character, exerted wide influence.[43] It was only too easy from there to make the convenient, vulgar deduction that creoles, born in a savage hemisphere, were by nature different from, and inferior to, the metropolitans – and thus unfit for higher office.[44]

---

40. Ibid., p. 253.

41. Rona Fields, *The Portuguese Revolution and the Armed Forces Movement*, p. 15.

42. Boxer, *The Portuguese Seaborne Empire*, pp. 257–58.

43. Kemiläinen, *Nationalism*, pp. 72–73.

44. I have emphasized here the racialist distinctions drawn between *peninsulares* and creoles because the main topic under review is the rise of creole nationalism. This should not be understood as minimizing the parallel growth of creole racism towards mestizos, Negroes, and Indians; nor the willingness of an unthreatened metropole to protect (up to a certain point) these unfortunates.

Our attention thus far has been focussed on the worlds of functionaries in the Americas – strategically important, but still small worlds. Moreover, they were worlds which, with their conflicts between *peninsulares* and creoles, predated the appearance of American national consciousnesses at the end of the eighteenth century. Cramped viceregal pilgrimages had no decisive consequences until their territorial stretch could be imagined as nations, in other words until the arrival of print-capitalism.

Print itself spread early to New Spain, but for two centuries it remained under the tight control of crown and church. Till the end of the seventeenth century, presses existed only in Mexico City and Lima, and their output was almost exclusively ecclesiastical. In Protestant North America printing scarcely existed at all in that century. In the course of the eighteenth, however, a virtual revolution took place. Between 1691 and 1820, no less than 2,120 'newspapers' were published, of which 461 lasted more than ten years.[45]

The figure of Benjamin Franklin is indelibly associated with creole nationalism in the northern Americas. But the importance of his trade may be less apparent. Once again, Febvre and Martin are enlightening. They remind us that 'printing did not really develop in [North] America during the eighteenth century until printers discovered a new source of income – the newspaper.'[46] Printers starting new presses always included a newspaper in their productions, to which they were usually the main, even the sole, contributor. Thus the printer-journalist was initially an essentially North American phenomenon. Since the main problem facing the printer-journalist was reaching readers, there developed an alliance with the post-master so intimate that often each became the other. Hence, the printer's office emerged as the key to North American communications and community intellectual life. In Spanish America, albeit more slowly and intermittently, similar processes

---

45. Febvre and Martin, *The Coming of the Book*, pp. 208–11.
46. Ibid., p. 211.

produced, in the second half of the eighteenth century, the first local presses.[47]

What were the characteristics of the first American newspapers, North or South? They began essentially as appendages of the market. Early gazettes contained – aside from news about the metropole – commercial news (when ships would arrive and depart, what prices were current for what commodities in what ports), as well as colonial political appointments, marriages of the wealthy, and so forth. In other words, what brought together, on the same page, *this* marriage with *that* ship, *this* price with *that* bishop, was the very structure of the colonial administration and market-system itself. In this way, the newspaper of Caracas quite naturally, and even apolitically, created an imagined community among a specific assemblage of fellow-readers, to whom *these* ships, brides, bishops and prices belonged. In time, of course, it was only to be expected that political elements would enter in.

One fertile trait of such newspapers was always their provinciality. A colonial creole might read a Madrid newspaper if he got the chance (but it would say nothing about his world), but many a peninsular official, living down the same street, would, if he could help it, *not* read the Caracas production. An asymmetry infinitely replicable in other colonial situations. Another such trait was plurality. The Spanish-American journals that developed towards the end of the eighteenth century were written in full awareness of provincials in worlds parallel to their own. The newspaper-readers of Mexico City, Buenos Aires, and Bogota, even if they did not read each other's newspapers, were nonetheless quite conscious of their existence. Hence a well-known doubleness in early Spanish-American nationalism, its alternating grand stretch and particularistic localism. The fact that early Mexican nationalists wrote of themselves as *nosotros los Americanos* and of their country as *nuestra América*, has been interpreted as revealing the vanity of the local creoles who, because Mexico was far the most valuable of Spain's American possessions, saw themselves as the centre of the New World.[48] But, in

---

47. Franco, *An Introduction*, p. 28.
48. Lynch, *The Spanish-American Revolutions*, p. 33.

fact, people all over Spanish America thought of themselves as 'Americans,' since this term denoted precisely the shared fatality of extra-Spanish birth.[49]

At the same time, we have seen that the very conception of the newspaper implies the refraction of even 'world events' into a specific imagined world of vernacular readers; and also how important to that imagined community is an idea of steady, solid simultaneity through time. Such a simultaneity the immense stretch of the Spanish American Empire, and the isolation of its component parts, made difficult to imagine.[50] Mexican creoles might learn months later of developments in Buenos Aires, but it would be through Mexican newspapers, not those of the Rio de la Plata; and the events would appear as 'similar to' rather than 'part of' events in Mexico.

In this sense, the 'failure' of the Spanish-American experience to generate a permanent Spanish-America-wide nationalism reflects both the general level of development of capitalism and technology in the late eighteenth century and the 'local' backwardness of Spanish capitalism and technology in relation to the administrative stretch of the empire. (The world-historical era in which each nationalism is born probably has a significant impact on its scope. Is Indian nationalism not inseparable from colonial administrative-market unification, after the Mutiny, by the most formidable and advanced of the imperial powers?)

The Protestant, English-speaking creoles to the north were much more favourably situated for realizing the idea of 'America' and indeed eventually succeeded in appropriating the everyday title of 'Americans'. The original Thirteen Colonies comprised an area

---

49. 'A peon came to complain that the Spanish overseer of his estancia had beaten him. San Martín was indignant, but it was a nationalist rather than socialist indignation. "What do you think? After three years of revolution, a *maturrango* [vulg., Peninsular Spaniard] dares to raise his hand against an American!"' Ibid., p. 87.

50. A spell-binding evocation of the remoteness and isolation of the Spanish-American populations is Márquez's picture of the fabulous Macondo in *One Hundred Years of Solitude*.

smaller than Venezuela, and one third the size of Argentina.[51] Bunched geographically together, their market-centres in Boston, New York, and Philadelphia were readily accessible to one another, and their populations were relatively tightly linked by print as well as commerce. The 'United States' could gradually multiply in numbers over the next 183 years, as old and new populations moved westwards out of the old east coast core. Yet even in the case of the USA there are elements of comparative 'failure' or shrinkage – non-absorption of English-speaking Canada, Texas's decade of independent sovereignty (1835–46). Had a sizeable English-speaking community existed in California in the eighteenth century, is it not likely that an independent state would have arisen there to play Argentina to the Thirteen Colonies' Peru? Even in the USA, the affective bonds of nationalism were elastic enough, combined with the rapid expansion of the western frontier and the contradictions generated between the economies of North and South, to precipitate a war of secession *almost a century after the Declaration of Independence*; and this war today sharply reminds us of those that tore Venezuela and Ecuador off from Gran Colombía, and Uruguay and Paraguay from the United Provinces of the Rio de la Plata.[52]

By way of provisional conclusion, it may be appropriate to re-emphasize the limited and specific thrust of the argument so far. It is intended less to explain the socio-economic bases of anti-metropolitan resistance in the Western hemisphere between say, 1760 and 1830, than why the resistance was conceived in plural, 'national' forms – rather than in others. The economic interests at stake are well-known and obviously of fundamental importance.

---

51. The total area of the Thirteen Colonies was 322,497 square miles. That of Venezuela was 352,143; of Argentina, 1,072,067; and of Spanish South America, 3,417,625 square miles.

52. Paraguay forms a case of exceptional interest. Thanks to the relatively benevolent dictatorship established there by the Jesuits early in the seventeenth century, the indigenes were better treated than elsewhere in Spanish America, and Guaraní achieved the status of print-language. The Crown's expulsion of the Jesuits from Spanish America in 1767 brought the territory into the Rio de la Plata, but very late in the day, and for little more than a generation. See Seton-Watson, *Nations and States*, pp. 200–201.

Liberalism and the Enlightenment clearly had a powerful impact, above all in providing an arsenal of ideological criticisms of imperial and *anciens régimes*. What I am proposing is that neither economic interest, Liberalism, nor Enlightenment could, or did, create *in themselves* the *kind*, or shape, of imagined community to be defended from these regimes' depredations; to put it another way, none provided the framework of a new consciousness – the scarcely-seen periphery of its vision – as opposed to centre-field objects of its admiration or disgust.[53] In accomplishing *this* specific task, pilgrim creole functionaries and provincial creole printmen played the decisive historic role.

---

53. It is instructive that the Declaration of Independence in 1776 speaks only of 'the people', while the word 'nation' makes its debut only in the Constitution of 1789. Kemiläinen, *Nationalism*, p. 105.

5

Old Languages, New Models

The close of the era of successful national liberation movements in the Americas coincided rather closely with the onset of the age of nationalism in Europe. If we consider the character of these newer nationalisms which, between 1820 and 1920, changed the face of the Old World, two striking features mark them off from their ancestors. First, in almost all of them 'national print-languages' were of central ideological and political importance, whereas Spanish and English were never issues in the revolutionary Americas. Second, all were able to work from visible models provided by their distant, and after the convulsions of the French Revolution, not so distant, predecessors. The 'nation' thus became something capable of being consciously aspired to from early on, rather than a slowly sharpening frame of vision. Indeed, as we shall see, the 'nation' proved an invention on which it was impossible to secure a patent. It became available for pirating by widely different, and sometimes unexpected, hands. In this chapter, therefore, the analytical focus will be on print-language and piracy.

In blithe disregard of some obvious extra-European facts, the great Johann Gottfried von Herder (1744–1803) had declared, towards the end of the eighteenth century, that: 'Denn *jedes* Volk ist Volk; es hat *seine* National Bildung wie *seine* Sprache.'[1] This splendidly *eng*-European conception of nation-ness as linked to a private-property language had wide influence in nineteenth-century Europe and, more narrowly, on subsequent theorizing about the nature of nationalism. What were the origins of this dream? Most probably, they lay in the profound shrinkage of the European world in time and space that began already in the fourteenth century, and was caused initially by the Humanists' excavations and later, paradoxically enough, by Europe's planetary expansion.

As Auerbach so well expresses it:[2]

> With the first dawn of humanism, there began to be a sense that the events of classical history and legend and also those of the Bible were not separated from the present simply by an extent of time but also by *completely different conditions of life*. Humanism with its program of renewal of antique forms of life and expression creates a historical perspective in depth such as no previous epoch known to us possessed: the humanists see antiquity in historical depth, and, against that background, the dark epochs of the intervening Middle Ages. . . . [This made impossible] re-establishing the autarchic life natural to antique culture or the historical naiveté of the twelfth and thirteenth centuries.

The growth of what might be called 'comparative history' led in time to the hitherto unheard-of conception of a 'modernity' explicitly juxtaposed to 'antiquity,' and by no means necessarily to the latter's advantage. The issue was fiercely joined in the 'Battle of Ancients and Moderns' which dominated French intellectual life in the last quarter of the seventeenth century.[3] To quote Auerbach again, 'Under Louis XIV the French had the courage to consider their own

---

1. Kemiläinen, *Nationalism*, p. 42. Emphases added.
2. *Mimesis*, p. 282. Emphasis added.
3. The battle opened in 1689 when the 59-year old Charles Perrault published his poem *Siècle de Louis le Grand*, which argued that the arts and sciences had come to their full flowering in his own time and place.

culture a valid model on a par with that of the ancients, and they imposed this view upon the rest of Europe.'[4]

In the course of the sixteenth century, Europe's 'discovery' of grandiose civilizations hitherto only dimly rumoured – in China, Japan, Southeast Asia, and the Indian subcontinent – or completely unknown – Aztec Mexico and Incan Peru – suggested an irremediable human pluralism. Most of these civilizations had developed quite separate from the known history of Europe, Christendom, Antiquity, indeed man: their genealogies lay outside of and were unassimilable to Eden. (Only homogeneous, empty time would offer them accommodation.) The impact of the 'discoveries' can be gauged by the peculiar geographies of the imaginary polities of the age. More's *Utopia*, which appeared in 1516, purported to be the account of a sailor, encountered by the author in Antwerp, who had participated in Amerigo Vespucci's 1497–1498 expedition to the Americas. Francis Bacon's *New Atlantis* (1626) was perhaps new above all because it was situated in the Pacific Ocean. Swift's magnificent Island of the Houyhnhnms (1726) came with a bogus map of its South Atlantic location. (The meaning of these settings may be clearer if one considers how unimaginable it would be to place Plato's Republic on any map, sham or real.) All these tongue-in-cheek utopias, 'modelled' on real discoveries, are depicted, not as lost Edens, but as *contemporary* societies. One could argue that they had to be, since they were composed as criticisms *of* contemporary societies, and the discoveries had ended the necessity for seeking models in a vanished antiquity.[5] In the wake of the utopians came the luminaries of the Enlightenment, Vico, Montesquieu, Voltaire, and Rousseau, who increasingly exploited a 'real' non-Europe for a barrage of subversive writings directed against current European social and political institutions. In effect, it became possible to think of Europe as only one

---

4. *Mimesis*, p. 343. Notice that Auerbach says 'culture', not 'language'. We should also be chary of attributing 'nation-ness' to 'their own.'

5. Similarly, there is a nice contrast between the two famous Mongols of English drama. Marlowe's *Tamburlaine the Great* (1587–1588) describes a famous dynast dead since 1407. Dryden's *Aurangzeb* (1676) depicts a contemporary reigning Emperor (1658–1707).

among many civilizations, and not necessarily the Chosen or the best.[6]

In due course, discovery and conquest also caused a revolution in European ideas about language. From the earliest days, Portuguese, Dutch, and Spanish seamen, missionaries, merchants and soldiers had, for practical reasons – navigation, conversion, commerce and war – gathered word-lists of non-European languages to be assembled in simple lexicons. But it was only in the later eighteenth century that the scientific comparative study of languages really got under way. Out of the English conquest of Bengal came William Jones's pioneering investigations of Sanskrit (1786), which led to a growing realization that Indic civilization was far older than that of Greece or Judaea. Out of Napoléon's Egyptian expedition came Jean Champollion's decipher-ment of hieroglyphics (1835), which pluralized that extra-European antiquity.[7] Advances in Semitics undermined the idea that Hebrew was either uniquely ancient or of divine provenance. Once again, genea-logies were being conceived which could only be accommodated by homogeneous, empty time. 'Language became less of a continuity between an outside power and the human speaker than an internal field created and accomplished by language users among themselves.'[8] Out of these discoveries came philology, with its studies of comparative grammar, classification of languages into families, and reconstructions by scientific reasoning of 'proto-languages' out of oblivion. As Hobs-bawm rightly observes, here was 'the first science which regarded evolution as its very core.'[9]

From this point on the old sacred languages – Latin, Greek, and Hebrew – were forced to mingle on equal ontological footing with a motley plebeian crowd of vernacular rivals, in a movement which complemented their earlier demotion in the market-place by print-capitalism. If all languages now shared a common (intra-)mundane

---

6. So, as European imperialism smashed its insouciant way around the globe, other civilizations found themselves traumatically confronted by pluralisms which annihilated their sacred genealogies. The Middle Kingdom's marginalization to the Far East is emblematic of this process.

7. Hobsbawm, *The Age of Revolution*, p. 337.

8. Edward Said, *Orientalism*, p. 136.

9. Hobsbawm, *The Age of Revolution*, p. 337.

status, then all were in principle equally worthy of study and admiration. But by who? Logically, since now none belonged to God, by their new owners: each language's native speakers – and readers.

As Seton-Watson most usefully shows, the nineteenth century was, in Europe and its immediate peripheries, a golden age of vernacularizing lexicographers, grammarians, philologists, and litterateurs.[10] The energetic activities of these professional intellectuals were central to the shaping of nineteenth-century European nationalisms in complete contrast to the situation in the Americas between 1770 and 1830. Monolingual dictionaries were vast compendia of each language's print-treasury, portable (if sometimes barely so) from shop to school, office to residence. Bilingual dictionaries made visible an approaching egalitarianism among languages – whatever the political realities outside, within the covers of the Czech-German/German-Czech dictionary the paired languages had a common status. The visionary drudges who devoted years to their compilation were of necessity drawn to or nurtured by the great libraries of Europe, above all those of the universities. And much of their immediate clientele was no less inevitably university and pre-university students. Hobsbawm's dictum that 'the progress of schools and universities measures that of nationalism, just as schools and especially universities became its most conscious champions,' is certainly correct for nineteenth-century Europe, if not for other times and places.[11]

---

10. 'Just because the history of language is usually in our time kept so rigidly apart from conventional political, economic and social history, it has seemed to me desirable to bring it together with these, even at the cost of less expertise.' *Nations and States*, p. 11. In fact, one of the most valuable aspects of Seton-Watson's text is precisely his attention to language history – though one can disagree with the way he employs it.

11. *The Age of Revolution*, p. 166. Academic institutions were insignificant to the American nationalisms. Hobsbawm himself notes that though there were 6,000 students in Paris at the time, they played virtually no role in the French Revolution (p. 167). He also usefully reminds us that although education spread rapidly in the first half of the nineteenth century, the number of adolescents in schools was still minuscule by modern standards: a mere 19,000 *lycée* students in France in 1842; 20,000 high school pupils among the 68,000,000 population of Imperial Russia in 1850; a likely total of 48,000 university students in all Europe in 1848. Yet in the revolutions of *that* year, this tiny, but strategic, group played a pivotal role. (pp. 166–67).

One can thus trace this lexicographic revolution as one might the ascending roar in an arsenal alight, as each small explosion ignites others, till the final blaze turns night into day.

By the middle of the eighteenth century, the prodigious labours of German, French and English scholars had not only made available in handy printed form virtually the entire extant corpus of the Greek classics, along with the necessary philological and lexicographic adjuncts, but in dozens of books were recreating a glittering, and firmly pagan, ancient Hellenic civilization. In the last quarter of the century, this 'past' became increasingly accessible to a small number of young Greek-speaking Christian intellectuals, most of whom had studied or travelled outside the confines of the Ottoman Empire.[12] Exalted by the philhellenism at the centres of Western European civilization, they undertook the 'debarbarizing' of the modern Greeks, i.e., their transformation into beings worthy of Pericles and Socrates.[13] Emblematic of this change in consciousness are the following words of one of these young men, Adamantios Koraes (who later became an ardent lexicographer!), in an address to a French audience in Paris in 1803:[14]

For the first time the nation surveys the hideous spectacle of its ignorance and trembles in measuring with the eye the distance separating it from its ancestors' glory. This painful *discovery*, however, does not precipitate the Greeks into despair: We are the descendants of Greeks, they implicitly told themselves, we must either try to become again worthy of this name, or we must not bear it.

Similarly in the late eighteenth century, grammars, dictionaries and histories of Rumanian appeared, accompanied by a drive, successful at first in the Habsburg realms, later in the Ottoman, for the replacement of Cyrillic by the Roman alphabet (marking

---

12. The first Greek newspapers appeared in 1784 in Vienna. Philike Hetairia, the secret society largely responsible for the 1821 anti-Ottoman uprising, was founded in the 'great new Russian grain port of Odessa' in 1814.

13. See Elie Kedourie's introduction to *Nationalism in Asia and Africa*, p. 40.

14. Ibid., pp. 43–44. Emphasis added. The full text of Koraes's 'The Present State of Civilization in Greece' is given in pp. 157–82. It contains a stunningly modern analysis of the sociological bases for Greek nationalism.

Rumanian sharply off from its Slavic-Orthodox neighbours).[15] Between 1789 and 1794, the Russian Academy, modelled on the Académie Française, produced a six-volume Russian dictionary, followed by an official grammar in 1802. Both represented a triumph of the vernacular over Church Slavonic. Although right into the eighteenth century Czech was the language only of the peasantry in Bohemia (the nobility and rising middle classes spoke German), the Catholic priest Josef Dobrovský (1753–1829) produced in 1792 his *Geschichte der böhmischen Sprache und ältern Literatur*, the first systematic history of the Czech language and literature. In 1835–39 appeared Josef Jungmann's pioneering five-volume Czech-German dictionary.[16]

Of the birth of Hungarian nationalism Ignotus writes that it is an event 'recent enough to be dated: 1772, the year of publication of some unreadable works by the versatile Hungarian author György Bessenyei, then a resident in Vienna and serving in Maria Theresa's bodyguard. . . . Bessenyei's *magna opera* were meant to prove that the Hungarian language was suitable for the very highest literary genre.'[17] Further stimulus was provided by the extensive publications of Ferenc Kazinczy (1759–1831), 'the father of Hungarian literature,' and by the removal, in 1784, of what became the University of Budapest to that city from the small provincial town of Trnava. Its first political expression was the Latin-speaking Magyar nobility's hostile reaction in the 1780s to Emperor Joseph II's decision to replace Latin by German as the prime language of imperial administration.[18]

In the period 1800–1850, as the result of pioneering work by native

---

15. Not pretending to any expert knowledge of Central and Eastern Europe, I have relied heavily on Seton-Watson in the analysis that follows. On Rumanian, see *Nations and States*, p. 177.

16. Ibid., pp. 150–153.

17. Paul Ignotus, *Hungary*, p. 44. 'He did prove it, but his polemical drive was more convincing than the aesthetic value of the examples he produced.' It is perhaps worth noting that this passage occurs in a subsection entitled 'The Inventing of the Hungarian Nation,' which opens with this pregnant phrase: 'A nation is born when a few people decide that it should be.'

18. Seton-Watson, *Nations and States*, pp. 158–61. The reaction was violent enough to persuade his successor Leopold II (r. 1790–1792) to reinstate Latin. See also below, Chapter VI. It is instructive that Kazinczy sided politically with Joseph II on this issue. (Ignotus, *Hungary*, p. 48).

scholars, three distinct literary languages were formed in the northern Balkans: Slovene, Serbo-Croat, and Bulgarian. If, in the 1830s, 'Bulgarians' had been widely thought to be of the same nation as the Serbs and Croats, and had in fact shared in the Illyrian Movement, a separate Bulgarian national state was to come into existence by 1878. In the eighteenth century, Ukrainian (Little Russian) was contemptuously tolerated as a language of yokels. But in 1798 Ivan Kotlarevsky wrote his *Aeneid*, an enormously popular satirical poem on Ukrainian life. In 1804, the University of Kharkov was founded and rapidly became the centre for a boom in Ukrainian literature. In 1819 appeared the first Ukrainian grammar – only 17 years after the official Russian one. And in the 1830s followed the works of Taras Shevchenko, of whom Seton-Watson observes that 'the formation of an accepted Ukrainian literary language owes more to him than to any other individual. The use of this language was the decisive stage in the formation of an Ukrainian national consciousness.'[19] Shortly thereafter, in 1846, the first Ukrainian nationalist organization was founded in Kiev – by a historian!

In the eighteenth century the language-of-state in today's Finland was Swedish. After the territory's union with Czardom in 1809, the official language became Russian. But an 'awakening' interest in Finnish and the Finnish past, first expressed through texts written in Latin and Swedish in the later eighteenth century, by the 1820s was increasingly manifested in the vernacular.[20] The leaders of the burgeoning Finnish nationalist movement were 'persons whose profession largely consisted of the handling of language: writers, teachers, pastors, and lawyers. The study of folklore and the rediscovery and piecing together of popular epic poetry went together with the publication of grammars and dictionaries, and led to the appearance of periodicals which served to standardize Finnish literary [i.e. print-] language, on behalf of which stronger

---

19. *Nations and States*, p. 187. Needless to say, Czarism gave these people short shrift. Shevchenko was broken in Siberia. The Habsburgs, however, gave some encouragement to Ukrainian nationalists in Galicia – to counterbalance the Poles.

20. Kemiläinen, *Nationalism*, pp. 208–15.

political demands could be advanced.'[21] In the case of Norway, which had long shared a written language with the Danes, though with a completely different pronunciation, nationalism emerged with Ivar Aasen's new Norwegian grammar (1848) and dictionary (1850), texts which responded to and stimulated demands for a specifically Norwegian print-language.

Elsewhere, in the latter portion of the nineteenth century, we find Afrikaner nationalism pioneered by Boer pastors and litterateurs, who in the 1870s were successful in making the local Dutch patois into a literary language and naming it something no longer European. Maronites and Copts, many of them products of Beirut's American College (founded in 1866) and the Jesuit College of St. Joseph (founded in 1875) were major contributors to the revival of classical Arabic and the spread of Arab nationalism.[22] And the seeds of Turkish nationalism are easily detectable in the appearance of a lively vernacular press in Istanbul in the 1870s.[23]

Nor should we forget that the same epoch saw the vernacularization of another form of printed page: the score. After Dobrovský came Smetana, Dvořák, and Janáček; after Aasen, Grieg; after Kazinczy, Béla Bártok; and so on well into our century.

At the same time, it is self-evident that all these lexicographers, philologists, grammarians, folklorists, publicists, and composers did not carry on their revolutionary activities in a vacuum. They were, after all, producers for the print-market, and they were linked, via that silent bazaar, to consuming publics. Who were these consumers? In the most general sense: the families of the reading classes – not merely the 'working father,' but the servant-girded wife and the school-age children. If we note that as late as 1840, even in Britain and France, the most advanced states in Europe, almost half the population was still illiterate (and in backward Russia almost 98 per

---

21. Seton-Watson, *Nations and States*, p. 72.

22. Ibid., pp. 232 and 261.

23. Kohn, *The Age of Nationalism*, pp. 105–7. This meant rejection of 'Ottoman', a dynastic officialese combining elements of Turkish, Persian, and Arabic. Characteristically, Ibrahim Sinasi, founder of the first such newspaper, had just returned from five years study in France. Where he led, others soon followed. By 1876, there were seven Turkish-language dailies in Constantinople.

cent), 'reading classes' meant people of some power. More concretely, they were, in addition to the old ruling classes of nobilities and landed gentries, courtiers and ecclesiastics, rising middle strata of plebeian lower officials, professionals, and commercial and industrial bourgeoisies.

Mid-nineteenth-century Europe witnessed a rapid increase in state expenditures and the size of state bureaucracies (civil and military), despite the absence of any major local wars. 'Between 1830 and 1850 public expenditure per capita increased by 25 per cent in Spain, by 40 per cent in France, by 44 per cent in Russia, by 50 per cent in Belgium, by 70 per cent in Austria, by 75 per cent in the USA, and by over 90 per cent in The Netherlands.'[24] Bureaucratic expansion, which also meant bureaucratic specialization, opened the gates of official preferment to much greater numbers and of far more varied social origins than hitherto. Take even the decrepit, sinecure-filled, nobility-ridden Austro-Hungarian state machinery: the percentage of men of middle class origins in the top echelons of its civil half rose from 0 in 1804, through 27 in 1829, 35 in 1859, to 55 in 1878. In the armed services, the same trend appeared, though characteristically at a slower, later pace: the middle class component of the officer corps rose from 10 per cent to 75 per cent between 1859 and 1918.[25]

If the expansion of bureaucratic middle classes was a relatively even phenomenon, occurring at comparable rates in both advanced and backward states of Europe, the rise of commercial and industrial bourgeoisies was of course highly uneven – massive and rapid in some places, slow and stunted in others. But no matter where, this 'rise' has to be understood in its relationship to vernacular print-capitalism.

The pre-bourgeois ruling classes generated their cohesions in some sense outside language, or at least outside print-language. If the ruler of Siam took a Malay noblewoman as a concubine, or if the King of England married a Spanish princess – did they ever talk seriously together? Solidarities were the products of kinship, clientship, and

---

24. Hobsbawm, *The Age of Revolution*, p. 229.
25. Peter J. Katzenstein, *Disjoined Partners, Austria and Germany since 1815*, pp. 74, 112.

personal loyalties. 'French' nobles could assist 'English' kings against 'French' monarchs, not on the basis of shared language or culture, but, Machiavellian calculations aside, of shared kinsmen and friendships. The relatively small size of traditional aristocracies, their fixed political bases, and the personalization of political relations implied by sexual intercourse and inheritance, meant that their cohesions as classes were as much concrete as imagined. An illiterate nobility could still act as a nobility. But the bourgeoisie? Here was a class which, figuratively speaking, came into being as a class only in so many replications. Factory-owner in Lille was connected to factory-owner in Lyon only by reverberation. They had no necessary reason to know of one another's existence; they did not typically marry each other's daughters or inherit each other's property. But they did come to visualize in a general way the existence of thousands and thousands like themselves through print-language. For an illiterate bourgeoisie is scarcely imaginable. Thus in world-historical terms bourgeoisies were the first classes to achieve solidarities on an essentially imagined basis. But in a nineteenth-century Europe in which Latin had been defeated by vernacular print-capitalism for something like two centuries, these solidarities had an outermost stretch limited by vernacular legibilities. To put it another way, one can sleep with anyone, but one can only read some people's words.

Nobilities, landed gentries, professionals, functionaries, and men of the market – these then were the *potential* consumers of the philological revolution. But such a clientele was almost nowhere fully realized, and the combinations of actual consumers varied considerably from zone to zone. To see why, one has to return to the basic contrast drawn earlier between Europe and the Americas. In the Americas there was an almost perfect isomorphism between the stretch of the various empires and that of their vernaculars. In Europe, however, such coincidences were rare, and intra-European dynastic empires were basically polyvernacular. In other words, power and print-language mapped different realms.

The general growth in literacy, commerce, industry, communications and state machineries that marked the nineteenth century created powerful new impulses for vernacular linguistic unification within each *language as power*

dynastic realm. Latin hung on as a language-of-state in Austro-Hungary as late as the early 1840s, but it disappeared almost immediately thereafter. Language-of-state it might be, but it could not, in the nineteenth century, be the language of business, of the sciences, of the press, or of literature, especially in a world in which these languages continuously interpenetrated one another.

Meantime, vernacular languages-of-state assumed ever greater power and status in a process which, at least at the start, was largely unplanned. Thus English elbowed Gaelic out of most of Ireland, French pushed Breton to the wall, and Castilian reduced Catalan to marginality. In those realms, such as Britain and France, where, for quite extraneous reasons, there happened to be, by mid-century, a relatively high coincidence of language-of-state and language of the population,[26] the general interpenetration alluded to above did not have dramatic political effects. (These cases are closest to those of the Americas.) In many other realms, of which Austro-Hungary is probably the polar example, the consequences were inevitably explosive. In its huge, ramshackle, polyglot, but increasingly literate, domain the replacement of Latin by *any* vernacular, in the mid nineteenth century, promised enormous advantages to those of its subjects who *already* used that print-language, and appeared correspondingly menacing to those who did not. I emphasize the word *any*, since, as we shall be discussing in greater detail below, German's nineteenth century elevation by the Habsburg court, German as some might think it, had nothing whatever to do with German nationalism. (Under these circumstances, one would expect a self-conscious nationalism to arise *last* in each dynastic realm among the native-readers of the official vernacular. And such expectations are borne out by the historical record.)

In terms of our lexicographers' clienteles, it is therefore not surprising to find very different bodies of customers according to different political conditions. In Hungary, for example, where virtually

---

26. As we have seen, vernacularization of the languages-of-state in these two realms was under way very early. In the case of the UK, the military subjugation of the Gaeltacht early in the eighteenth century and the Famine of the 1840s were powerful contributory factors.

no Magyar bourgeoisie existed, but one out of eight claimed some aristocratic status, the parapets of print-Hungarian were defended against the German tide by segments of the petty nobility and an impoverished landed gentry.[27] Much the same could be said of Polish-readers. More typical, however, was a coalition of lesser gentries, academics, professionals, and businessmen, in which the first often provided leaders of 'standing,' the second and third myths, poetry, newspapers, and ideological formulations, and the last money and marketing facilities. The amiable Koraes offers us a fine vignette of the early clientele for Greek nationalism, in which intellectuals and entrepreneurs predominated:[28]

> In those towns which were less poor, which had some well-to-do inhabitants and a few schools, and therefore a few individuals who could at least read and understand the ancient writers, the revolution began earlier and could make more rapid and more comforting progress. In some of these towns, schools are already being enlarged, and the study of *foreign* languages and even of those sciences which are taught in Europe [sic] is being introduced into them. The wealthy sponsor the printing of books translated from Italian, French, German, and English; they send to Europe at their expense young men eager to learn; they give their children a better education, not excepting girls . . .

Reading coalitions, with compositions that lay variously on the spectrum between Hungarian and Greek, developed similarly throughout Central and Eastern Europe, and into the Near East as the century proceeded.[29] How far the urban and rural masses shared in the new vernacularly imagined communities naturally also varied a great deal.

---

27. Hobsbawm, *The Age of Revolution*, p. 165. For an excellent, detailed discussion, see Ignotus, *Hungary*, pp. 44–56; also Jászi, *The Dissolution*, pp. 224–25.

28. Kedourie, *Nationalism in Asia and Africa*, p. 170. Emphasis added. Everything here is exemplary. If Koraes looks to 'Europe,' it is over his shoulder; he faces Constantinople. Ottoman is not yet a foreign language. And non-labouring future wives are entering the print-market.

29. For examples, see Seton-Watson, *Nations and States*, pp. 72 (Finland), 145 (Bulgaria), 153 (Bohemia), and 432 (Slovakia); Kohn, *The Age of Nationalism*, pp. 83 (Egypt) and 103 (Persia).

Much depended on the relationship between these masses and the missionaries of nationalism. At one extreme, perhaps, one might point to Ireland, where a Catholic priesthood drawn from the peasantry and close to it played a vital mediating role. Another extreme is suggested by Hobsbawm's ironic comment that: 'The Galician peasants in 1846 opposed the Polish revolutionaries even though these actually proclaimed the abolition of serfdom, preferring to massacre gentlemen and trust to the Emperor's officials.'[30] But everywhere, in fact, as literacy increased, it became easier to arouse popular support, with the masses discovering a new glory in the print elevation of languages they had humbly spoken all along.

Up to a point, then, Nairn's arresting formulation – 'The new middle-class intelligentsia of nationalism had to invite the masses into history; and the invitation-card had to be written in a language they understood'[31] – is correct. But it will be hard to see why the invitation came to seem so attractive, and why such different alliances were able to issue it (Nairn's middle-class intelligentsia was by no means the only host), unless we turn finally to piracy.

Hobsbawm observes that 'The French Revolution was not made or led by a formed party or movement in the modern sense, nor by men attempting to carry out a systematic programme. It hardly even threw up "leaders" of the kind to which twentieth century revolutions have accustomed us, until the post-revolutionary figure of Napoléon.'[32] But once it had occurred, it entered the accumulating memory of print. The overwhelming and bewildering concatenation of events experienced by its makers and its victims became a 'thing' – and with its own name: The French Revolution. Like a vast shapeless rock worn to a rounded boulder by countless drops of water, the experience was shaped by millions of printed words into a 'concept' on the printed page, and, in due course, into a model. Why 'it' broke out, what 'it' aimed for, why 'it' succeeded or failed, became subjects for endless polemics on the part of friends and foes:

---

30. *The Age of Revolution*, p. 169.
31. *The Break-up of Britain*, p. 340.
32. *The Age of Revolution*, p. 80.

but of its 'it-ness', as it were, no one ever after had much doubt.[33]

In much the same way, the independence movements in the Americas became, as soon as they were printed about, 'concepts,' 'models', and indeed 'blueprints.' In 'reality', 'Bolívar's fear of Negro insurrections and San Martín's summoning of his indigenes to Peruvianness jostled one another chaotically. But printed words washed away the former almost at once, so that, if recalled at all, it appeared an inconsequential anomaly. Out of the American welter came these imagined realities: nation-states, republican institutions, common citizenships, popular sovereignty, national flags and anthems, etc., and the liquidation of their conceptual opposites: dynastic empires, monarchical institutions, absolutisms, subjecthoods, inherited nobilities, serfdoms, ghettoes, and so forth. (Nothing more stunning, in this context, than the general 'elision' of massive slavery from the 'modal' USA of the nineteenth century, and of the shared language of the 'modal' Southern republics.) Furthermore, the validity and generalizability of the blueprint were undoubtedly confirmed by the *plurality* of the independent states.

In effect, by the second decade of the nineteenth century, if not earlier, a 'model' of 'the' independent national state was available for pirating.[34] (The first groups to do so were the marginalized vernacular-based coalitions of the educated on which this chapter has been focused.) But precisely because it was by then a known model, it imposed certain 'standards' from which too-marked deviations were impermissible. Even backward and reactionary Hungarian and Polish gentries were hard put to it not to make a show of 'inviting in' (if only to the pantry) their oppressed compatriots. If you like, the logic of San Martín's Peruvianization was at work. If 'Hungarians' deserved a

---

33. Compare: 'The very name of the Industrial Revolution reflects its relatively tardy impact on Europe. The thing [*sic*] existed in Britain before the word. Not until the 1820s did English and French socialists – themselves an unprecedented group – invent it, probably by analogy with the political revolution of France.' Ibid., p. 45.

34. It would be more precise, probably to say that the model was a complex composite of French and American elements. But the 'observable reality' of France until after 1870 was restored monarchies and the ersatz dynasticism of Napoléon's great-nephew.

national state, then that *meant* Hungarians, all of them;[35] it meant a state in which the ultimate locus of sovereignty had to be the collectivity of Hungarian-speakers and readers; and, in due course, the liquidation of serfdom, the promotion of popular education, the expansion of the suffrage, and so on. Thus the 'populist' character of the early European nationalism, even when led, demagogically, by the most backward social groups, was deeper than in the Americas: serfdom *had* to go, legal slavery was unimaginable – not least because the conceptual model was set in ineradicable place.

---

35. Not that this was a clear-cut matter. Half the subjects of the Kingdom of Hungary were non-Magyar. Only one third of the serfs were Magyar-speakers. In the early nineteenth century, the high Magyar aristocracy spoke French or German; the middle and lower nobility 'conversed in a dog-Latin strewn with Magyar, but also with Slovak, Serb, and Romanian expressions as well as vernacular German . . . .' Ignotus, *Hungary*, pp. 45–46, and 81.

6

Official Nationalism
and Imperialism

In the course of the nineteenth century, and especially in its latter half, the philological-lexicographic revolution and the rise of intra-European nationalist movements, themselves the products, not only of capitalism, but of the elephantiasis of the dynastic states, created increasing cultural, and therefore political, difficulties for many dynasts. For, as we have seen, the fundamental legitimacy of most of these dynasties had nothing to do with nationalness. Romanovs ruled over Tatars and Letts, Germans and Armenians, Russians and Finns. Habsburgs were perched high over Magyars and Croats, Slovaks and Italians, Ukrainians and Austro-Germans. Hanoverians presided over Bengalis and Québecois, as well as Scots and Irish, English and Welsh.[1] On the continent, furthermore, members of the same dynastic families often ruled in different, sometimes rivalrous, states. What nationality should be assigned to Bourbons ruling in France and

---

1. It is nice that what eventually became the late British Empire has not been ruled by an 'English' dynasty since the early eleventh century: since then a motley parade of Normans (Plantagenets), Welsh (Tudors), Scots (Stuarts), Dutch (House of Orange) and Germans (Hanoverians) have squatted on the imperial throne. No one much cared until the philological revolution and a paroxysm of English nationalism in World War I. House of Windsor rhymes with House of Schönbrunn or House of Versailles.

Spain, Hohenzollerns in Prussia and Rumania, Wittelsbachs in Bavaria and Greece?

We have also seen that for essentially administrative purposes these dynasties had, at different speeds, settled on certain print-vernaculars as languages-of-state – with the 'choice' of language essentially a matter of unselfconscious inheritance or convenience.

The lexicographic revolution in Europe, however, created, and gradually spread, the conviction that languages (in Europe at least) were, so to speak, the personal property of quite specific groups – their daily speakers and readers – and moreover that these groups, imagined as communities, were entitled to their autonomous place in a fraternity of equals. The philological incendiaries thus presented the dynasts with a disagreeable dilemma which did not fail to sharpen over time. Nowhere is this dilemma clearer than in the case of Austro-Hungary. When the enlightened absolutist Joseph II decided early in the 1780s to switch the language of state from Latin to German, 'he did not fight, for instance, against the Magyar language, but he fought against the Latin. . . . He thought that, on the basis of the mediaeval Latin administration of the nobility, no effective work in the interest of the masses could have been carried on. The necessity of a unifying language connecting all parts of his empire seemed to him a peremptory claim. Under this necessity he could not choose any other language than German, the only one which had a vast culture and literature under its sway and which had a considerable minority in all his provinces.'[2] Indeed, 'the Habsburgs were *not* a consciously and consequentially Germanizing power. . . . There were *Habsburgs who did not even speak German*. Even those Habsburg emperors who sometimes fostered a policy of Germanization were not led in their efforts by any nationalistic point of view, but their measures were dictated by the intent of unification and universalism of their empire.'[3] Their essential aim was Hausmacht. After the middle of the nineteenth century, however, German

---

2. Jászi, *The Dissolution*, p. 71. It is interesting that Joseph had refused to take the coronation oath as King of Hungary because this would have committed him to respecting the 'constitutional' privileges of the Magyar nobility. Ignotus, *Hungary*, p. 47.

3. Ibid., p. 137. Emphasis added.

increasingly acquired a double status: 'universal–imperial' and 'particular–national'. The more the dynasty pressed German in its first capacity, the more it appeared to be siding with its German-speaking subjects, and the more it aroused antipathy among the rest. Yet if it did not so press, indeed made concessions to other languages, above all Hungarian, not only was unification set back, but its German-speaking subjects allowed themselves to feel affronted. Thus it threatened to be hated simultaneously as champion of the Germans and traitor to them. (In much the same way, the Ottomans came to be hated by Turkish-speakers as apostates and by non-Turkish-speakers as Turkifiers.)

Insofar as all dynasts by mid-century were using *some* vernacular as language-of-state,[4] and also because of the rapidly rising prestige all over Europe of the national idea, there was a discernible tendency among the Euro-Mediterranean monarchies to sidle towards a beckoning national identification. Romanovs discovered they were Great Russians, Hanoverians that they were English, Hohenzollerns that they were Germans – and with rather more difficulty their cousins turned Romanian, Greek, and so forth. On the one hand, these new identifications shored up legitimacies which, in an age of capitalism, scepticism, and science, could less and less safely rest on putative sacrality and sheer antiquity. On the other hand, they posed new dangers. If Kaiser Wilhelm II cast himself as 'No. 1 German,' he implicitly conceded that he was *one among many of the same kind as himself*, that he had a representative function, and therefore could, in principle, be a *traitor* to his fellow-Germans (something inconceivable in the dynasty's heyday. Traitor to whom or to what?). In the wake of the disaster that overtook Germany in 1918, he was taken at his implied word. Acting in the name of the German nation, civilian politicians (publicly) and the General Staff (with its usual courage, secretly) sent him packing from the Fatherland to an obscure Dutch suburb. So too Mohammad-Reza Pahlavi, having cast himself,

---

4. One could argue that a long era closed in 1844, when Magyar finally replaced Latin as language-of-state in the Kingdom of Hungary. But, as we have seen, dog-Latin was in fact the *vernacular* of the Magyar middle and lower nobility until well into the nineteenth century.

not as Shah, but as Shah of Iran, came to be branded traitor. That he himself accepted, not the verdict, but, as it were, the jurisdiction of the national court, is shown by a small comedy at the moment of his departure into exile. Before climbing the ramp of his jet, he kissed the earth for the photographers and announced that he was taking a small quantity of sacred Iranian soil with him. This take is lifted from a film about Garibaldi, not the Sun King.[5]

The 'naturalizations' of Europe's dynasties – maneuvers that required in many cases some diverting acrobatics – eventually led to what Seton-Watson bitingly calls 'official nationalisms,'[6] of which Czarist Russification is only the best-known example. These 'official nationalisms' can best be understood as a means for combining naturalization with retention of dynastic power, in particular over the huge polyglot domains accumulated since the Middle Ages, or, to put it another way, for stretching the short, tight, skin of the nation over the gigantic body of the empire. 'Russification' of the heterogeneous population of the Czar's subjects thus represented a violent, conscious welding of two opposing political orders, one ancient, one quite new. (While there is a certain analogy with, say, the Hispanization of the Americas and the Philippines, one central difference remains. The cultural conquistadors of late-nineteenth-century Czardom were proceeding from a selfconscious Machiavellism, while their sixteenth-century Spanish ancestors acted out of an unselfconscious everyday pragmatism. Nor was it for them really 'Hispanization' – rather it was simply *conversion* of heathens and savages.)

The key to situating 'official nationalism' – willed merger of nation and dynastic empire – is to remember that it developed *after*, and *in reaction to*, the popular national movements proliferating in Europe since the 1820s. If these nationalisms were modelled on

---

5. From Professor Chehabi of Harvard University I have learned that the Shah was in the first instance imitating his father, Reza Pahlavi, who, on being exiled by London to Mauritius in 1941, included some Iranian soil in his luggage.

6. Seton-Watson, *Nations and States*, p. 148. Alas, the bite extends only to Eastern Europe. Seton-Watson is rightly sardonic at the expense of Romanov and Soviet regimes, but overlooks analogous policies being pursued in London, Paris, Berlin, Madrid and Washington.

American and French histories, so now they became modular in turn.[7] It was only that a certain inventive legerdemain was required to permit the empire to appear attractive in national drag.

To gain some perspective on this whole process of reactionary, secondary modelling, we may profitably consider some parallel, yet usefully contrasting cases.

How uneasy Romanov autocracy initially felt at 'taking to the streets' is excellently shown by Seton-Watson.[8] As noted earlier, the language of the court of St. Petersburg in the eighteenth century was French, while that of much of the provincial nobility was German. In the aftermath of Napoléon's invasion, Count Sergei Uvarov, in an official report of 1832, proposed that the realm should be based on the three principles of Autocracy, Orthodoxy, and Nationality (*natsionalnost*). If the first two were old, the third was quite novel – and somewhat premature in an age when half the 'nation' were still serfs, and more than half spoke a mother-tongue other than Russian. Uvarov's report won him the post of Minister of Education, but little more. For another half-century Czarism resisted Uvarovian enticements. It was not until the reign of Alexander III (1881–94) that Russification became official dynastic policy: long after Ukrainian, Finnish, Lett and other nationalisms had appeared within the Empire. Ironically enough, the first Russifying measures were taken against precisely those 'nationalities' which had been most *Kaisertreu* – such as the Baltic Germans. In 1887, in the Baltic provinces, Russian was made compulsory as the language of instruction in all state schools above the lowest primary classes, a measure later extended to private schools as well. In 1893, the University of Dorpat, one of the most distinguished colleges in the imperial domains, was closed down because it used German in the lecture-rooms. (Recall that hitherto German had been a provincial language-of-state, *not* the voice of a popular nationalist movement).

---

7. There is an instructive parallel to all this in the politico-military reforms of Scharnhorst, Clausewitz and Gneisenau who in a selfconsciously conservative spirit adapted many of the spontaneous innovations of the French Revolution for the erection of the great modular professionally-officered, standing, conscript army of the nineteenth century.

8. Ibid., pp. 83–87.

And so on. Seton-Watson even goes so far as to venture that the Revolution of 1905 was 'as much a revolution of non-Russians against Russification as it was a revolution of workers, peasants, and radical intellectuals against autocracy. The two revolts were of course connected: the social revolution was in fact most bitter in non-Russian regions, with Polish workers, Latvian peasants, and Georgian peasants as protagonists.'[9]

At the same time, it would be a big mistake to suppose that since Russification was a *dynastic* policy, it did not achieve one of its main purposes – marshalling a growing 'Great Russian' nationalism behind the throne. And not simply on the basis of sentiment. Enormous opportunities were after all available for Russian functionaries and entrepreneurs in the vast bureaucracy and expanding market that the empire provided.

No less interesting than Alexander III, Russifying Czar of All the Russias, is his contemporary Victoria von Saxe-Coburg-Gotha, Queen of England *and*, late in life, Empress of India. Actually her title is more interesting than her person, for it represents emblematically the thickened metal of a weld between nation and empire.[10] Her reign too marks the onset of a London-style 'official nationalism' which has strong affinities with the Russification being pursued in St. Petersburg. A good way to appreciate this affinity is by longitudinal comparison.

In *The Break-up of Britain*, Tom Nairn raises the problem of why there was no Scottish nationalist movement in the late eighteenth century, in spite of a rising Scots bourgeoisie and a very distinguished Scots intelligentsia.[11] Hobsbawm has peremptorily dismissed Nairn's thoughtful discussion with the remark: 'It is pure anachronism to expect [the Scots] to have demanded an independent state at this time.'[12] Yet if we recall that Benjamin Franklin, who co-signed the American Declaration of Independence, was born five years before

---

9. Ibid., p. 87.
10. This weld's disintegration is clocked by the procession from British Empire to British Commonwealth, to Commonwealth, to . . . .?
11. *The Break-up of Britain*, pp. 106ff.
12. 'Some Reflections', p. 5.

David Hume, we may be inclined to think this judgement itself a shade anachronistic.[13] It seems to me that the difficulties – and their resolution – lie elsewhere.

On the other hand, there is Nairn's good nationalist tendency to treat his 'Scotland' as an unproblematic, primordial given. Bloch reminds us of the chequered ancestry of this 'entity', observing that the ravages of the Danes and William the Conqueror destroyed forever the cultural hegemony of Northern, Anglo-Saxon Northumbria, symbolized by such luminaries as Alcuin and Bede:[14]

> A part of the northern zone was detached for ever from England proper. Cut off from other populations of Anglo-Saxon speech by the settlement of the Vikings in Yorkshire, the lowlands round about the Northumbrian citadel of Edinburgh fell under the domination of the Celtic chiefs of the hills. Thus the bilingual kingdom of Scotland was by a sort of backhanded stroke a creation of the Scandinavian invasions.

And Seton-Watson, for his part, writes that the Scottish language:[15]

> developed from the flowing together of Saxon and French, though with less of the latter and with rather more from Celtic and Scandinavian sources than in the south. This language was spoken not only in the east of Scotland but also in northern England. Scots, or 'northern English,' was spoken at the Scottish court and by the social elite (who might or might not also speak Gaelic), as well as by the Lowland population as a whole. It was the language of the poets Robert Henryson and William Dunbar. It might have developed as a distinct literary language into modern times had not the union of the crowns in 1603 brought the predominance of southern English through its extension to the court, administration and upper class of Scotland.

---

13. In a book significantly entitled *Inventing America: Jefferson's Declaration of Independence*, Gary Wills argues in fact that the nationalist Jefferson's thinking was fundamentally shaped, not by Locke, but by Hume, Hutcheson, Adam Smith, and other eminences of the Scottish Enlightenment.

14. *Feudal Society*, I, p. 42.

15. *Nations and States*, pp. 30–31.

The key point here is that already in the early seventeenth century large parts of what would one day be imagined as Scotland were English-speaking and had immediate access to print-English, provided a minimal degree of literacy existed. Then in the early eighteenth century the English-speaking Lowlands collaborated with London in largely exterminating the Gaeltacht. In neither 'northward thrust' was a selfconscious Anglicizing policy pursued – in both cases Anglicization was essentially a byproduct. But combined, they had effectively eliminated, 'before' the age of nationalism, any possibility of a European-style vernacular-specific nationalist movement. Why not one in the American style? Part of the answer is given by Nairn in passing, when he speaks of a 'massive intellectual migration' southwards from the mid eighteenth century onwards.[16] But there was more than an intellectual migration. Scottish politicians came south to legislate, and Scottish businessmen had open access to London's markets. In effect, in complete contrast to the Thirteen Colonies (and to a lesser extent Ireland), *there were no barricades* on all these pilgrims' paths towards the centre. (Compare the clear highway before Latin- and German-reading Hungarians to Vienna in the eighteenth century.) English had yet to become an 'English' language.

The same point can be made from a different angle. It is true that in the seventeenth century London resumed an acquisition of overseas territories arrested since the disastrous ending to the Hundred Years War. But the 'spirit' of these conquests was still fundamentally that of a prenational age. Nothing more stunningly confirms this than the fact that 'India' only became 'British' twenty years after Victoria's accession to the throne. In other words, until after the 1857 Mutiny, 'India' was ruled by a commercial enterprise – not by a state, and certainly not by a nation-state.

But change was on the way. When the East India Company's charter came up for renewal in 1813, Parliament mandated the allocation of 100,000 rupees a year for the promotion of native education, *both* 'oriental' and 'Western.' In 1823, a Committee of Public Instruction was set up in Bengal; and in 1834, Thomas

---

16. *The Break-up of Britain*, p. 123.

Babington Macaulay became president of this committee. Declaring that 'a single shelf of a good European library is worth the whole native literature of India and Arabia,'[17] he produced the following year his notorious 'Minute on Education.' Luckier than Uvarov, his recommendations went into immediate effect. A thoroughly English educational system was to be introduced which, in Macaulay's own ineffable words, would create 'a class of persons, Indian in blood and colour, but English in taste, in opinion, in morals and in intellect.'[18] In 1836, he wrote that:[19]

> No Hindu who has received an English education ever remains sincerely attached to his religion. It is my firm belief [so they always were] that if our plans of education are followed up, there will not be a single idolater among the respectable classes in Bengal thirty years hence.

There is here, to be sure, a certain naive optimism, which reminds us of Fermín in Bogotá half a century earlier. But the important thing is that we see a long-range (30 years!) policy, consciously formulated and pursued, to turn 'idolaters,' not so much into Christians, as into people culturally English, despite their irremediable colour and blood. A sort of mental miscegenation is intended, which, when compared with Fermín's physical one, shows that, like so much else in the Victorian age, imperialism made enormous progress in daintiness. In any event, it can be safely said that from this point on, all over the expanding empire, if at different speeds, Macaulayism was pursued.[20]

Like Russification, Anglicization naturally also offered rosy

---

17. We can be confident that this bumptious young middle-class English Uvarov knew nothing about either 'native literature'.

18. See Donald Eugene Smith, *India as a Secular State*, pp. 337–38; and Percival Spear, *India, Pakistan and the West*, p. 163.

19. Smith, *India*, p. 339.

20. See, for example, Roff's poker-faced account of the founding in 1905 of the Kuala Kangsar Malay College, which quickly became known, wholly without irony, as 'the Malay Eton.' True to Macaulay's prescriptions, its pupils were drawn from the 'respectable classes' – i.e. the compliant Malay aristocracy. Half the early boarders were direct descendants of various Malay sultans. William R. Roff, *The Origins of Malay Nationalism*, pp. 100–105.

opportunities to armies of middle-class metropolitans (not least Scots-men!) – functionaries, schoolmasters, merchants, and planters – who quickly fanned out over the vast, permanently sunlit realm. Nonetheless there was a central difference between the empires ruled from St. Petersburg and London. Czardom remained a 'continuous' continental domain, confined to the temperate and arctic zones of Eurasia. One could, so to speak, walk from one end of it to the other. Linguistic kinship with the Slavic populations of Eastern Europe, and – to put it pleasantly – historical, political, religious and economic ties with many non-Slavic peoples, meant that *relatively* speaking, the barriers on the road to St. Petersburg were not impermeable.[21] The British Empire, on the other hand, was a grab-bag of primarily tropical possessions scattered over every continent. Only a minority of the subjected peoples had any long-standing religious, linguistic, cultural, or even political and eco-nomic, ties with the metropole. Juxtaposed to one another in the Jubilee Year, they resembled those random collections of Old Masters hastily assembled by English and American millionaires which eventually turn into solemnly imperial state museums.

The consequences are well illustrated by the bitter recollections of Bipin Chandra Pal, who, in 1932, a century after Macaulay's 'Minute', still felt angry enough to write that Indian Magistrates:[22]

had not only passed a very rigid test on the same terms as British members of the service, but had spent the very best years of the formative period of their youth in England. Upon their return to their homeland, they practically lived in the same style as their brother Civilians, and *almost religiously* followed the social conventions and the ethical standards of the latter. In those days the India-born [sic – compare our Spanish-American creoles] Civilian practically cut himself off from his parent society, and lived and moved and had his being in the atmosphere so beloved of his British colleagues. *In mind and manners he was as much an Englishman as any Englishman.* It was no small sacrifice for him, because in this way he completely estranged himself from the society of his own people and became socially and morally a pariah

21. The trans-Ural populations were another story.
22. See his *Memories of My Life and Times*, pp. 331–32. Emphases added.

among them. . . . He was as much a *stranger in his own native land* as the
European residents in the country.

So far, so Macaulay. Much more serious, however, was that such
strangers in their native land were *still* condemned – no less fatally than
the American creoles – to an 'irrational' permanent subordination to the
English maturrangos. It was not simply that, no matter how Anglicized a
Pal became, he was always barred from the uppermost peaks of the Raj.
He was also barred from movement outside its perimeter – laterally, say,
to the Gold Coast or Hong Kong, and vertically to the metropole.
'Completely estranged from the society of his own people' he might be,
but he was under life sentence to serve among them. (To be sure, who
'they' included varied with the stretch of British conquests on the
subcontinent.[23])

We shall be looking later at the consequences of official nationalisms for the rise of twentieth-century Asian and African nationalisms.
For our purposes here, what needs to be stressed is that Anglicization
produced thousands of Pals all over the world. Nothing more sharply
underscores the fundamental contradiction of English official
nationalism, i.e. the inner incompatibility of empire and nation. I
say 'nation' advisedly, because it is always tempting to account for
these Pals in terms of racism. No one in their right mind would deny the
profoundly racist character of nineteenth-century English imperialism. But the Pals also existed in the *white* colonies – Australia, New
Zealand, Canada and South Africa. English and Scottish schoolmasters also swarmed there, and Anglicization was also cultural
policy. As to Pal, to them too the looping upward path still open to
the Scots in the eighteenth century was closed. Anglicized Australians
did not serve in Dublin or Manchester, and not even in Ottawa or
Capetown. Nor, until quite late on, could they become Governors-

---

23. It is true that Indian officials were employed in Burma; but Burma was
administratively part of British India until 1937. Indians also served in subordinate
capacities – especially in the police – in British Malaya and Singapore, but they served as
'locals' and 'immigrants', i.e. were not transferable 'back' to India's police forces. Note
that the emphasis here is on officials: Indian labourers, merchants, and even professionals, moved in sizeable numbers to British colonies in Southeast Asia, South and East
Africa, and even the Caribbean.

General in Canberra.[24] Only 'English English' did, i.e. members of a half-concealed English nation.

Three years before the East India Company lost its Indian hunting-ground, Commodore Perry with his black ships peremptorily battered down the walls that for so long had kept Japan in self-imposed isolation. After 1854, the self-confidence and inner legitimacy of the Bakufu (Tokugawa Shogunate regime) were rapidly undermined by a conspicuous impotence in the face of the penetrating West. Under the banner of Sonnō Jōi (Revere the Sovereign, Expel the Barbarians), a small band of middle-ranking samurai, primarily from the Satsuma and Chōshū han, finally overthrew it in 1868. Among the reasons for their success was an exceptionally creative absorption, especially after 1860, of the new Western military science systematized since 1815 by Prussian and French staff professionals. They were thus able to make effective use of 7,300 ultra-modern rifles (most of them American Civil War scrap), purchased from an English arms-merchant.[25] 'In the use of guns . . .

---

24. To be sure, by late Edwardian times, a few 'white colonials' did migrate to London and become members of Parliament or prominent press-lords.

25. Here the key figure was Ōmura Masujirō (1824–1869), the so-called 'Father of the Japanese Army'. A low-ranking Chōshū samurai, he started his career by studying Western medicine through Dutch-language manuals. (It will be recalled that until 1854 the Dutch were the only Westerners permitted access to Japan, and this access was limited essentially to the island of Deshima off the Bakufu-controlled port of Nagasaki.) On graduating from the Tekijyuku in Osaka, then the best Dutch-language training centre in the country, he returned home to practise medicine – but without much success. In 1853, he took a position in Uwajima as instructor in Western learning, with a foray to Nagasaki to study naval science. (He designed and supervised the building of Japan's first steamship on the basis of written manuals.) His chance came after Perry's arrival; he moved to Edo in 1856 to work as an instructor at what would become the National Military Academy and at the Bakufu's top research office for the study of Western texts. His translations of European military works especially on Napoléon's innovations in strategy and tactics, won him fame and recall to Chōshū in 1860 to serve as military adviser. In 1864–65, he proved the relevance of his writing as a successful commander in the Chōshū civil war. Subsequently he became the first Meiji Minister of War, and drew up the regime's revolutionary plans for mass conscription and elimination of the samurai as a legal caste. For his pains he was assassinated by an outraged samurai. See Albert M. Craig, *Chōshū in the Meiji Restoration*, especially pp. 202–204, 267–280.

the men of Chōshū had such mastery that the old blood and thunder slash and cut methods were quite useless against them.'[26]

Once in power, however, the rebels, whom we remember today as the Meiji oligarchs, found that their military prowess did not automatically guarantee political legitimacy. If the Tennō ('Emperor') could quickly be restored with the abolition of the Bakufu, the barbarians could not so easily be expelled.[27] Japan's geopolitical security remained just as fragile as before 1868. One of the basic means adopted for consolidating the oligarchy's domestic position was thus a variant of mid-century 'official nationalism,' rather consciously modelled on Hohenzollern Prussia-Germany. Between 1868 and 1871, all residual local 'feudal' military units were dissolved, giving Tokyo a centralized monopoly of the means of violence. In 1872, an Imperial Rescript ordered the promotion of universal literacy among adult males. In 1873, well before the United Kingdom, Japan introduced conscription. At the same time, the regime liquidated the samurai as a legally-defined and privileged class, an essential step not only for (slowly) opening the officer corps to all talents, but also to fit the now 'available' nation-of-citizens model. The Japanese peasantry was freed from subjection to the feudal *han*-system and henceforth exploited directly by the state and commercial-agricultural landowners.[28] In 1889, there followed a Prussian-style constitution and eventually universal male suffrage.

In this orderly campaign the men of Meiji were aided by three half-fortuitous factors. First was the relatively high degree of Japanese ethnocultural homogeneity resulting from two and a half centuries of isolation and internal pacification by the Bakufu. While the Japanese spoken in Kyūshū was largely incomprehensible in Honshū, and

---

26. A contemporary Japanese observer, quoted in E. Herbert Norman, *Soldier and Peasant in Japan*, p. 31.

27. They knew this from bitter personal experience. In 1862, an English squadron had levelled half the Satsuma port of Kagoshima; in 1864, a joint American, Dutch, and English naval unit destroyed the Chōshū coastal fortifications at Shimonoseki. John M. Maki, *Japanese Militarism*, pp. 146–47.

28. All this reminds one of those reforms accomplished in Prussia after 1810 in response to Blücher's impassioned plea to Berlin: 'Get us a national army!' Vagts, *A History of Militarism*, p. 130; Cf. Gordon A. Craig, *The Politics of the Prussian Army*, ch. 2.

even Edo-Tokyo and Kyoto-Ōsaka found verbal communication problematic, the half-Sinified ideographic reading-system was long in place throughout the islands, and thus the development of mass literacy through schools and print was easy and uncontroversial. Second, the unique antiquity of the imperial house (Japan is the only country whose monarchy has been monopolized by a single dynasty throughout recorded history), and its emblematic Japanese-ness (contrast Bourbons and Habsburgs), made the exploitation of the Emperor for official-nationalist purposes rather simple.[29] Third, the penetration of the barbarians was abrupt, massive, and menacing enough for most elements of the politically-aware population to rally behind a programme of self-defence conceived in the new national terms. It is worth emphasizing that this possibility had everything to do with the timing of Western penetration, i.e. the 1860s as opposed to the 1760s. For by then, in dominant Europe, the 'national community' had been coming into its own for half a century, in both popular and official versions. In effect, self-defence could be fashioned along lines and in accordance with what were coming to be 'international norms.'

That the gamble paid off, in spite of the terrible sufferings imposed on the peasantry by the ruthless fiscal exactions required to pay for a munitions-based programme of industrialization, was certainly due in part to the single-minded determination of the oligarchs themselves. Fortunate to come to power in an era in which numbered accounts in Zürich lay in an undreamed-of future, they were not tempted to move the exacted surplus outside Japan. Fortunate to rule in an age when military technology was still advancing at a relative amble, they were able, with their catch-up armaments programme, to turn Japan into an independent military power by the end of the century. Spectacular successes by Japan's conscript army against China in 1894–5, and by her navy against Czardom in 1905, plus the annexation of Taiwan (1895) and Korea (1910), all consciously

---

29. But I have been informed by scholars of Japan that recent excavations of the earliest royal tombs suggest strongly that the family may originally have been – horrors! – Korean. The Japanese government has strongly discouraged further research on these sites.

propagandized through schools and print, were extremely valuable in creating the general impression that the conservative oligarchy was an authentic representative of the nation of which Japanese were coming to imagine themselves members.

That this nationalism took on an aggressive imperialist character, even outside ruling circles, can best be accounted for by two factors: the legacy of Japan's long isolation and the power of the official-national model. Maruyama shrewdly points out that all nationalisms in Europe arose in the context of a traditional pluralism of interacting dynastic states – as I put it earlier, Latin's European universalism never had a political correlate:[30]

> National consciousness in Europe therefore bore from its inception the imprint of a consciousness of international society. It was a self-evident premise that disputes among sovereign states were conflicts among independent members of this international society. Precisely for this reason war, since Grotius, has come to occupy an important and systematic place in international law.

Centuries of Japanese isolation, however, meant that:[31]

> an awareness of equality in international affairs was totally absent. The advocates of expulsion [of the barbarians] viewed international relations from positions within the national hierarchy based on the supremacy of superiors over inferiors. Consequently, when the premises of the national hierarchy were transferred horizontally into the international sphere, international problems were reduced to a single alternative: conquer or be conquered. In the absence of any higher normative standards with which to gauge international relations, power politics is bound to be the rule and yesterday's timid defensiveness will become today's unrestrained expansionism.

Secondly, the oligarchy's prime models were the self-naturalizing dynasties of Europe. Insofar as these dynasties were more and more defining themselves in national terms, while at the same time

---

30. Maruyama Masao, *Thought and Behaviour in Modern Japanese Politics*, p. 138.
31. Ibid., pp. 139–40.

expanding their power outside Europe, it is not surprising that the model should have been understood imperially.[32] As the parcellization of Africa at the Congress of Berlin (1885) showed, great nations were global conquerors. How plausible then to argue that, for Japan to be accepted as 'great,' she too should turn Tennō into Emperor and launch overseas adventures, even if she was late to the game and had a lot of catching up to do. Few things give one a sharper sense of the way these residues impinged on the consciousness of the reading population than the following formulation by the radical-nationalist ideologue and revolutionary Kita Ikki (1884–1937), in his very influential *Nihon Kaizō Hōan Taikō* [Outline for the Reconstruction of Japan], published in 1924:[33]

As the class struggle within a nation is waged for the readjustment of unequal distinctions, so war between nations for an honorable cause will reform the present unjust distinctions. The British Empire is a millionaire possessing wealth all over the world; and Russia is a great landowner in occupation of the northern half of the globe. Japan with her scattered fringe [sic] of islands is one of the proletariat, and she has the right to declare war on the big monopoly powers. The socialists of the West contradict themselves when they admit the right of class struggle to the proletariat at home and at the same time condemn war, waged by a proletariat among nations, as militarism and aggression . . . If it is permissible for the working class to unite to overthrow unjust authority by bloodshed, then unconditional approval should be given to Japan to perfect her army and navy and make war for the rectification of unjust international frontiers. In the name of rational social democracy Japan claims possession of Australia and Eastern Siberia.

It remains only to add that, as the empire expanded after 1900, Japanification à la Macaulay was selfconsciously pursued as state policy. In the interwar years Koreans, Taiwanese and Manchurians,

---

32. Unluckily, the only alternative to the officially-nationalizing *dynastic* states of the time – Austro-Hungary – was not among the powers with a significant presence in the Far East.

33. As translated and cited in Richard Storry, *The Double Patriots*, p. 38.

and, after the outbreak of the Pacific War, Burmese, Indonesians and Filipinos, were subjected to policies for which the European model was an established working practice. And just as in the British Empire, Japanified Koreans, Taiwanese or Burmese had their passages to the metropole absolutely barred. They might speak and read Japanese perfectly, but they would never preside over prefectures in Honshū, or even be posted outside their zones of origin.

Having considered these three varied cases of 'official nationalism', it is important to stress that the model could be selfconsciously followed by states with no serious great power pretensions, so long as they were states in which the ruling classes or leading elements in them felt threatened by the world-wide spread of the nationally-imagined community. A comparison between two such states, Siam and Hungary-within-Austro-Hungary, may prove instructive.

Meiji's contemporary, the long-reigning Chulalongkorn (r. 1868–1910), defended his realm from Western expansionism in a style that differed markedly from that of his Japanese opposite number.[34] Squeezed between British Burma and Malaya, and French Indochina, he devoted himself to a shrewd manipulative diplomacy rather than attempting to build up a serious war machine. (A Ministry of War was not established until 1894.) In a way that reminds one of eighteenth-century Europe, his armed forces were primarily a motley array of Vietnamese, Khmer, Lao, Malay, and Chinese mercenaries and tributaries. Nor was anything much done to push an official nationalism through a modernized educational system. Indeed, primary education was not made compulsory till more than a decade after his death, and the country's first university was not set up until 1917, four decades after the founding of the Imperial University in Tokyo. Nonetheless, Chulalongkorn regarded himself as a modernizer. But his prime models were not the United Kingdom or Germany, but rather the colonial *beamtenstaaten* of the Dutch East

---

34. The following section is a condensed version of part of my 'Studies of the Thai State: the State of Thai Studies', in Eliezer B. Ayal (ed.), *The State of Thai Studies*.

Indies, British Malaya, and the Raj.[35] Following these models meant rationalizing and centralizing royal government, eliminating traditional semi-autonomous tributary statelets, and promoting economic development somewhat along colonial lines. The most striking example of this – an example which in its odd way looks forward to contemporary Saudi Arabia – was his encouragement of a massive immigration of young, single, male foreigners to form the disoriented, politically powerless workforce needed to construct port facilities, build railway lines, dig canals, and expand commercial agriculture. This importing of *gastarbeiter* paralleled, indeed was modelled on, the policies of the authorities in Batavia and Singapore. And as in the case of the Netherlands Indies and British Malaya, the great bulk of the labourers imported during the nineteenth century were from southeastern China. It is instructive that this policy caused him neither personal qualms nor political difficulties – no more than it did the colonial rulers on whom he modelled himself. Indeed the policy made good short term sense for a *dynastic* state, since it created an impotent working class 'outside' Thai society and left that society largely 'undisturbed.'

Wachirawut, his son and successor (r. 1910–1925), had to pick up the pieces, modelling himself this time on the self-naturalizing dynasts of Europe. Although – and because – he was educated in late Victorian England, he dramatized himself as his country's 'first nationalist.'[36] The target of this nationalism, however, was neither the United Kingdom, which controlled 90 per cent of Siam's trade, nor France, which had recently made off with easterly segments of the old realm: it was the Chinese whom his father had so recently and blithely imported. The style of his anti-Chinese stance is suggested by the titles of two of his most famous pamphlets: *The Jews of the Orient* (1914), and *Clogs on Our Wheels* (1915).

---

35. Battye nicely shows that the purpose of the young monarch's visits to Batavia and Singapore in 1870 and to India in 1872 was, in Chulalongkorn's own sweet words, 'selecting what may be safe models.' See 'The Military, Government and Society in Siam, 1868–1910,' p. 118.

36. 'The inspiration of Vajiravudh's [Wachirawut's] nationalist program was, first and foremost, Great Britain, the Western nation Vajiravudh knew best, at this time a nation caught up in imperialist enthusiasm.' Walter F. Vella, *Chaiyo! King Vajiravudh and the Development of Thai Nationalism*, p. xiv. See also pp. 6 and 67–68.

Why the change? Doubtless dramatic events immediately preceding and following his coronation in November 1910 had their effect. The previous June the police had had to be called out to suppress a general stike by Bangkok's Chinese merchants (upwardly mobile children of early immigrants) and workers, marking their initiation into Siamese politics.[37] The following year, the Celestial Monarchy in Peking was swept away by a heterogeneous assortment of groups from which merchants were by no means absent. 'The Chinese' thus appeared as harbingers of a popular *republicanism* profoundly threatening to the dynastic principle. Second, as the words 'Jews' and 'Orient' suggest, the Anglicized monarch had imbibed the particular racisms of the English ruling class. But, in addition, there was the fact that Wachirawut was a sort of Asian Bourbon. In a pre-national era his ancestors had readily taken attractive Chinese girls as wives and concubines, with the result that, Mendelianly-speaking, he himself had more Chinese 'blood' than Thai.[38]

Here is a fine example of the character of official nationalism – an anticipatory strategy adopted by dominant groups which are threatened with marginalization or exclusion from an emerging nationally-imagined community. (It goes without saying that Wachirawut also began moving all the policy levers of official nationalism: compulsory state-controlled primary education, state-organized propaganda, official rewriting of history, militarism – here more visible show than the real thing – and endless affirmations of the identity of dynasty and nation.[39])

The development of Hungarian nationalism in the nineteenth century shows in a different way the imprint of the 'official' model. We noted

---

37. The strike was occasioned by the government's decision to exact the same head-tax on the Chinese as on the native Thai. Hitherto it had been lower, as an inducement to immigration. See Bevars D. Mabry, *The Development of Labor Institutions in Thailand*, p. 38. (Exploitation of the Chinese came mainly via the opium-farm.)

38. For genealogical details, see my 'Studies of the Thai State,' p. 214.

39. He also coined the slogan, *Chat, Sasana, Kasat* (Nation, Religion, Monarch) which has been the shibboleth of rightwing regimes in Siam for the last quarter of a century. Here Uvarov's Autocracy, Orthodoxy, Nationality appear in reversed Thai order.

earlier the Latin-speaking Magyar nobility's enraged opposition to Joseph II's attempt in the 1780s to make German the sole imperial language-of-state. The more advantaged segments of this class feared losing their sinecures under a centralized, streamlined administration dominated by imperial-German bureaucrats. The lower echelons were panicked by the possibility of losing their exemptions from taxes and compulsory military service, as well as their control over the serfs and rural counties. Yet alongside the defence of Latin, Magyar was, quite opportunistically, spoken for, 'since in the long run a Magyar administration seemed the only workable alternative to a German one.'[40] Béla Grünwald sardonically noted that 'the same counties which (arguing against the decree of the Emperor) emphasized the possibility of an administration in the Magyar tongue, decared it in 1811 – that is, twenty-seven years later – an impossibility.' Two decades later still, in a very 'nationalistic' Hungarian county it was said that 'the introduction of the Magyar language would endanger our constitution and all our interests.'[41] It was really only in the 1840s that the Magyar nobility – a class consisting of about 136,000 souls monopolizing land and political rights in a country of eleven million people[42] – became seriously committed to Magyarization, and then only to prevent its own historic marginalization.

At the same time, slowly increasing literacy (by 1869 one third of the adult population), the spread of print-Magyar, and the growth of a small, but energetic, liberal intelligentsia all stimulated

---

40. Ignotus, *Hungary*, pp. 47–48. Thus in 1820 the *Tiger in Schlafrock* (Tiger in a Nightgown), Emperor Franz II, made a fine impression with his Latin address to the Hungarian magnates assembled in Pest. In 1825, however, the romantic-radical grand seigneur Count István Széchenyi 'staggered his fellow-magnates' in the Diet by addressing them in Magyar! Jászi, *The Dissolution*, p. 80; and Ignotus, *Hungary*, p. 51.

41. Translated citation from his *The Old Hungary* (1910) in Jászi, *The Dissolution*, pp. 70–71. Grünwald (1839–1891) was an interesting and tragic figure. Born to a Magyarized noble family of Saxon descent, he became both a superb administrator and one of Hungary's earliest social scientists. The publication of his research demonstrating that the famous Magyar gentry-controlled 'counties' were parasites on the nation evoked a savage campaign of public obloquy. He fled to Paris and there drowned himself in the Seine. Ignotus, *Hungary*, pp. 108–109.

42. Jászi, *The Dissolution*, p. 299.

a *popular* Hungarian nationalism conceived very differently from that of the nobility. This popular nationalism, symbolized for later generations by the figure of Lajos Kossuth (1802–1894), had its hour of glory in the Revolution of 1848. The revolutionary regime not only got rid of the imperial governors appointed by Vienna, but abolished the supposedly Ur-Magyar feudal Diet of Noble Counties, and proclaimed reforms to put an end to serfdom and noblemen's tax-exempt status, as well as to curb drastically the entailment of estates. In addition, it was decided that all Hungarian-speakers should be Hungarian (as only the privileged had been before) and every Hungarian should speak Magyar (as only some Magyars had hitherto been accustomed to do). As Ignotus drily comments, 'The "nation" was, by the standard of that time (which viewed the rise of the twin stars of Liberalism and Nationalism with boundless optimism), justified in feeling itself extremely generous when it "admitted" the Magyar peasant with no discrimination save for that relating to property;[43] and the non-Magyar Christians on condition they became Magyar; and eventually, with some reluctance and a delay of twenty years, the Jews.'[44] Kossuth's own position, in his fruitless negotiations with leaders of the various non-Magyar minorities, was that these peoples should have exactly the same civil rights as the Magyars, but that since they lacked 'historical personalities' they could not form nations on their own. Today, this position may seem a trifle arrogant. It will appear in a better light if we recall that the brilliant, young, radical-nationalist poet Sándor Petöfi (1823–1849), a leading spirit of 1848, on one occasion referred to the minorities as 'ulcers on the body of the motherland.'[45]

After the suppression of the revolutionary regime by Czarist armies in August 1849, Kossuth went into life-long exile. The stage was now set for a revival of 'official' Magyar nationalism, epitomized by the reactionary regimes of Count Kálmán Tisza

---

43. The Kossuth regime instituted adult male suffrage, but with such high property qualifications that relatively few persons were in a position to vote.
44. Ignotus, *Hungary*, p. 56.
45. Ibid., p. 59.

(1875–1890) and his son István (1903–1906). The reasons for this revival are very instructive. During the 1850s, the authoritarian-bureaucratic Bach administration in Vienna combined severe political repression with a firm implementation of certain social and economic policies proclaimed by the revolutionaries of 1848 (most notably the abolition of serfdom and noblemen's tax-exempt status) and the promotion of modernized communications and large-scale capitalist enterprise.[46] Largely deprived of its feudal privileges and security, and incapable of competing economically with the great latifundists and energetic German and Jewish entrepreneurs, the old middle and lower Magyar nobility declined into an angry, frightened rural gentry.

Luck, however, was on their side. Humiliatingly defeated by Prussian armies on the field of Königgrätz in 1866, Vienna was forced to accede to the institution of the Dual Monarchy in the Ausgleich (Compromise) of 1867. From them on, the Kingdom of Hungary enjoyed a very considerable autonomy in the running of its internal affairs. The initial beneficiaries of the Ausgleich were a group of liberal-minded high Magyar aristocrats and educated professionals. In 1868, the administration of the cultivated magnate Count Gyula Andrássy enacted a Nationalities Law which gave the non-Magyar minorities 'every right they had ever claimed or could have claimed – short of turning Hungary into a federation.'[47] But Tisza's accession to the premiership in 1875 opened an era in which the reactionary gentry successfully reconstituted their position, relatively free from Viennese interference.

In the economic field, the Tisza regime gave the great agrarian magnates a free hand,[48] but political power was essentially monopolized by the gentry. For,

---

46. Ignotus observes that Bach did provide the noblemen with some financial compensation for the loss of their privileges, 'probably neither more nor less than they would have got under Kossuth' (pp. 64–65).

47. Ibid., p. 74.

48. As a result, the number of entailed estates trebled between 1867 and 1918. If one includes Church property, fully one third of all land in Hungary was entailed by the end of the Dual Monarchy. German and Jewish capitalists also did well under Tisza.

there remained only one refuge for the dispossessed: the administrative network of national and local government and the army. For
these, Hungary needed a tremendous staff; and if she did not she
could at least pretend to. Half the country consisted of 'nationalities'
to be kept in check. To pay a host of reliable, Magyar, gentlemanly
country magistrates to control them, so the argument ran, was a
modest price for the national interest. The problem of multi-
nationalities was also a godsend; it excused the proliferation of
sinecures.

Thus 'the magnates held their entailed estates; the gentry held their
entailed jobs.'[49] Such was the social basis for a pitiless policy of enforced
Magyarization which after 1875 made the Nationalities Law a dead
letter. Legal narrowing of the suffrage, proliferation of rotten boroughs,
rigged elections, and organized political thuggery in the rural areas[50]
simultaneously consolidated the power of Tisza and his constituency
and underscored the 'official' character of their nationalism.

Jászi rightly compares this late-nineteenth-century Magyarization to
'the policy of Russian Tsardom against the Poles, the Finns, and the
Ruthenians; the policy of Prussia against the Poles and Danes; and the
policy of feudal England against the Irish.'[51] The nexus of reaction and
official nationalism is nicely illustrated by these facts: while linguistic
Magyarization was a central element of regime policy, by the end of
the 1880s only 2 per cent of the officials in the more important
branches of central and local governments were Romanian, although
Romanians constituted 20 per cent of the population, and 'even these
2 per cent are employed in the lowest grades.'[52] On the other hand, in

---

49. Ibid., pp. 81 and 82.
50. The thuggery was mainly the work of the notorious 'pandoors,' part of the
army put at the disposal of the county administrators and deployed as a violent rural
police.
51. *The Dissolution*, p. 328.
52. According to the calculations of Lajos Mocsáry (*Some Words on the Nationality
Problem*, Budapest, 1886), cited in ibid., pp. 331–332. Mocsáry (1826–1916) had in
1874 established a small Independence Party in the Hungarian parliament to fight for
Kossuth's ideas, particularly on the minorities question. His speeches denouncing
Tisza's blatant violations of the 1868 Nationalities Law led first to his physical
extrusion from parliament and then expulsion from his own party. In 1888, he

the Hungarian parliament prior to World War I, there was 'not a single representative of the working classes and of the landless peasantry (the great majority of the country) . . . and there were only 8 Romanians and Slovaks out of a total membership of 413 in a country in which only 54 per cent of the inhabitants spoke Magyar as their mother-tongue.'[53] Small wonder, then, that when Vienna sent in troops to dissolve this parliament in 1906, 'not even a single mass-meeting, a single placard, or a single popular proclamation protested against the new era of "Viennese absolutism." On the contrary the working masses and nationalities regarded with malicious joy the impotent struggle of the national oligarchy.'[54]

The triumph of the reactionary Magyar gentry's 'official national-ism' after 1875 cannot, however, be explained solely by that group's own political strength, nor by the freedom of manoeuvre it inherited from the Ausgleich. The fact is that until 1906 the Habsburg court did not feel in a position to assert itself decisively against a regime which in many respects remained a pillar of the empire. Above all, the dynasty was incapable of superimposing a strenuous official nationalism of its own. Not merely because the regime was, in the words of the eminent socialist Viktor Adler, *'Absolutismus gemildert durch Schlamperei* [absolutism tempered by slovenliness].'[55] Later

---

was returned to parliament from a wholly Romanian constituency and became largely a political outcast. Ignotus, *Hungary*, p. 109.

53. Jászi, *The Dissolution*, p. 334.

54. Ibid., p. 362. Right into the twentieth century there was a spurious quality to this 'national oligarchy.' Jászi reports the diverting story of one correspondent of a famous Hungarian daily who during World War I interviewed the wounded officer who would become the reactionary dictator of Hungary in the inter-war years. Horthy was enraged by the article's description of his thoughts 'winging back to the Hungarian father land, home of the ancestors.' 'Remember,' he said 'that, if my chief warlord is in Baden, then my fatherland is also there!' *The Dissolution*, p. 142.

55. Ibid., p. 165. 'And in the good old days when there was still such a place as Imperial Austria, one could leave the train of events, get into an ordinary train on an ordinary railway-line, and travel back home. . . . Of course cars also drove along those roads – but not too many cars! The conquest of the air had begun here too; but not too intensively. Now and then a ship was sent off to South America or the Far East; but not too often. There was no ambition to have world markets and world power. Here one was in the centre of Europe, at the focal point of the world's old axes; the words 'colony' and 'overseas' had the ring of something as yet utterly untried and remote. There was

than almost anywhere else, the dynasty clung to vanished conceptions. 'In his *religious* mysticism, each Habsburg felt himself connected by a special tie with divinity, as an executor of the divine
will. This explains their almost unscrupulous attitude in the midst of
historical catastrophes, and their proverbial ungratefulness. *Der Dank
vom Hause Habsburg* became a widely spread slogan.'[56] In addition,
bitter jealousy of Hohenzollern Prussia, which increasingly made off
with the plate of the Holy Roman Empire *and* turned itself into
Germany, kept the dynasty insisting on Franz II's splendid 'patriotism for me.'

At the same time, it is interesting that in its last days the dynasty
discovered, perhaps to its own surprise, affinities with its Social
Democrats, to the point that some of their common enemies spoke
sneeringly of 'Burgsozialismus [Court Socialism]'. In this tentative
coalition there was doubtless a mixture of Machiavellism and idealism
on each side. One can see this mixture in the vehement campaign led by
the Austrian Social Democrats against the economic and military
'separatism' pressed by the regime of Count István Tisza in 1905. Karl
Renner, for example, 'chastized the cowardice of the Austrian bourgeoisie who began to acquiesce in the separatistic plans of the Magyars,
though "the Hungarian market is incomparably more significant *for
Austrian capital* than [the] Moroccan is for the German," which German
foreign policy defends so energetically. In the claim for an independent
Hungarian customs territory he saw nothing else than the clamouring of
city sharks, swindlers, and political demagogues, against the *very interests
of Austrian industry*, of the Austrian working-classes, and of the Hungarian agricultural population.'[57] Similarly, Otto Bauer wrote that:[58]

---

some display of luxury, but it was not, of course as oversophisticated as the French. One
went in for sport; but not in madly Anglo-Saxon fashion. One spent tremendous sums
on the army; but only just enough to assure one of remaining the second weakest among
the great powers.' Robert Musil, *The Man Without Qualities*, I, pp. 31–32. This book is
the great comic novel of our century.

· 56. Jászi, *The Dissolution*, p. 135. Author's emphasis. When Metternich was
dismissed after the 1848 insurrections and had to flee, 'nobody in the whole court
asked him where he would go and how he could live.' Sic transit.

57. Ibid., p. 181. Emphases added.

58. Otto Bauer, *Die Nationalitätenfrage und die Sozialdemocratie* (1907), as found in

In the era of the Russian revolution [of 1905], no one will dare to use naked military force to subjugate the country [Hungary], rent as it is by class and national antagonisms. But the inner conflicts of the country will provide the Crown with another instrument of power which it will have to exploit if it does not wish to suffer the fate of the House of Bernadotte. It can not be the organ of two wills and yet still intend to rule over Hungary and Austria. Hence it must take steps to ensure that Hungary and Austria have a common will, and that it constructs a *single* realm [*Reich*]. Hungary's inward fragmentation offers her the possibility to achieve this goal. She will dispatch her army to Hungary to recapture it for the realm, but she will inscribe on her banners: Uncorrupted, universal and equal suffrage! Right of coalition for the agricultural laborer! National autonomy! She will counterpose to the idea of an independent Hungarian nation-state [*Nationalstaat*] the idea of the *United States of Great Austria* [sic], the idea of a federative state [*Bundesstaat*], in which each nation will administer independently its own national affairs, and all the nations will unite in one state for the preservation of their common interests. Inevitably and unavoidably, the idea of a federative state of nation-alities [*Nationalitätenbundesstaat*] will become an instrument of the Crown [sic! – *Werkzeug der Krone*], whose realm is being destroyed by the decay of Dualism.

It seems reasonable to detect in this United States of Great Austria (USGA) residues of the USA and the United Kingdom of Great Britain and Northern Ireland (one day to be ruled by a Labour Party), as well as a foreshadowing of a Union of Soviet Socialist Republics whose stretch is strangely reminiscent of Czardom's. The fact is that this USGA seemed, in its imaginer's mind, the necessary heir of a *particular* dynastic dominion (Great Austria) – with its enfranchised components exactly those produced by centuries of Habsburg 'hucksterings'.

Such 'imperial' imaginings were partly the misfortune of a socialism born in the capital of one of Europe's great dynastic

---

his *Werkausgabe*, I, p. 482. Italics in the original. Comparison of this translation with that of Jászi, given in the original version of this book, offers food for thought.

empires.[59] As we have noted earlier, the new imagined communities (including the still-born, but still imagined USGA) conjured up by lexicography and print-capitalism always regarded themselves as somehow ancient. In an age in which 'history' itself was still widely conceived in terms of 'great events' and 'great leaders', pearls strung along a thread of narrative, it was obviously tempting to decipher the community's past in antique dynasties. Hence a USGA in which the membrane separating empire from nation, crown from proletariat, is almost transparent. Nor was Bauer unusual in all this. A William the Conqueror and a George I, neither of whom could speak English, continue to appear unproblematically as beads in the necklace 'Kings of England'. 'Saint' Stephen (r. 1001–1038) might admonish his successor that:[60]

> The utility of foreigners and guests is so great that they can be given a place of sixth importance among the royal ornaments. . . . For, as the guests come from various regions and provinces, they bring with them various languages and customs, various knowledges and arms. All these adorn the royal court, heighten its splendour, and terrify the haughtiness of foreign powers. For a country unified in language and customs is fragile and weak. . . .

But such words would not in the least prevent his subsequent apotheosis as the First King of Hungary.

In conclusion, then it has been argued that from about the middle of the nineteenth century there developed what Seton-Watson terms 'official nationalisms' inside Europe. These nationalisms were historically 'impossible' until after the appearance of popular linguistic-nationalisms, for, at bottom, they were *responses* by power-groups – primarily, but not exclusively, dynastic and

---

59. Surely they also reflect the characteristic mindset of a well-known type of leftwing European intellectual, proud of his command of the civilized languages, his Enlightenment heritage, and his penetrating understanding of everyone else's problems. In this pride, internationalist and aristocratic ingredients are rather evenly mixed.
60. Jászi, *The Dissolution*, p. 39.

aristocratic – threatened with exclusion from, or marginalization in, popular imagined communities. A sort of tectonic upheaval was beginning, which, after 1918 and 1945, tipped these groups towards drainages in Estoril and Monte Carlo. Such official nationalisms were conservative, not to say reactionary, *policies*, adapted from the model of the largely spontaneous popular nationalisms that preceded them.[61] Nor were they ultimately confined to Europe and the Levant. In the name of imperialism, very similar policies were pursued by the same sorts of groups in the vast Asian and African territories subjected in the course of the nineteenth century.[62] Finally, refracted into non-European cultures and histories, they were picked up and imitated by indigenous ruling groups in those few zones (among them Japan and Siam) which escaped direct subjection.

In almost every case, official nationalism concealed a discrepancy between nation and dynastic realm. Hence a world-wide contradiction: Slovaks were to be Magyarized, Indians Anglicized, and Koreans Japanified, but they would not be permitted to join pilgrimages which would allow them to administer Magyars, Englishmen, or Japanese. The banquet to which they were invited always

---

61. Half a century ago Jászi had already suspected as much: 'One may ask whether the late imperialist developments of nationalism do really emanate from the genuine sources of the national idea and not from the monopolistic interests of certain groups which were *alien* to the original conception of national aims.' Ibid., p. 286. Emphasis added.

62. The point is nicely underlined by inversion in the case of the Netherlands Indies, which in its last days was still to a large extent ruled through a language which we know today as 'Indonesian.' This is, I think, the only case of a large colonial possession in which to the end a non-European language remained a language-of-state. The anomaly is primarily to be explained by the sheer antiquity of the colony, which was founded early in the seventeenth century by a corporation (the Vereenigde Oostindische Compagnie) – long before the age of official nationalism. Doubtless there was also a certain lack of confidence on the part of the Dutch in modern times that their language and culture had a European cachet comparable to that of English, French, German, Spanish, or Italian. (Belgians in the Congo would use French rather than Flemish.) Finally, colonial educational policy was exceptionally conservative: in 1940, when the indigenous population numbered well over 70 millions, there were only 637 'natives' in college, and only 37 graduated with BAs. See George McT. Kahin, *Nationalism and Revolution in Indonesia*, p. 32. For more on the Indonesian case, see below, Chapter VII.

turned out to be a Barmecide feast. The reason for all this was not simply racism; it was also the fact that at the core of the empires nations too were emerging – Hungarian, English, and Japanese. And these nations were also instinctively resistant to 'foreign' rule. Imperialist ideology in the post-1850 era thus typically had the character of a conjuring-trick. How much it was a conjuring-trick is suggested by the equanimity with which metropolitan popular classes eventually shrugged off the 'losses' of the colonies, even in cases like Algeria where the colony had been legally incorporated into the metropole. In the end, it is always the ruling classes, bourgeois certainly, but above all aristocratic, that long mourn the empires, and their grief always has a stagey quality to it.

7

The Last Wave

The First World War brought the age of high dynasticism to an end. By 1922, Habsburgs, Hohenzollerns, Romanovs and Ottomans were gone. In place of the Congress of Berlin came the League of *Nations*, from which non-Europeans were not excluded. From this time on, the legitimate international norm was the nation-state, so that in the League even the surviving imperial powers came dressed in national costume rather than imperial uniform. After the cataclysm of World War II the nation-state tide reached full flood. By the mid-1970s even the Portuguese Empire had become a thing of the past.

The new states of the post-World War II period have their own character, which nonetheless is incomprehensible except in terms of the succession of models we have been considering. One way of underlining this ancestry is to remind ourselves that a very large number of these (mainly non-European) nations came to have European languages-of-state. If they resembled the 'American' model in this respect, they took from linguistic European nationalism its ardent populism, and from official nationalism its Russifying policy-orientation. They did so because Americans and Europeans had lived through complex historical experiences which were now everywhere modularly imagined, and because the European languages-of-state they employed were the legacy of imperialist official nationalism. This is why so often in the 'nation-building' policies of the new states one sees both a genuine, popular nationalist enthusiasm and a systematic, even Machiavellian, instilling of nationalist ideology through the mass media, the educational system, administrative regulations, and so forth. In turn, this blend of popular and official nationalism has been the product of anomalies created by European imperialism: the well-known arbitrariness of frontiers, and bilingual intelligentsias poised precariously over diverse monoglot populations. One can thus think of many of these nations as projects the achievement of which is still in progress, yet projects conceived more in the spirit of Mazzini than that of Uvarov.

In considering the origins of recent 'colonial nationalism', one central similarity with the colonial nationalisms of an earlier age immediately strikes the eye: the isomorphism between each nationalism's territorial stretch and that of the previous imperial administrative unit. The similarity is by no means fortuitous; it is clearly related to the geography of all colonial pilgrimages. The difference lies in the fact that the contours of eighteenth-century creole pilgrimages were shaped not only by the centralizing ambitions of metropolitan absolutism, but by real problems of communication and transportation, and a general technological primitiveness. In the twentieth century, these problems had largely been overcome, and in their place came a Janus-faced 'Russification'.

I argued earlier that in the late eighteenth century the imperial administrative unit came to acquire a national meaning in part because it circumscribed the ascent of creole functionaries. So too in the twentieth century. For even in cases where a young brown or black Englishman came to receive some education or training in the metropole, in a way that few of his creole progenitors had been able to do, that was typically the last time he made this bureaucratic pilgrimage. From then on, the apex of his looping flight was *the highest administrative centre to which he could be assigned*: Rangoon, Accra, Georgetown, or Colombo. Yet in each constricted journey he found bilingual travelling companions with whom he came to feel a growing communality. In his journey he understood rather quickly that his point of origin – conceived either ethnically, linguistically, or geographically – was of small significance. At most it started him on this pilgrimage rather than that: it did not fundamentally determine his destination or his companions. Out of this pattern came that subtle, half-concealed transformation, step by step, of the colonial-state into the national-state, a transformation made possible not only by a solid continuity of personnel, but by the established skein of journeys through which each state was experienced by its functionaries.[1]

Yet increasingly after the middle of the nineteenth century, and above all in the twentieth, the journeys were no longer made by a mere handful of travellers, but rather by huge and variegated crowds. The central factors at work were three. First and foremost was the enormous increase in physical mobility made possible by the aston-ishing achievements of industrial capitalism – railways and steamships in the last century, motor transport and aviation in this. The interminable journeys of the old Americas were quickly becoming things of the past.

Second, imperial 'Russification' had its practical as well as ideo-logical side. The sheer size of the global European empires, and the vast populations subjected, meant that purely metropolitan, or even creole, bureaucracies were neither recruitable nor affordable. The colonial state, and, somewhat later, corporate capital, needed armies of clerks, who to be useful had to be bilingual, capable of mediating linguistically between the metropolitan nation and the colonized peoples. The need was all the greater as the specialized functions of the state everywhere multiplied after the turn of the century. Alongside the old district officer appeared the medical officer, the irrigation engineer, the agricultural extension-worker, the school-teacher, the policeman, and so on. With every enlargement of the state, the swarm of its inner pilgrims swelled.[2]

---

1. Not only, of course by functionaries, though they were the main group. Consider, for example, the geography of *Noli Me Tangere* (and many other nationalist novels). Though some of the most important characters in Rizal's text are Spanish, and some of the Filipino characters have been to Spain (off the novel's stage), the circumambience of travel by any of the characters is confined to what, eleven years after its publication and two years after its author's execution, would become the Republic of the Philippines.

2. To give only one example: by 1928, there were almost 250,000 indigenes on the payroll of the Netherlands East Indies, and these formed 90% of all state functionaries. (Symptomatically, the widely discrepant salaries and pensions of Dutch

Third was the spread of modern-style education, not only by the colonial state, but also by private religious and secular organizations. This expansion occurred not simply to provide cadres for governmental and corporate hierarchies, but also because of the growing acceptance of the moral importance of modern knowledge even for colonized populations.[3] (Indeed the phenomenon of the educated unemployed was already beginning to be apparent in a variety of colonial states.)

It is generally recognized that the intelligentsias were central to the rise of nationalism in the colonial territories, not least because colonialism ensured that native agrarian magnates, big merchants, industrial entrepreneurs, and even a large professional class were relative rarities. Almost everywhere economic power was either monopolized by the colonialists themselves, or unevenly shared with a politically impotent class of pariah (non-native) businessmen – Lebanese, Indian and Arab in colonial Africa, Chinese, Indian, and Arab in colonial Asia. It is no less generally recognized that the intelligentsias' vanguard role derived from their bilingual literacy, or rather literacy and bilingualism. Print-literacy already made possible the imagined community floating in homogeneous, empty time of which we have spoken earlier. Bilingualism meant access, through the European language-of-state, to modern Western culture in the broadest sense, and, in particular, to the models of nationalism, nation-ness, and nation-state produced elsewhere in the course of the nineteenth century.[4]

In 1913, the Dutch colonial regime in Batavia, taking its lead from

---

and native officials, when combined, ate up 50% of state expenditures!). See Amry Vandenbosch, *The Dutch East Indies*, pp. 171–73. Yet Dutchmen were proportionately nine times as thick on the bureaucratic ground as were Englishmen in British (non-'native state') India.

3. Even in the ultra-conservative Netherlands Indies, the number of natives receiving a primary Western-style education shot up from an average of 2,987 in the years 1900–04 to 74,697 in 1928; while those receiving a Western-style secondary education increased in the same span of time from 25 to 6,468. Kahin, *Nationalism*, p. 31.

4. To borrow from Anthony Barnett, it also 'allowed the intellectuals to *say* to their fellow-speakers [of the indigenous vernaculars] that "we" can be like "them" '.

The Hague, sponsored massive colony-wide festivities to celebrate the centennial of the 'national liberation' of the Netherlands from French imperialism. Orders went out to secure physical participation and financial contributions, not merely from the local Dutch and Eurasian communities, but also from the subject native population. In protest, the early Javanese–Indonesian nationalist Suwardi Surjaningrat (Ki Hadjar Dewantoro) wrote his famous Dutch-language newspaper article 'Als ik eens Nederlander was' (If I were for once to be a Dutchman).[5]

> In my opinion, there is something out of place – something indecent – if we (I still being a Dutchman in my imagination) ask the natives to join the festivities which celebrate our independence. Firstly, we will hurt their sensitive feelings because we are here celebrating our own independence in their native country which we colonize. At the moment we are very happy because a hundred years ago we liberated ourselves from foreign domination; and all of this is occurring in front of the eyes of those who are still under our domination. Does it not occur to us that these poor slaves are also longing for such a moment as this, when they like us will be able to celebrate their independence? Or do we perhaps feel that because of our soul-destroying policy we regard all human souls as dead? If that is so, then we are deluding ourselves, because no matter how primitive a community is, it is against any type of oppression. If I were a Dutchman, I would not organize an independence celebration in a country where the independence of the people has been stolen.

With these words Suwardi was able to turn Dutch history against the Dutch, by scraping boldly at the weld between Dutch nationalism and imperialism. Furthermore, by the imaginary transformation of

---

5. It appeared originally in *De Expres* on July 13, 1913, but was quickly translated into 'Indonesian' and published in the native press. Suwardi was then 24 years old. An unusually well-educated and progressive aristocrat, he had in 1912 joined with a Javanese commoner, Dr. Tjipto Mangoenkoesoemo, and a Eurasian, Eduard Douwes Dekker, to from the Indische Partij, the colony's first political party. For a brief, but useful, study of Suwardi, see Savitri Scherer, 'Harmony and Dissonance: Early Nationalist Thought in Java', chapter 2. Her Appendix I gives an English translation of the famous article, from which this passage is drawn.

himself into a temporary Dutchman (which invited a reciprocal transformation of his Dutch readers into temporary Indonesians), he undermined all the racist fatalities that underlay Dutch colonial ideology.[6]

Suwardi's broadside – which delighted his Indonesian as much as it irritated his Dutch audience – is exemplary of a world-wide twentieth-century phenomenon. For the paradox of imperial official nationalism was that it inevitably brought what were increasingly thought of and written about as European 'national histories' into the consciousnesses of the colonized – not merely via occasional obtuse festivities, but also through reading-rooms and classrooms.[7] Viet-namese youngsters could not avoid learning about the *philosophes* and the Revolution, and what Debray calls 'our secular antagonism to Germany'.[8] Magna Carta, the Mother of Parliaments, and the Glorious Revolution, glossed as English national history, entered schools all over the British Empire. Belgium's independence struggle against Holland was not erasable from schoolbooks Congolese children would one day read. So also the histories of the USA in the Philippines and, last of all, Portugal in Mozambique and Angola. The irony, of course, is that these histories were written out of a historiographical consciousness which by the turn of the century was, all over Europe, becoming nationally defined. (The barons who imposed Magna Carta on John Plantagenet did not speak 'English,' and had no conception of themselves as 'Englishmen,' but they were firmly defined as early patriots in the classrooms of the United Kingdom 700 years later.)

Yet there is a characteristic feature of the emerging nationalist intelligentsias in the colonies which to some degree marks them off

---

6. Notice the educational linkage here between 'imagined' and 'imaginary' communities.

7. The celebrations of 1913 were agreeably emblematic of official nationalism in another sense. The 'national liberation' commemorated was in fact the restoration of the House of Orange by the victorious armies of the Holy Alliance (not the establishment of the Batavian Republic in 1795); and half the liberated nation soon seceded to form the Kingdom of Belgium in 1830. But the 'national liberation' gloss was certainly what Suwardi imbibed in his colonial classroom.

8. 'Marxism and the National Question,' p. 41.

from the vernacularizing nationalist intelligentsias of nineteenth-century Europe. Almost invariably they were very young, and attached a complex political significance to their youth – a significance which, though it has changed over time, remains important to this day. The rise of (modern/organized) Burmese nationalism is often dated to the founding in 1908 of the Young Men's Buddhist Association in Rangoon; and of Malayan by the establishment in 1938 of the Kesatuan Melayu Muda (Union of Malay Youth). Indonesians annually celebrate the *Sumpah Pemuda* (Oath of Youth) drawn up and sworn by the nationalist youth congress of 1928. And so on. It is perfectly true that in one sense Europe had been there before – if we think of Young Ireland, Young Italy, and the like. Both in Europe and in the colonies 'young' and 'youth' signified dynamism, progress, self-sacrificing idealism and revolutionary will. But in Europe 'young' had little in the way of definable sociological contours. One could be middle-aged and still part of Young Ireland; one could be illiterate and still part of Young Italy. The reason, of course, was that the language of these nationalisms was either a vernacular mother-tongue to which the members had spoken access from the cradle, or, as in the case of Ireland, a metropolitan language which had sunk such deep roots in sections of the population over centuries of conquest that it too could manifest itself, creole-style, as a vernacular. There was thus no necessary connection between language, age, class, and status.

In the colonies things were very different. Youth meant, above all, the *first* generation in any significant numbers to have acquired a European education, marking them off linguistically and culturally from their parents' generation, as well from the vast bulk of their colonized agemates (cf. B. C. Pal). Burma's 'English-language' YMBA, modelled in part on the YMCA, was built by English-reading schoolboys. In the Netherlands Indies one finds, *inter alia*, Jong Java (Young Java), Jong Ambon (Young Amboina), and Jong Islamietenbond (League of Young Muslim) – titles incomprehensible to any young native unacquainted with the colonial tongue. In the colonies, then, by 'Youth' we mean 'Schooled Youth,' at least at the start. This in turn reminds us again of the unique role played by colonial school-systems in promoting colonial nationalisms.[9]

The case of Indonesia affords a fascinatingly intricate illustration of this process, not least because of its enormous size, huge population (even in colonial times), geographical fragmentation (about 3,000 islands), religious variegation (Muslims, Buddhists, Catholics, assorted Protestants, Hindu-Balinese, and 'animists'), and ethnolinguistic diversity (well over 100 distinct groups). Furthermore, as its hybrid pseudo-Hellenic name suggests, its stretch does not remotely correspond to any precolonial domain; on the contrary, at least until General Suharto's brutal invasion of ex-Portuguese East Timor in 1975, its boundaries have been those left behind by the last Dutch conquests (c. 1910).

Some of the peoples on the eastern coast of Sumatra are not only physically close, across the narrow Straits of Malacca, to the populations of the western littoral of the Malay Peninsula, but they are ethnically related, understand each other's speech, have a common religion, and so forth. These same Sumatrans share neither mother-tongue, ethnicity, nor religion with the Ambonese, located

---

9. Our focus here will be on civilian schools. But their military counterparts were often important too. The professionally officered standing army pioneered by Prussia early in the nineteenth century has required an educational pyramid in some ways more elaborate, if not more specialized, than its civilian analogue. Young officers ('Turks') produced by new military academies have often played significant roles in the development of nationalism. Emblematic is the case of Major Chukuma Nzeogwu, who masterminded the January 15, 1966 coup in Nigeria. A Christian Ibo, he was among the first group of young Nigerians sent for training to Sandhurst to make possible the transformation of a white-officered colonial mercenary force into a national army, on Nigeria's attainment of independence in 1960. (If he attended Sandhurst with the future Brigadier Afrifa, who, also in 1966, was to overthrow *his* government, each native was destined to return to his own imperial habitat). It is striking evidence of the power of the Prussian model that he was able to lead Muslim Hausa troops in assassinating the Sardauna of Sokoto and other Muslim Hausa aristocrats, and, consequently, destroy the Muslim-Hausa-dominated government of Abubakar Tafawa Balewa. It is no less striking a sign of colonial-school-generated nationalism that over Radio Kaduna he assured his countrymen that 'you will no more be ashamed to say that you are Nigerian.' (Quotation taken from Anthony H.M. Kirk-Greene, *Crisis and Conflict in Nigeria: A Documentary Source Book*, p. 126.) Yet nationalism was thinly enough then spread in Nigeria for Nzeogwu's nationalist coup to be quickly interpreted as an Ibo plot; hence the military mutinies of July, the anti-Ibo pogroms of September and October, and Biafra's secession in May 1967. (See Robin Luckham's superb *The Nigerian Military*, passim.)

on islands thousands of miles away to the east. Yet during this century they have come to understand the Ambonese as fellow-Indonesians, the Malays as foreigners.

Nothing nurtured this bonding more than the schools that the regime in Batavia set up in increasing numbers after the turn of the century. To see why, one has to remember that in complete contrast to traditional, indigenous schools, which were always local and personal enterprises (even if, in good Muslim fashion, there was plenty of horizontal movement of students from one particularly well-reputed ulama-teacher to another), the government schools formed a colossal, highly rationalized, tightly centralized hierarchy, structurally analogous to the state bureaucracy itself. Uniform textbooks, standardized diplomas and teaching certificates, a strictly regulated gradation of age-groups,[10] classes and instructional materials, in themselves created a self-contained, coherent universe of experience. But no less important was the hierarchy's geography. Standardized elementary schools came to be scattered about in villages and small townships of the colony; junior and senior middle-schools in larger towns and provincial centres; while tertiary education (the pyramid's apex) was confined to the colonial capital of Batavia and the Dutch-built city of Bandung, 100 miles southwest in the cool Priangan highlands. Thus the twentieth-century colonial school-system brought into being pilgrimages which paralleled longer-established functionary journeys. The Rome of these pilgrimages was Batavia: not Singapore, not Manila, not Rangoon, not even the old Javanese royal capitals of Jogjakarta and Surakarta.[11] From all over the vast colony, but from nowhere outside it, the tender pilgrims made their inward, upward way, meeting fellow-pilgrims from different, perhaps once hostile, villages in primary school; from different ethnolinguistic groups in middle-school; and from every

---

10. The idea of a student being 'too old' to be in class X or Y, unthinkable in a traditional Muslim school, was an unselfconscious axiom of the colonial Western-style school.

11. Ultimately, of course, the apices were The Hague, Amsterdam, and Leiden; but those who could seriously dream of studying there were a tiny handful.

part of the realm in the tertiary institutions of the capital.[12] And they knew that from wherever they had come they still had read the same books and done the same sums. They also knew, even if they never got so far – and most did not – that Rome was Batavia, and that all these journeyings derived their 'sense' from the capital, in effect explaining why 'we' are 'here' 'together.' To put it another way, their common experience, and the amiably competitive comradeship of the classroom, gave the maps of the colony which they studied (always coloured differently from British Malaya or the American Philippines) a territorially specific imagined reality which was every day confirmed by the accents and physiognomies of their classmates.[13]

And what were they all together? The Dutch were quite clear on this point: whatever mother-tongue they spoke, they were irremediably *inlanders*, a word which, like the English 'natives' and the French '*indigènes*,' always carried an unintentionally paradoxical semantic load. In this colony, as in each separate, other colony, it meant that the persons referred to were both 'inferior' *and 'belonged there'* (just as the Dutch, being 'natives' of Holland, belonged *there*). Conversely, the Dutch by such language assigned themselves, along with superiority, 'not-belonging-there'. The word also implied that in their common inferiority, the *inlanders* were *equally* contemptible, no matter what ethnolinguistic group or class they came from. Yet even this miserable equality of condition had a definite perimeter. For *inlander* always raised the question 'native of what?'. If the Dutch sometimes spoke as if *inlanders* were a world-category, experience showed that this notion was hardly sustainable in practice. *Inlanders* stopped at the coloured colony's drawn edge. Beyond that were, variously, 'natives', *indigènes* and *indios*. Moreover, colonial legal terminology included the category *vreemde oosterlingen* (foreign Orientals), which had the dubious ring of false coin – as it were 'foreign natives.' Such 'foreign Orientals,' mainly Chinese, Arabs and Japanese, though they might live in the colony, had a politico-

12. Being secular, twentieth-century schools they were usually co-educational, though with boys the preponderant majority. Hence love-affairs, and quite often marriages, 'off the school-bench,' which crossed all traditional lines.
    13. Sukarno never saw the West Irian for which he fought so hard till he was over 60. Here, as in the schoolroom maps, we see fiction seeping into reality – cf. *Noli* and *El Periquillo Sarniento*.

122

legal legal status superior to that of the 'native natives'. Furthermore, tiny Holland was sufficiently awed by the Meiji oligarchs' economic strength and military prowess for Japanese in the colony to be legally promoted, from 1899 on, to 'honorary Europeans'. From all this, by a sort of sedimentation, *inlander* – excluding whites, Dutchmen, Chinese, Arabs, Japanese, 'natives,' *indigènes*, and *indios* – grew ever more specific in content; until, like a ripe larva, it was suddenly transmogrified into the spectacular butterfly called 'Indonesian'.

While it is true that the concepts *inlander* and 'native' could never be truly generalized racist notions, since they always implied roots in some specific habitat,[14] the case of Indonesia should not lead us to assume that each 'native' habitat had preordained or immutable frontiers. Two examples will show the contrary: French West Africa and French Indochina.

In its heyday, the École Normale William Ponty in Dakar, though only a secondary school, was still the apex of the colonial educational pyramid in French West Africa.[15] To William Ponty came intelligent students from what we know today as Guinea, Mali, the Ivory Coast, Senegal, and so on. We should not be surprised therefore if the pilgrimages of these boys, terminating in Dakar, were initially read in French [West] African terms, of which the paradoxical concept *négritude* – essence of African-ness expressible only in French, language of the William Ponty classrooms – is an unforgettable symbol. Yet the apicality of William Ponty was accidental and evanescent. As more secondary schools were constructed in French West Africa, it was no longer necessary for bright boys to make so distant a

---

14. Compare, by contrast, 'half-breeds' or 'niggers,' who, beginning at Calais, could crop up anywhere on the planet outside the United Kingdom.

15. On the origins and development of this famous school, see Abdou Moumouni, *L'Education en Afrique*, pp. 41–49; on its political significance, Ruth Schachter Morgenthau, *Political Parties in French-Speaking West Africa*, pp. 12–14, 18–21. Originally an untitled *école normale* located in Saint-Louis, it was moved to Gorée, just outside Dakar, in 1913. Subsequently it was named after William Merlaud-Ponty, the fourth governor-general (1908–15) of French West Africa. Serge Thion informs me that the name William (as opposed to Guillaume) has long been in vogue in the area around Bordeaux. He is surely right in attributing this popularity to the historic ties with England created by the wine trade; but it seems just possible that it goes back to the era when Bordeaux (Guyenne) was still a solid part of the realm ruled from London.

pilgrimage. And in any case the educational centrality of William Ponty was never matched by a comparable administrative centrality of Dakar. The interchangeability of French West African boys on the benches of William Ponty was not paralleled by their later bureau-cratic substitutability in the French West African colonial adminis-tration. Hence, the school's Old Boys went home to become, eventually, Guinean or Malian nationalist leaders, while retaining a 'West African' camaraderie and solidary intimacy lost to succeeding generations.[16]

In much the same way, for one generation of relatively well educated adolescents, the curious hybrid 'Indochine' had a real, experienced, imagined meaning.[17] This entity, it will be recalled, was not legally proclaimed until 1887, and did not acquire its fullest territorial form until 1907, though active French meddling in the general area went back a century earlier.

Broadly speaking, the educational policy pursued by the colonial rulers of 'Indochine' had two fundamental purposes[18] – both of which, as it turned out, contributed to the growth of an 'Indochinese' consciousness. One aim was to break existing politico-cultural ties between the colonized peoples and the immediate extra-Indochinese

---

16. There seems to have been nothing similar in British West Africa, whether because the British colonies were non-contiguous, or because London was wealthy and liberal enough to start secondary schools almost simultaneously in the major territories, or because of the localism of rival Protestant missionary organizations. Achimota School, a secondary school founded by the colonial state in Accra in 1927, quickly became the main peak of a Gold Coast-specific educational pyramid, and after independence it was where the children of cabinet ministers began learning how to succeed their fathers. A rival peak, Mfantsipim Secondary School, had the advantage of seniority (it was founded in 1876), but the weaknesses of locale (Cape Coast) and semi-detachment from the state (it was in denominational hands till well after independence). I owe this information to Mohamed Chambas.

17. It led, *inter alia*, to a one-generation (1930–1951?) Indochinese Communist Party in which, for a time, youngsters whose mother tongues might be Vietnamese, Khmer, or Lao participated. Today, the formation of this party is sometimes viewed merely as an expression of 'age-old Vietnamese expansionism.' In fact, it was sired by the Comintern out of the educational (and to a lesser extent administrative) system of French Indochina.

18. This policy is ably and thoroughly discussed in Gail Paradise Kelly, 'Franco-Vietnamese Schools, 1918 to 1938'. Unluckily, the author concentrates exclusively on the Vietnamese-speaking population of Indochina.

world. As far as 'Cambodge' and 'Laos' were concerned,[19] the target was Siam, which had previously exercised a variable suzerainty over them and shared with both the rituals, institutions, and sacred language of Hinayana Buddhism. (In addition, the language and script of the lowland Lao were, and are, closely related to those of the Thai). It was precisely out of this concern that the French experimented first in those zones *last* seized from Siam with the so-called 'renovated pagoda schools,' which were designed to move Khmer monks and their pupils out of the Thai orbit into that of Indochina.[20]

In eastern Indochina (my shorthand for 'Tonkin,' 'Annam,' and 'Cochin China'), the target was China and Chinese civilization. Although the dynasties ruling in Hanoi and Hué had for centuries defended their independence from Peking, they came to rule through a mandarinate consciously modelled on that of the Chinese. Recruitment into the state machinery was geared to written examinations in the Confucian classics; dynastic documents were written in Chinese characters; and the ruling class was heavily Sinicized in culture. These long-standing ties assumed an additionally unwelcome character after about 1895, when the writings of such Chinese reformers as K'ang Yu-wei and Liang Ch'i-ch'ao, and nationalists like Sun Yat-sen, began seeping across the northern frontier of the colony.[21]

---

19. I use this perhaps clumsy terminology to emphasize the colonial origins of these entities. 'Laos' was assembled out of a cluster of rival principalities, leaving more than half of the Lao-speaking population in Siam. The boundaries of 'Cambodge' conformed neither to any particular historical stretch of the precolonial realm, nor to the distribution of the Khmer-speaking peoples. Some hundreds of thousands of such people ended up trapped in 'Cochin China,' producing in time that distinct community known as the Khmer Krom (down-river Khmer).

20. They pursued this aim by establishing in the 1930s an Ecole Supérieure de Pali in Phnom Penh, an ecclesiastical college attended by both Khmer- and Lao-speaking monks. The attempt to turn Buddhist eyes away from Bangkok seems not to have been wholly successful. In 1942 (shortly after Siam regained control of much of northwestern 'Cambodge' with Japanese assistance), the French arrested a venerable professor of the Ecole for possession and distribution of 'subversive' Thai educational materials. (Most likely, these materials were some of the strongly nationalist school-texts produced by the vociferously anti-French regime of Field-Marshal Plaek Phibunsongkhram (1938–1944).

21. David G. Marr, *Vietnamese Tradition on Trial, 1920–1945*, p. 146. No less alarming were smuggled Chinese translations of such troubling French authors as Rousseau. (Kelly, 'Franco-Vietnamese Schools', p. 19).

Accordingly, Confucian examinations were successively abolished in 'Tonkin' in 1915 and in 'Annam' in 1918. Henceforth, recruitment into the civil services of Indochina was to take place exclusively through a developing French colonial education system. Furthermore, *quốc ngữ*, a romanized phonetic script originally devised by Jesuit missionaries in the seventeenth century,[22] and adopted by the authorities for use in 'Cochin China' as early as the 1860s, was consciously promoted to break the links with China – and perhaps also with the indigenous past – by making dynastic records and ancient literatures inaccessible to a new generation of colonized Vietnamese.[23]

The second aim of educational policy was to produce a carefully-calibrated quantum of French-speaking and French-writing Indochinese to serve as a politically reliable, grateful, and acculturated indigenous elite, filling the subordinate echelons of the colony's bureaucracy and larger commercial enterprises.[24]

The intricacies of the colonial educational system need not detain us here. For our present purposes, the key characteristic of the system was that it formed a single, if ramshackle, pyramid, of which, until the mid-1930s, the upper terraces all lay in the east. Up until then, for

---

22. In its final form, this script is usually attributed to the gifted lexicographer Alexandre de Rhodes, who in 1651 published his remarkable *Dictionarium annamiticum, lusitanum et latinum.*

23. '[Most] French colonial officials of the late nineteenth century . . . were convinced that to achieve permanent colonial success required the harsh curtailment of Chinese influences, including the writing system. Missionaries often saw the Confucian literati as the main obstacle to the general Catholic conversion of Vietnam. Hence, in their view, to eliminate the Chinese language was simultaneously to isolate Vietnam from its heritage and to neutralize the traditional elite.' (Marr, *Vietnamese Tradition*, p. 145). Kelly quotes one colonial writer thus: 'in effect, the teaching of quoc ngu alone . . . will have the result of communicating to Vietnamese only the French writing, literature, and philosophy which we wish them [to be exposed to]. That is those [works] which we judge useful to them and easily assimilable: only the texts which we transcribe into quoc ngu.' 'Franco-Vietnamese Schools', p. 22.

24. See ibid., pp. 14–15. For a wider, lower stratum of the Indochinese population Governor-General Albert Sarraut (author of the 1917 Code of Public Instruction) urged: 'a simple education, reduced to essentials, permitting the child to learn all that will be useful to him to know in his humble career of farmer or artisan to ameliorate the natural and social conditions of his existence.' Ibid., p. 17.

example, the only state-sponsored *lycées* were located in Hanoi and Saigon; and throughout the prewar colonial period, the sole university in Indochina was located in Hanoi, so to speak 'just down the street' from the palace of the Governor-General.[25] The climbers of these terraces included all the major vernacular-speakers of the French domain: Vietnamese, Chinese, Khmer, and Lao (and not a few young French colonials). For the climbers, coming from, shall we say, My Tho, Battambang, Vientiane, and Vinh, the meaning of their convergence had to be 'Indochinese,' in the same way that the polyglot and polyethnic student body of Batavia and Bandung had to read theirs as 'Indonesian.'[26] This Indochinese-ness, although it was quite real, was nonetheless imagined by a tiny group, and not for very long. Why did it turn out to be so evanescent, while Indonesian-ness survived and deepened?

First there was a marked change of course in colonial education, above all as applied in eastern Indochina, from about 1917 on. The actual, or immediately impending, liquidation of the traditional Confucian examination system persuaded more and more members of the Vietnamese elite to try to place their children in the best French schools available, so as to ensure their bureaucratic futures. The resulting competition for places in the few good schools available

---

25. In 1937, a total of 631 students were enrolled, 580 of them in the faculties of law and medicine. Ibid., p. 79; see also pp. 69–79, for the bizarre history of this institution, founded in 1906, closed in 1908, reopened in 1918, and never, till the late 1930s, much more than a glorified vocational college.

26. As I shall be concentrating on Khmers and Vietnamese below, this may be the place to make a brief reference to some prominent Lao. The present Prime Minister of Laos, Kaysone Phoumvihan attended the University of Hanoi's medical faculty in the late 1930s. The head of state, Prince Souphanouvong, graduated from Hanoi's Lycée Albert Sarraut before obtaining an engineering degree in metropolitan France. His elder brother, Prince Phetsarath Ratanavongsa, who headed the short-lived Lao Issara (Free Lao) anticolonial government in Vientiane from October 1945 to April 1946, had as a youth been graduated from Saigon's Lycée Chasseloup-Laubat. Prior to World War II, the highest educational institution in 'Laos' was the small Collège [i.e. junior high school] Pavie in Vientiane. See Joseph J. Zasloff, *Pathet Lao*, pp. 104–105; and '3349' [pseudonym of Phetsarath Ratanavongsa], *Iron Man of Laos*, pp. 12 and 46. It is revealing, I think, that in his account of his later schooldays in Paris, Phetsarath regularly and unselfconsciously speaks of his identifiably Lao, Khmer, and Vietnamese classmates as 'the Indochinese students.' See, e.g., ibid., pp. 14–15.

aroused a particularly strong reaction from the *colons*, who regarded these schools as by right a largely French preserve. The colonial regime's solution to the problem was to create a separate and subordinate 'Franco-Vietnamese' educational structure which placed special emphasis, in its lower grades, on Vietnamese-language instruction in *quốc ngữ* (with French taught as a second language via the medium of *quốc ngữ*).[27] This policy shift had two complementary results. On the one hand, government publication of hundreds of thousands of *quốc ngữ* primers significantly accelerated the spread of this European-invented script, unintentionally helping to turn it, between 1920 and 1945, into *the* popular medium for the expression of Vietnamese cultural (and national) solidarity.[28] For even if only 10 per cent of the Vietnamese-speaking population was literate by the late 1930s, this was a proportion unprecedented in the history of this people. Moreover, these literates were, unlike the Confucian literati, deeply committed to a rapid increase in their own numbers. (Similarly, in 'Cambodge' and 'Laos', if on a more limited scale, the authorities promoted the *printing* of elementary school-texts in the vernaculars, initially and mainly in the traditional orthographies, later and more feebly in romanized scripts).[29] On the other hand, the policy worked to exclude non-native-Vietnamese-speakers residing in eastern Indochina. In the case of the Khmer Krom of 'Cochin

---

27. Thus in the previously 'integrated' *lycées* Chasseloup-Laubat and Albert Sarraut, sub-standard 'native sections' were established in 1917–1918. These 'native sections' eventually turned respectively into the Lycée Petrus Ky and the Lycée du Protectorat. (Ibid., pp. 60–63). Nonetheless, a minority of privileged *indigènes* continued to attend the 'real French' *lycées* (the adolescent Norodom Sihanouk graced Chasseloup-Laubat), while a minority of 'French' (mainly Eurasians and natives with French legal status) attended Petrus Ky and its sister institution in Hanoi.

28. Marr notes that in the 1920s 'even the most optimistic member of the intelligentsia [committed to *quốc ngữ*] could not have guessed that only two decades later, citizens of a Democratic Republic of Vietnam would be able to conduct all important affairs – political, military, economic, scientific and academic – in spoken Vietnamese linked to the *quốc ngữ* writing system.' *Vietnamese Tradition*, p. 150. It was also a disagreeable surprise to the French.

29. It is instructive that one of the first issues raised by the early Khmer nationalists of the late 1930s was the 'menace' of a so-called 'quoc ngu-ization' of the Khmer script by the colonial authorities.

China,' it worked, in combination with the colonial regime's willingness to permit them to have 'Franco-Khmer' elementary schools like those being encouraged in the Protectorate, to re-orient ambitions *back* up the Mekong. Thus those Khmer Krom adolescents who aspired to higher education in the administrative capital of Indochina (and, for a select few, even in metropolitan France) increasingly took the detour via Phnom Penh rather than the highway through Saigon.

Second, in 1935 the Collège Sisowath in Phnom Penh was upgraded into a full-fledged state *lycée*, with a status equal to, *and a curriculum identical with*, those of the existing state *lycées* in Saigon and Hanoi. Although its students were at first drawn heavily (in the tradition of the Collège) from local Sino-Khmer merchant families and those of resident Vietnamese functionaries, the proportion of native Khmers steadily increased.[30] It is probably fair to say that, after 1940, the great bulk of Khmer-speaking adolescents who achieved a solid French high-school education did so in the neat colonial capital the colonialists had built for the Norodoms.

Third was the fact that there was no real isomorphism between the educational and administrative pilgrimages in Indochina. The French made no bones about expressing the view that if the Vietnamese were untrustworthy and grasping, they were nonetheless decisively more energetic and intelligent than the 'child-like' Khmer and Lao. Accordingly, they made extensive use of Vietnamese functionaries in western Indochina.[31] The 176,000 Vietnamese residing in 'Cambodge' in 1937 – representing less than one per cent of the 19 million Vietnamese-speakers of the colony, but about 6 per cent of the Protectorate's population – formed a relatively successful group, for whom therefore Indochina had a rather solid meaning, as it did for

---

30. The pattern was not immediately followed in Vientiane. Toye reports that in the course of the 1930s only 52 Lao were graduated from the Collège [he wrongly terms it Lycée] Pavie, as opposed to 96 Vietnamese. *Laos*, p. 45.

31. It is possible that this influx paralleled the institution of the Franco-Vietnamese school system, in that it deflected Vietnamese from competing with French nationals in the more advanced, eastern parts of Indochina. In 1937, there were 39,000 Europeans living in 'Cochin China,' 'Annam' and 'Tonkin,' and only 3,100 in 'Cambodge' and 'Laos' combined. Marr, *Vietnamese Tradition*, p. 23.

the 50,000 sent into 'Laos' prior to 1945. Particularly the function-aries among them, who might be posted from place to place in *all* five subsections of the colony, could well imagine Indochina as the wide stage on which they would continue to perform.

Such imagining was much less easy for Lao and Khmer functionaries, although there was no formal or legal prohibition on fully-Indochinese careers for them. Even the more ambitious youngsters coming from the *c.*326,000 (1937) Khmer Krom community in eastern Indochina (representing perhaps 10 per cent of the entire Khmer-speaking population) found that *in practice* they had very limited career prospects outside 'Cambodge'. Thus Khmer and Lao might sit alongside Vietna-mese in French-language secondary and tertiary schools in Saigon and Hanoi, but they were unlikely to go on to share administrative offices there. Like youngsters from Cotonou and Abidjan in Dakar, they were destined to go back, on graduation, to the 'homes' colonialism had demarcated for them. To put it another way, if their educational pilgrimages were directed towards Hanoi, their administrative journeys ended in Phnom Penh and Vientiane.

Out of these contradictions emerged those Khmer-speaking students who subsequently came to be remembered as the first Cambodian nationalists. The man who can reasonably be regarded as the 'father' of Khmer nationalism, Son Ngoc Thanh, was, as his Vietnamized name suggests, a Khmer Krom who was educated in Saigon and for a while held a minor judicial post in that city. But in the mid-1930s he abandoned the Paris of the Mekong Delta to seek a more promising future in its Blois. Prince Sisowath Youtevong attended secondary school in Saigon before leaving for France for further study. When he returned to Phnom Penh fifteen years later, after World War II, he helped to found the (Khmer) Democratic Party and served as Prime Minister in 1946–1947. His Defence Minister, Sonn Voeunnsai, under-took virtually the same journeys. Huy Kanthoul, Democratic Prime Minister in 1951–1952, had graduated from an *école normale* in Hanoi in 1931, and was then returned to Phnom Penh, where he eventually joined the Lycée Sisowath's teaching staff.[32] Perhaps most exemplary of

32. Biographical materials on these men were kindly provided to me by Steve Heder.

all is the figure of Ieu Koeus, first of a melancholy line of assassinated Khmer political leaders.[33] Born in the province of Battambang in 1905 – when it was still ruled from Bangkok – he attended a local 'reformed pagoda school' before entering an 'Indochinese' elementary school in Battambang town. In 1921, he proceeded to the Collège Sisowath in the Protectorate's capital, and then to a *collège de commerce* in Hanoi, from which he graduated in 1927 at the top of his French-reading class. Hoping to study chemistry in Bordeaux, he took and passed the scholarship examination. But the colonial state blocked his way abroad. He returned to his native Battambang, where he ran a pharmacy, continuing to do so even after Bangkok regained the province in 1941. After the Japanese collapse in August 1945, he reappeared in 'Cambodge' as a Democratic parliamentarian. It is notable that he was in his way a lineal descendant of the illustrious philologists of an earlier Europe, insofar as he designed a typewriter keyboard for the Khmer script and published a weighty two-volume *Pheasa Khmer* [The Khmer Language], or as the misleading title-page of the 1967 edition has it, *La Langue Cambodgienne (Un Essai d'étude raisonné).*[34] But this text made its first appearance – volume 1 only – in 1947, when its author was Chairman of the Constituent Assembly in Phnom Penh, not in 1937, when he was vegetating in Battambang, when as yet no Khmer-speaking *lycéens* had been produced by the Lycée Sisowath, and when Indochina still had an ephemeral reality. By 1947, Khmer-speakers – at least those from 'Cambodge' – were no longer attending classes in Saigon or Hanoi. A new generation was coming on the scene for whom 'Indochine' was history and 'Vietnam' now a real and foreign country.

It is true that brutal invasions and occupations during the nineteenth century, ordered by the Nguyên dynasts in Hué, left bitter folk-memories among the Khmer, including those in that 'Cochin China' fated to become part of Vietnam. But comparable bitternesses

---

33. He died in 1950, in a grenade attack on the Democratic Party headquarters organized by an unknown, but probably princely, hand.

34. Published in Phnom Penh by the Librairie Mitserei [Free Friends]. 'Misleading' because the entire text is in Khmer. Biographical details on Ieu Koeus, drawn from his 1964 cremation volume, were generously passed on to me by Steve Heder.

existed in the Netherlands Indies: Sundanese against Javanese; Batak against Minangkabau; Sasak against Balinese; Toraja against Buginese; Javanese against Ambonese, and so on. The so-called 'federalist policy' pursued between 1945 and 1948 by the formidable Lieutenant Governor-General Hubertus van Mook to outflank the infant Indonesian Republic attempted precisely to exploit such bitternesses.[35] But in spite of a spate of ethnic rebellions in almost all parts of independent Indonesia between 1950 and 1964, 'Indonesia' survived. In part it survived because Batavia remained the educational apex to the end, but also because colonial administrative policy did not rusticate educated Sundanese to the 'Sundalands,' or Batak to their place of origin in the highlands of North Sumatra. Virtually all the major ethnolinguistic groups were, by the end of the colonial period, accustomed to the idea that there was an archipelagic stage on which they had parts to play. Thus, only one of the rebellions of 1950–64 had *separatist* ambitions; all the rest were competitive within a single Indonesian political system.[36]

In addition, one can not ignore the curious accident that by the 1920s an 'Indonesian language' had come into self-conscious existence. How this accident came about is so instructive that it seems worth a brief digression. Earlier, mention was made of the fact that only to a limited and late extent were the Indies ruled through Dutch. How could it not be so, when the Dutch had begun their local conquests in the early seventeenth century, while Dutch-language instruction for *inlanders* was not seriously undertaken until the early twentieth? What happened instead was that by a slow, largely unplanned process, a strange language-of-state evolved on the basis of an ancient inter-insular lingua franca.[37] Called *dienstmaleisch* (perhaps 'service-Malay' or

35. See Kahin, *Nationalism*, chapter 12; Anthony Reid, *The Indonesian National Revolution, 1945–50*, chapter 6; and Henri Alers, *Om een rode of groene Merdeka*, passim.

36. The exception was the abortive Republic of the South Moluccas. Christianized Ambonese had long been heavily recruited for the repressive colonial army. Many fought under van Mook against the new-born revolutionary Indonesian Republic; after Holland's recognition of Indonesian independence in 1950, they had some reason to expect an unpleasant future.

37. See the valuable account in John Hoffman, 'A Foreign Investment: Indies Malay to 1902,' *Indonesia*, 27 (April 1979), pp. 65–92.

'administrative-Malay'), it belonged typologically with 'Ottoman' and that 'fiscal German' which emerged from the polyglot barracks of the Habsburg empire.[38] By the early nineteenth century it was solidly in place inside officialdom. When print-capitalism arrived on the scene in a sizeable way after mid-century, the language moved out into the marketplace and the media. Used at first mainly by Chinese and Eurasian newspapermen and printers, it was picked up by *inlanders* at the century's close. Quickly the *dienst* branch of its family tree was forgotten and replaced by a putative ancestor in the Riau Islands (of which the most important had – perhaps fortunately – since 1819 become British Singapore). By 1928, shaped by two generations of urban writers and readers, it was ready to be adopted by Young Indonesia as the national(-ist) language *bahasa Indonesia*. Since then, it has never looked back.

Yet, in the end, the Indonesian case, interesting as it is, should not mislead us into thinking that, if Holland had been a bigger power,[39] and had arrived in 1850 rather than 1600, the national language could not just as well have been Dutch. Nothing suggests that Ghanaian nationalism is any less real than Indonesian simply because its national language is English rather than Ashanti. It is always a mistake to treat languages in the way that certain nationalist ideologues treat them – as *emblems* of nation-ness, like flags, costumes, folk-dances, and the rest. Much the most important thing about language is its capacity for generating imagined communities, building in effect *particular solidarities*. After all, imperial languages are still *vernaculars*, and thus

---

38. The military 'constituted something like an *anational caste*, the members of which lived even in their private lives ordinarily distinct from their national environments and spoke very often a special language, the so-called *ärarisch deutsch* ("fiscal German"), as it was ironically named by the representatives of the literary German, meaning by it a strange linguistic mixture which does not take the rules of grammar very seriously.' Jászi, *The Dissolution*, p. 144. Author's emphases.

39. Not merely in the obvious sense. Because, in the eighteenth and nineteenth centuries, Holland had, for all intents and purposes, only one colony, and a huge, profitable one at that, it was quite practical to train its functionaries in a (single) non-European *diensttaal*. Over time, special schools and faculties grew up in the metropole to prepare future functionaries linguistically. For multi-continental empires like the British, no single locally-based *diensttaal* would have sufficed.

particular vernaculars among many. If radical Mozambique speaks Portuguese, the significance of this is that Portuguese is the medium through which Mozambique is imagined (and at the same time limits its stretch into Tanzania and Zambia). Seen from this perspective the use of Portuguese in Mozambique (or English in India) is basically no different than the use of English in Australia or Portuguese in Brazil. Language is not an instrument of exclusion: in principle, anyone can learn any language. On the contrary, it is fundamentally inclusive, limited only by the fatality of Babel: no one lives long enough to learn *all* languages. Print-language is what invents nationalism, not *a* particular language per se.[40] The only question-mark standing over languages like Portuguese in Mozambique and English in India is whether the administrative and educational systems, particularly the latter, can generate a politically sufficient diffusion of bilingualism. Thirty years ago, almost no Indonesian spoke *bahasa Indonesia* as his or her mother-tongue; virtually everyone had their own 'ethnic' language and some, especially people in the nationalist movement, *bahasa Indonesia/dienstmaleisch* as well. Today there are perhaps millions of young Indonesians, from dozens of ethnolinguistic backgrounds, who speak Indonesian as their mother-tongue.

It is not clear yet whether thirty years from now there will be a generation of Mozambiquians who speak only Mozambique-Portuguese. But, in this late twentieth century, it is not necessarily the case that the emergence of such a generation is a *sine qua non* for

---

40. Marr's account of language-development in eastern Indochina is very revealing on this point. He notes that as late as *c.* 1910 'most educated Vietnamese assumed that Chinese or French, or both, were essential modes of "higher" communication.' (*Vietnamese Tradition*, p. 137). After 1920, however, and partly as a result of state promotion of the phonetic *quốc ngữ* script, things changed quickly. By then 'the belief was growing that spoken Vietnamese was an important and perhaps [sic] essential component of national identity. Even intellectuals more at home in French than in their mother tongue came to appreciate the significance of the fact that at least 85% of their fellow-countrymen spoke the same language.' (p. 138) They were by then fully aware of the role of mass literacy in advancing the nation-states of Europe and Japan. Yet Marr also shows that for a long time there was no clear correlation between language-preference and political stance: 'Upholding the Vietnamese mother tongue was not inherently patriotic, any more than promoting the French language was inherently collaborationist.' (p. 150).

Mozambiquian national solidarity. In the first place, advances in communications technology, especially radio and television, give print allies unavailable a century ago. Multilingual broadcasting can conjure up the imagined community to illiterates and populations with different mother-tongues. (Here there are resemblances to the conjuring up of mediaeval Christendom through visual representations and bilingual literati.) In the second place, twentieth-century nationalisms have, as I have been arguing, a profoundly modular character. They can, and do, draw on more than a century and a half of human experience and three earlier models of nationalism. Nationalist leaders are thus in a position consciously to deploy civil and military educational systems modelled on official nationalism's; elections, party organizations, and cultural celebrations modelled on the popular nationalisms of ninteenth-century Europe; and the citizen-republican idea brought into the world by the Americas. Above all, the very idea of 'nation' is now nestled firmly in virtually all print-languages; and nation-ness is virtually inseparable from political consciousness.

In a world in which the national state is the overwhelming norm, all of this means that nations can now be imagined without linguistic communality – not in the native spirit of *nosotros los Americanos*, but out of a general awareness of what modern history has demonstrated to be possible.[41] It seems fitting, in this context, to conclude this chapter by returning to Europe and considering briefly that nation whose linguistic diversity has so often been used as a cudgel to club proponents of language-based theories of nationalism.

In 1891, amidst novel jubilees marking the 600th anniversary of the Confederacy of Schwyz, Obwalden, and Nidwalden, the Swiss state 'decided on' 1291 as the date of the 'founding' of Switzerland.[42] Such a decision, waiting 600 years to be made, has its diverting aspects, and suggests already that modernity rather than antiquity characterizes

---

41. I say 'can' because there are obviously plenty of cases where the possibility has been, and is being, rejected. In such cases, for example Old Pakistan, the explanation is not ethno-cultural pluralism, but barred pilgrimages.

42. Christopher Hughes, *Switzerland*, p. 107. This excellent text, for which Seton-Watson rightly expresses his admiration, is the basis for the argument that follows.

Swiss nationalism. Indeed, Hughes goes so far as to argue that the 1891 jubilees mark the birth of this nationalism, commenting that 'in the first half of the nineteenth century . . . nationhood sat rather lightly on the shoulders of the cultivated middle classes: Mme de Staël [1766–1817], Fuseli [1741–1825], Angelica Kauffmann [1741–1807], Sismondi [1773–1842], Benjamin Constant [1767–1830], are they all Swiss?'[43] If the implied answer is 'hardly,' its significance derives from the fact that, all over the Europe surrounding Switzerland, the first half of the nineteenth century saw the burgeoning of vernacular nationalist movements in which 'cultivated middle classes' (as it were, philologists + capitalists) played central parts. Why then did nationalism come so late to Switzerland, and what consequences did that lateness have for its ultimate shaping (in particular, its contemporary multiplicity of 'national languages')?

Part of the answer lies in the youth of the Swiss state, which, Hughes drily observes, is difficult to trace back beyond 1813–15 'without the aid of some prevarication.'[44] He reminds us that the first real Swiss citizenship, the introduction of direct (male) suffrage, and the ending of 'internal' tolls and customs areas were achievements of the Helvetic Republic forcibly brought into being by the French occupation of 1798. Only in 1803 did the state include significant numbers of Italian-speakers, with the acquisition of Ticino. Only in 1815 did it gain the populous French-speaking areas of Valais, Geneva, and Neuchâtel from a vengefully anti-French Holy Alliance – in exchange for neutrality and a highly conservative constitution.[45] In effect, today's multilingual Switzerland is a product of the early nineteenth century.[46]

A second factor was the country's backwardness (which, combined

---

43. Ibid., p. 218. The dates are my interpolations.

44. Ibid., p. 85.

45. Plus Aargau, St. Gallen and Grisons. This last is of special interest since today it is the surviving home of Romansch, the most echt-Swiss of the country's national languages – a status it achieved, however, only in 1937! Ibid., pp. 59 and 85.

46. We might note in passing that Mme. de Staël barely survived long enough to see its birth. Besides, her family, like that of Sismondi, came from Geneva, which was an independent statelet outside 'Switzerland' until 1815. Small wonder that Swiss nationhood rested 'rather lightly' on their shoulders.

with its forbidding topography and lack of exploitable resources, helped to keep it from absorption by more powerful neighbours). Today it may be difficult to remember that until World War II Switzerland was a poor country, with a standard of living half that of England's, and an overwhelmingly *rural* country. In 1850, barely 6 per cent of the population lived in minimally urban areas, and as late as 1920 the figure had risen only to 27.6 per cent.[47] Throughout the nineteenth century, then, the bulk of the population was an immobile (except for the age-old export of hardy youths as mercenaries and Papal Guards) peasantry. The country's backwardness was not merely economic, it was also political and cultural. 'Old Switzerland,' the area of which did not change between 1515 and 1803, and most of whose inhabitants spoke one or other of numerous German patois, was ruled by a loose coalition of cantonal aristocratic oligarchies. 'The secret of the long duration of the Confederacy was its double nature. Against outside enemies it produced a sufficient unity of peoples. Against internal rebellion, it produced a sufficient unity of oligarchies. If peasants rebelled, as they did three times or so in every century, then differences would be put aside and the *governments* of other cantons would lend their assistance, mediating often, but not always, in favour of their fellow-ruler.'[48] Except for the absence of monarchical institutions, the picture is not much different from that of the innumerable petty principalities within the Holy Roman Empire, of which Liechtenstein, on Switzerland's eastern border, is a last odd relic.[49]

It is instructive that as late as 1848, almost two generations after the Swiss state came into being, ancient religious cleavages were much more politically salient than linguistic ones. Remarkably enough, in territories unalterably-denoted Catholic Protestantism was *unlawful*, and in those so-denoted Protestant Catholicism was

47. Ibid., pp. 173 and 274. Any nineteenth-century 'cultivated middle class' had to be very small.

48. Ibid., p. 86. Emphasis added.

49. An absence of monarchies also characterized the Hanseatic League, a loose political coalition to which it would be problematic to attribute either statehood or nationhood.

illegal; and these laws were strictly enforced. (Language was a matter of personal choice and convenience). Only after 1848, in the back-wash of Europe-wide revolutionary upheavals and the general spread of vernacularizing national movements, did language take religion's place, and the country become segmented into unalterably-denoted linguistic zones. (Religion now became a matter of personal choice).[50]

Finally, the persistence – in such a small country – of a large variety of sometimes mutually-unintelligible German idiolects suggests the late arrival of print-capitalism and standardized modern education to much of Swiss peasant society. Thus *Hochsprache* (print-German) has had, until rather recently, the language-of-state status of *ärarisch deutsch* and *dienstmaleisch*. Furthermore, Hughes remarks that today 'higher' officials are expected to have a working knowledge of two federal languages, implying that the same competence is not expected of their subordinates. Indirectly, a similar point is made by the Federal Directive of 1950 which insists that '*Educated* German Swiss are certainly able to work in French, as are *educated* Italian Swiss.'[51] We have, in effect, a situation which at bottom is not too different from Mozambique's – a bilingual political class ensconced over a variety of monolingual populations, with only this dissimilarity: the 'second language' is that of a powerful neighbour rather than of a former colonial ruler.

Nonetheless, in view of the fact that in 1910 the maternal language of almost 73 per cent of the population was German, 22 per cent French, 4 per cent Italian, and 1 per cent Romansch (these proportions have scarcely varied over the intervening decades), it is perhaps surprising that in the second half of the nineteenth century – era of official nationalisms – Germanification was not attempted. Certainly up to 1914 strong pro-German sympathies existed. Between Germany and German Switzerland borders were porous in the extreme. Trade and investment, as well as aristocrats and professionals, moved back and forth quite freely. But Switzerland also abutted on two other major European powers, France and Italy,

---

50. Ibid., p. 274.
51. Ibid., pp. 59–60. Emphases added.

and the political risks of Germanizing were plain. Legal parity between German, French, and Italian was thus the obverse side of the coin of Swiss neutrality.[52]

All of the preceding evidence indicates that Swiss nationalism is best understood as part of the 'last wave'. If Hughes is right in dating its birth to 1891, it is not much more than a decade older than Burmese or Indonesian nationalism. In other words, it arose in that period of world history in which the nation was becoming an international norm, and in which it was possible to 'model' nationness in a much more complex way than hitherto. If the conservative political, and backward socio-economic, structure of Switzerland 'delayed' the rise of nationalism,[53] the fact that its pre-modern political institutions were non-dynastic and non-monarchical helped to prevent the excesses of official nationalism (contrast the case of Siam discussed in Chapter 6). Finally, as in the case of the Southeast Asian examples, the appearance of Swiss nationalism on the eve of the communications revolution of the twentieth century made it possible and practical to 'represent' the imagined community in ways that did not require linguistic uniformity.

In conclusion, it may be worth restating the general argument of this chapter. The 'last wave' of nationalisms, most of them in the colonial territories of Asia and Africa, was in its origins a response to the new-style global imperialism made possible by the achievements of industrial capitalism. As Marx put it in his inimitable way: 'The need of a constantly expanding market for its products chases the bourgeoisie over the whole face of the globe.'[54] But capitalism had also, not least by its dissemination of print, helped to create popular, vernacular-based nationalisms in Europe, which to different degrees undermined the age-old dynastic principle, and egged into self-

---

52. Romansch's elevation in 1937 scarcely disguised the original calculation.

53. The social structure of Hungary was also backward, but Magyar aristocrats sat inside a huge polyethnic dynastic empire, in which their putative language-group formed merely a minority, albeit a very important one. Small, republican Switzerland's aristocratic oligarchy was never threatened in the same way.

54. Marx and Engels, *The Communist Manifesto*, p. 37. Who but Marx would have described this world-transforming class as being 'chased'?

naturalization every dynasty positioned to do so. Official nationalism – weld of the new national and old dynastic principles (the *British Empire*) – led in turn to what, for convenience, one can call 'Russification' in the extra-European colonies. This ideological tendency meshed neatly with practical exigencies. The late-nineteenth-century empires were too large and too far-flung to be ruled by a handful of nationals. Moreover, in tandem with capitalism the state was rapidly multiplying its functions, in both the metropoles and the colonies. Combined, these forces generated 'Russifying' school-systems intended in part to produce the required subordinate cadres for state and corporate bureaucracies. These school-systems, centralized and standardized, created quite new pilgrimages which typically had their Romes in the various colonial capitals, for the nations hidden at the core of the empires would permit no more inward ascension. Usually, but by no means always, these educational pilgrimages were paralleled, or replicated, in the administrative sphere. The interlock between particular educational and administrative pilgrimages provided the territorial base for new 'imagined communities' in which natives could come to see themselves as 'nationals'. The expansion of the colonial-state which, so to speak, invited 'natives' into schools and offices, and of colonial capitalism which, as it were, excluded them from boardrooms, meant that to an unprecedented extent the key early spokesmen for colonial nationalism were lonely, bilingual intelligentsias unattached to sturdy local bourgeoisies.

As bilingual intelligentsias, however, and above all as early-twentieth-century intelligentsias, they had access, inside the classroom and outside, to models of nation, nation-ness, and nationalism distilled from the turbulent, chaotic experiences of more than a century of American and European history. These models, in turn, helped to give shape to a thousand inchoate dreams. In varying combinations, the lessons of creole, vernacular and official nationalism were copied, adapted, and improved upon. Finally, as with increasing speed capitalism transformed the means of physical and intellectual communication, the intelligentsias found ways to bypass print in propagating the imagined community, not merely to illiterate masses, but even to literate masses *reading* different languages.

8

Patriotism and Racism

In the preceding chapters I have tried to delineate the processes by which the nation came to be imagined, and, once imagined, modelled, adapted and transformed. Such an analysis has necessarily been concerned primarily with social change and different forms of consciousness. But it is doubtful whether either social change or transformed consciousnesses, in themselves, do much to explain the *attachment* that peoples feel for the inventions of their imaginations – or, to revive a question raised at the beginning of this text – why people are ready to die for these inventions.

In an age when it is so common for progressive, cosmopolitan intellectuals (particularly in Europe?) to insist on the near-pathological character of nationalism, its roots in fear and hatred of the Other, and its affinities with racism,[1] it is useful to remind ourselves that nations inspire love, and often profoundly self-sacrificing love. The cultural products of nationalism – poetry, prose fiction, music, plastic arts – show this love very clearly in thousands of different forms and styles. On the other hand, how truly rare it is to find

---

1. Cf. the passage in Nairn's *Break-up of Britain*, pp. 14–15 above, and Hobsbawm's somewhat Biedermeier dictum: 'the basic fact [is] that Marxists as such are not nationalists.' 'Some Reflections,' p. 10.

analogous nationalist products expressing fear and loathing.[2] Even in the case of colonized peoples, who have every reason to feel hatred for their imperialist rulers, it is astonishing how insignificant the element of hatred is in these expressions of national feeling. Here, for example, are the first and last stanzas of *Último Adiós*, the famous poem written by Rizal as he awaited execution at the hands of Spanish imperialism:[3]

1. Adiós, Patria adorada, región del sol querida,
    Perla del Mar de Oriente, nuestro perdido edén,
    A darte voy, alegre, la triste mustia vida;
    Y fuera más brillante, más fresca, más florida,
    También por ti la diera, la diera por tu bien . . .

12. Entonces nada importa me pongas en olvido:
    Tu atmósfera, tu espacio, tus valles cruzaré;
    Vibrante y limpia nota seré par tu oído;
    Aroma, luz, colores, rumor, canto, gemido,
    Constante repitiendo la esencia de mi fe.

13. Mi Patria idolatrada, dolor de mis dolores,
    Querida Filipinas, oye el postrer adiós.
    Ahí, te dejo todo: mis padres, mis amores.
    Voy donde no hay esclavos, verdugos ni opresores;
    Donde la fe no mata, donde el que reina es Dios.

14. Adiós, padres y hermanos, trozos del alma mía,
    Amigos de la infancia, en el perdido hogar;
    Dad gracias, que descanso del fatigoso día;
    Adiós, dulce extranjera, mi amiga, mi alegría;
    Adiós, queridos séres. Morir es descansar.

---

2. Can the reader think immediately of even three Hymns of Hate? The second stanza of God Save the Queen/King is worded instructively: 'O Lord our God, arise/ Scatter her/his enemies,/And make them fall;/Confound their politics,/ Frustrate their knavish tricks;/On Thee our hopes we fix;/God save us all.' Notice that these enemies have no identity and could as well be Englishmen as anyone else since they are 'her/his' enemies *not* 'ours.' The entire anthem is a paean to monarchy, not to the/a nation – which is not once mentioned.

3. Or in the translation of Trinidad T. Subido:

Notice not only that the nationality of the 'tyrants' goes unmentioned, but that Rizal's passionate patriotism is expressed superbly in 'their' language.[4]

Something of the nature of this political love can be deciphered from the ways in which languages describe its object: either in the vocabulary of kinship (motherland, *Vaterland, patria*) or that of home (*heimat* or *tanah air* [earth and water, the phrase for the Indonesians' native archipelago]). Both idioms denote something to which one is naturally tied. As we have seen earlier, in everything 'natural' there is always something unchosen. In this way, nation-ness is assimilated to skin-colour, gender, parentage and birth-era – all those things one can not help. And in these 'natural ties' one senses what one might call 'the beauty of *gemeinschaft*'. To put it another way, precisely because such ties are not chosen, they have about them a halo of disinterestedness.

While it is true that in the past two decades the idea of the family-

---

1. Farewell, dear Land, beloved of the sun,
   Pearl of the Orient seas, lost Paradise!
   Gladly, I will to you this life undone;
   Were it a fairer, fresher, fuller one,
   I'd cede it still, your weal to realize . . .

12. What matters then that you forget me, when
    I might explore your ev'ry dear retreat?
    Be as a note, pulsing and pure; and then,
    Be scent, light, tone; be song or sign, again;
    And through it all, my theme of faith, repeat.

13. Land I enshrine, list to my last farewell!
    Philippines, Love, of pains my pain extreme,
    I leave you all, all whom I love so well,
    To go where neither slaves nor tyrants dwell,
    Where Faith kills not, and where God reigns supreme.

14. Farewell to all my soul does comprehend –
    O kith and kin in my home dispossessed;
    Give thanks my day oppressive is at end;
    Farewell, sweet stranger, my delight and friend;
    Farewell, dear ones. To die is but to rest.

Jaime C. de Veyra, El *'Último Adiós' de Rizal: estudio crítico-expositivo*, pp. 89–90, and 101–102 (the translation).

4. It was, however, quickly translated into Tagalog by the great Filipino revolutionary Andrés Bonifacio. His version is given in ibid., pp. 107–109.

as-articulated-power-structure has been much written about, such a conception is certainly foreign to the overwhelming bulk of mankind. Rather, the family has traditionally been conceived as the domain of disinterested love and solidarity. So too, if historians, diplomats, politicians, and social scientists are quite at ease with the idea of 'national interest,' for most ordinary people of whatever class the whole point of the nation is that it is interestless. Just for that reason, it can ask for sacrifices.

As noted earlier, the great wars of this century are extraordinary not so much in the unprecedented scale on which they permitted people to kill, as in the colossal numbers persuaded to lay down their lives. Is it not certain that the numbers of those killed vastly exceeded those who killed? The idea of the ultimate sacrifice comes only with an idea of purity, through fatality.

Dying for one's country, which usually one does not choose, assumes a moral grandeur which dying for the Labour Party, the American Medical Association, or perhaps even Amnesty International can not rival, for these are all bodies one can join or leave at easy will. Dying for the revolution also draws its grandeur from the degree to which it is felt to be something fundamentally pure. (If people imagined the proletariat *merely* as a group in hot pursuit of refrigerators, holidays, or power, how far would they, including members of the proletariat, be willing to die for it?)[5] Ironically enough, it may be that to the extent that Marxist interpretations of history are felt (rather than intellected) as representations of ineluctable necessity, they also acquire an aura of purity and disinterestedness.

Here we may usefully return once more to language. First, one notes the primordialness of languages, even those known to be modern. No one can give the date for the birth of any language. Each looms up imperceptibly out of a horizonless past. (Insofar as *homo sapiens* is *homo dicens*, it can seem difficult to imagine an origin of

---

5. This formulation should not at all be taken to mean that revolutionary movements do not pursue material objectives. But these objectives are envisioned, not as a congeries of individual acquisitions, but as the conditions of Rousseau's shared *bonheur*.

language newer than the species itself.) Languages thus appear rooted beyond almost anything else in contemporary societies. At the same time, nothing connects us affectively to the dead more than language. If English-speakers hear the words 'Earth to earth, ashes to ashes, dust to dust' – created almost four-and-a-half centuries ago – they get a ghostly intimation of simultaneity across homogeneous, empty time. The weight of the words derives only in part from their solemn meaning; it comes also from an as-it-were ancestral 'Englishness'.

Second, there is a special kind of contemporaneous community which language alone suggests – above all in the form of poetry and songs. Take national anthems, for example, sung on national holidays. No matter how banal the words and mediocre the tunes, there is in this singing an experience of simultaneity. At precisely such moments, people wholly unknown to each other utter the same verses to the same melody. The image: unisonance.[6] Singing the Marseillaise, Waltzing Matilda, and Indonesia Raya provide occasions for unisonality, for the echoed physical realization of the imagined community. (So does listening to [and maybe silently chiming in with] the recitation of ceremonial poetry, such as sections of *The Book of Common Prayer*.) How selfless this unisonance feels! If we are aware that others are singing these songs precisely when and as we are, we have no idea who they may be, or even where, out of earshot, they are singing. Nothing connects us all but imagined sound.

Yet such choruses are joinable in time. If I am a Lett, my daughter may be an Australian. The son of an Italian immigrant to New York will find ancestors in the Pilgrim Fathers. If nationalness has about it an aura of fatality, it is nonetheless a fatality embedded in *history*. Here San Martín's edict baptizing Quechua-speaking Indians as 'Peruvians' – a movement that has affinities with religious conversion – is exemplary. For it shows that from the start the nation was conceived in language, not in blood, and that one could be 'invited into' the imagined community. Thus today, even the most insular nations accept the principle of *naturalization* (wonderful word!), no matter how difficult in practice they may make it.

---

6. Contrast this *a capella* chorus with the language of everyday life, which is typically experienced decani/cantoris-fashion as dialogue and exchange.

Seen as both a *historical* fatality and as a community imagined through language, the nation presents itself as simultaneously open and closed. This paradox is well illustrated in the shifting rhythms of these famous lines on the death of John Moore during the battle of Coruña:[7]

1. Not a drum was heard, not a funeral note,
   As his corse to the rampart we hurried;
   Not a soldier discharged his farewell shot
   O'er the grave where our hero we buried.

2. We buried him darkly at dead of night,
   The sods with our bayonets turning;
   By the struggling moonbeams' misty light,
   And the lantern dimly burning.

3. No useless coffin enclosed his breast,
   Not in sheet or in shroud we wound him;
   But he lay like a warrior taking his rest,
   With his martial cloak around him . . .

5. We thought, as we hollowed his narrow bed,
   And smoothed down his lonely pillow,
   That the foe and the stranger would tread o'er his head
   And we far away on the billow . . .

8. Slowly and sadly we laid him down.
   From the field of his fame fresh and gory;
   We carved not a line, and we raised not a stone –
   But we left him alone with his glory!

The lines celebrate a heroic memory with a beauty inseparable from the English language – one untranslatable, audible only to its speakers and readers. Yet both Moore and his eulogist were Irishmen. And there is no reason why a descendant of Moore's French or Spanish 'foes' can not fully hear the poem's resonance: English, like any other language, is always open to new speakers, listeners, and readers.

---

7. 'The Burial of Sir John Moore,' in *The Poems of Charles Wolfe*, pp. 1–2.

Listen to Thomas Browne, encompassing in a pair of sentences the length and breadth of man's history:[8]

> Even the old ambitions had the advantage of ours, in the attempts of their vainglories, who acting early and before the probable Meridian of time, have by this time found great accomplishment of their designs, whereby the ancient Heroes have already out-lasted their Monuments, and Mechanicall preservations. But in this latter Scene of time we cannot expect such Mummies unto our memories, when ambition may fear the Prophecy of Elias, and Charles the Fifth can never hope to live within two Methusela's of Hector.

Here ancient Egypt, Greece, and Judaea are united with the Holy Roman Empire, but their unification across thousands of years and thousands of miles is accomplished within the particularity of Browne's seventeenth-century English prose.[9] The passage can, of course, up to a point be translated. But the eerie splendour of 'probable Meridian of time,' 'Mechanicall preservations,' 'such Mummies unto our memories,' and 'two Methusela's of Hector' can bring goose-flesh to the napes only of English-readers.

On this page, it opens itself wide to the reader. On the other hand, the no less eerie splendour of the final lines of 'Yang Sudah Hilang' by the great Indonesian author Pramoedya Ananta Toer:[10]

> Suara itu hanya terdengar beberapa detik saja dalam hidup. Getarannya sebentar berdengung, takkan terulangi lagi. Tapi seperti juga halnya dengan kali Lusi yang abadi menggarisi kota Blora, dan seperti kali itu juga, suara yang tersimpan menggarisi kenangan dan ingatan itu mengalir juga — mengalir kemuaranya, kelaut yang tak bertepi. Dan tak seorangpun tahu kapan laut itu akan kering dan berhenti berdeburan.

---

8. *Hydriotaphia, Urne-Buriall, or, A Discourse of the Sepulchrall Urnes lately found in Norfolk*, pp. 72–73. On 'the probable Meridian of time' compare Bishop Otto of Freising.

9. Yet 'England' goes unmentioned in this unification. We are reminded of those provincial newspapers which brought the whole world, through Spanish, into Caracas and Bogotá.

10. In *Tjerita dari Blora* [Tales from Blora], pp. 15–44, at p. 44.

Hilang.

Semua itu sudah hilang dari jangkauan panc[h]a-indera.

on the same print page, are most likely closed.[11]

If every language is acquirable, its acquisition requires a real portion of a person's life: each new conquest is measured against shortening days. What limits one's access to other languages is not their imperviousness but one's own mortality. Hence a certain privacy to all languages. French and American imperialists governed, exploited, and killed Vietnamese over many years. But whatever else they made off with, the Vietnamese language stayed put. Accordingly, only too often, a rage at Vietnamese 'inscrutability,' and that obscure despair which engenders the venomous argots of dying colonialisms: 'gooks,' '*ratons*', etc.[12] (In the longer run, the only responses to the vast privacy of the language of the oppressed are retreat or further massacre.)

Such epithets are, in their inner form, characteristically racist, and decipherment of this form will serve to show why Nairn is basically mistaken in arguing that racism and anti-semitism derive from nationalism – and thus that 'seen in sufficient historical depth, fascism tells us more about nationalism than any other episode.'[13] A word like 'slant,' for example, abbreviated from 'slant-eyed', does not simply express an ordinary political enmity. It erases nation-ness by reducing the adversary to his biological physiognomy.[14] It denies, by substituting for, 'Vietnamese;' just as *raton* denies, by substituting for, 'Algerian'. At the same time, it stirs 'Vietnamese' into a nameless sludge along with 'Korean,' 'Chinese,' 'Filipino,' and so on. The character of this vocabulary may become still more evident if it is contrasted with other Vietnam-War-period words like 'Charlie' and

---

11. Still, listen to them! I have adapted the original spelling to accord with current convention and to make the quotation completely phonetic.

12. The logic here is: 1. I will be dead before I have penetrated them. 2. My power is such that they have had to learn my language. 3. But this means that my privacy has been penetrated. Terming them 'gooks' is small revenge.

13. *The Break-up of Britain*, pp. 337 and 347.

14. Notice that there is no obvious, selfconscious antonym to 'slant.' 'Round'? 'Straight'? 'Oval'?

'V.C.', or from an earlier era, 'Boches,' 'Huns,' 'Japs' and 'Frogs,' all of which apply only to *one* specific nationality, and thus concede, in hatred, the adversary's membership in a league of nations.[15]

The fact of the matter is that nationalism thinks in terms of historical destinies, while racism dreams of eternal contaminations, transmitted from the origins of time through an endless sequence of loathsome copulations: outside history. Niggers are, thanks to the invisible tar-brush, forever niggers; Jews, the seed of Abraham, forever Jews, no matter what passports they carry or what languages they speak and read. (Thus for the Nazi, the *Jewish* German was always an impostor.)[16]

The dreams of racism actually have their origin in ideologies of *class*, rather than in those of nation: above all in claims to divinity among rulers and to 'blue' or 'white' blood and 'breeding' among aristocracies.[17] No surprise then that the putative sire of modern racism should be, not some petty-bourgeois nationalist, but Joseph Arthur, Comte de Gobineau.[18] Nor that, on the whole, racism and

---

15. Not only, in fact, in an earlier era. Nonetheless, there is a whiff of the antique-shop about these words of Debray: 'I can conceive of no hope for Europe save under the hegemony of a revolutionary France, firmly grasping the banner of independence. Sometimes I wonder if the whole "anti-Boche" mythology and our secular antagonism to Germany may not be one day indispensable for saving the revolution, or even our national-democratic inheritance.' 'Marxism and the National Question,' p. 41.

16. The significance of the emergence of Zionism and the birth of Israel is that the former marks the reimagining of an ancient religious community as a nation, down there among the other nations – while the latter charts an alchemic change from wandering devotee to local patriot.

17. 'From the side of the landed aristocracy came conceptions of inherent superiority in the ruling class, and a sensitivity to status, prominent traits well into the twentieth century. Fed by new sources, these conceptions could later be vulgarized [sic] and made appealing to the German population as a whole in doctrines of racial superiority.' Barrington Moore, Jr., *Social Origins of Dictatorship and Democracy*, p. 436.

18. Gobineau's dates are perfect. He was born in 1816, two years after the restoration of the Bourbons to the French throne. His diplomatic career, 1848–1877, blossomed under Louis Napoléon's Second Empire and the reactionary monarchist regime of Marie Edmé Patrice Maurice, Comte de MacMahon, former imperialist proconsul in Algiers. His *Essai sur l'Inégalité des Races Humaines* appeared in 1854 – should one say in response to the popular vernacular-nationalist insurrections of 1848?

anti-semitism manifest themselves, not across national boundaries, but within them. In other words, they justify not so much foreign wars as domestic repression and domination.[19]

Where racism developed outside Europe in the nineteenth century, it was always associated with European domination, for two converging reasons. First and most important was the rise of official nationalism and colonial 'Russification'. As has been repeatedly emphasized official nationalism was typically a response on the part of threatened dynastic and aristocratic groups – upper *classes* – to popular vernacular nationalism. Colonial racism was a major element in that conception of 'Empire' which attempted to weld dynastic legitimacy and national community. It did so by generalizing a principle of innate, inherited superiority on which its own domestic position was (however shakily) based to the vastness of the overseas possessions, covertly (or not so covertly) conveying the idea that if, say, English lords were naturally superior to other Englishmen, no matter: these other Englishmen were no less superior to the subjected natives. Indeed one is tempted to argue that the existence of late colonial empires even served to *shore up* domestic aristocratic bastions, since they appeared to confirm on a global, modern stage antique conceptions of power and privilege.

It could do so with some effect because – and here is our second reason – the colonial empire, with its rapidly expanding bureaucratic apparatus and its 'Russifying' policies, permitted sizeable numbers of bourgeois and petty bourgeois to play aristocrat off centre court: i.e. anywhere in the empire except at home. In each colony one found this grimly amusing *tableau vivant:* the bourgeois gentilhomme speaking poetry against a backcloth of spacious mansions and gardens filled with mimosa and bougainvillea, and a large supporting cast of houseboys, grooms, gardeners, cooks, amahs, maids, washer-

---

19. South African racism has not, in the age of Vorster and Botha, stood in the way of amicable relations (however discreetly handled) with prominent black politicians in certain independent African states. If Jews suffer discrimination in the Soviet Union, that did not prevent respectful working relations between Brezhnev and Kissinger.

women, and, above all, horses.[20] Even those who did not manage to live in this style, such as young bachelors, nonetheless had the grandly equivocal status of a French nobleman on the eve of a jacquerie:[21]

> In Moulmein, in lower Burma [this obscure town needs explaining to readers in the metropole], I was hated by large numbers of people – the only time in my life that I have been important enough for this to happen to me. I was sub-divisional police officer of the town.

This 'tropical Gothic' was made possible by the overwhelming power that high capitalism had given the metropole – a power so great that it could be kept, so to speak, in the wings. Nothing better illustrates capitalism in feudal-aristocratic drag than colonial militaries, which were notoriously distinct from those of the metropoles, often even in formal institutional terms.[22] Thus in Europe one had the 'First Army,' recruited by conscription on a mass, citizen, metropolitan base; ideologically conceived as the defender of the *heimat*; dressed in practical, utilitarian khaki; armed with the latest affordable weapons; in peacetime isolated in barracks, in war stationed in trenches or behind heavy field-guns. Outside Europe one had the 'Second Army,' recruited (below the officer level) from local religious or ethnic minorities on a mercenary basis; ideologically conceived as an internal police force; dressed to kill in bed- or ballroom; armed with swords and obsolete industrial weapons; in peace on display, in war on horseback. If the Prussian General Staff, Europe's military teacher, stressed the anonymous solidarity of a professionalized corps, ballistics, railroads, engineering, strategic planning, and the like, the colonial army stressed glory, epaulettes, personal heroism, polo, and an archaizing courtliness among its officers. (It could afford to do so

---

20. For a stunning collection of photographs of such tableaux vivants in the Netherlands Indies (and an elegantly ironical text), see 'E. Breton de Nijs,' *Tempo Doeloe.*

21. George Orwell, 'Shooting an Elephant,' in *The Orwell Reader*, p. 3. The words in square brackets are of course my interpolation.

22. The KNIL (Koninklijk Nederlandsch-Indisch Leger) was quite separate from the KL (Koninklijk Leger) in Holland. The Légion Étrangère was almost from the start legally prohibited from operations on continental French soil.

because the First Army and the Navy were there in the background.)
This mentality survived a long time. In Tonkin, in 1894, Lyautey
wrote:[23]

> Quel dommage de n'être pas venu ici dix ans plus tôt! Quelles
> carrières à y fonder et à y mener. Il n'y a pas ici un de ces petits
> lieutenants, chefs de poste et de reconnaissance, qui ne développe en
> 6 mois plus d'initiative, de volonté, d'endurance, de *personnalité*,
> qu'un officier *de* France en toute sa carrière.

In Tonkin, in 1951, Jean de Lattre de Tassigny, 'who liked officers
who combined guts with "style," took an immediate liking to the
dashing cavalryman [Colonel de Castries] with his bright-red Spahi
cap and scarf, his magnificent riding-crop, and his combination of
easy-going manners and *ducal* mien, which made him as irresistible to
women in Indochina in the 1950s as he had been to Parisiennes of the
1930s.'[24]

Another instructive indication of the aristocratic or pseudo-
aristocratic derivation of colonial racism was the typical 'solidarity

---

23. *Lettres du Tonkin et de Madagascar (1894–1899)*, p. 84. Letter of December 22, 1894, from Hanoi. Emphases added.

24. Bernard B. Fall, *Hell is a Very Small Place: The Siege of Dien Bien Phu*, p. 56. One can imagine the shudder of Clausewitz's ghost. [Spahi, derived like Sepoy from the Ottoman Sipahi, meant mercenary irregular cavalrymen of the 'Second Army' in Algeria.] It is true that the France of Lyautey and de Lattre was a Republican France. However, the often talkative Grande Muette had since the start of the Third Republic been an asylum for aristocrats increasingly excluded from power in all other important institutions of public life. By 1898, a full quarter of all Brigadier- and Major-Generals were aristocrats. Moreover, this aristocrat-dominated officer corps was crucial to nineteenth and twentieth-century French imperialism. 'The rigorous control imposed on the army in the *métropole* never extended fully to *la France d'outremer*. The extension of the French Empire in the nineteenth century was partially the result of uncontrolled initiative on the part of colonial military commanders. French West Africa, largely the creation of General Faidherbe, and the French Congo as well, owed most of their expansion to independent military forays into the hinterland. Military officers were also responsible for the *faits accomplis* which led to a French protectorate in Tahiti in 1842, and, to a lesser extent, to the French occupation of Tonkin in Indochina in the 1880's . . . In 1897 Galliéni summarily abolished the ˙monarchy in Madagascar and deported the Queen, all without consulting the French government, which later accepted the *fait accompli* . . .' John S. Ambler, *The French Army in Politics, 1945–1962*, pp. 10–11 and 22.

among whites,' which linked colonial rulers from different national metropoles, whatever their internal rivalries and conflicts. This solidarity, in its curious trans-state character, reminds one instantly of the class solidarity of Europe's nineteenth-century aristocracies, mediated through each other's hunting-lodges, spas, and ballrooms; and of that brotherhood of 'officers and gentlemen,' which in the Geneva convention guaranteeing privileged treatment to captured enemy *officers*, as opposed to partisans or civilians, has an agreeably twentieth-century expression.

The argument adumbrated thus far can also be pursued from the side of colonial populations. For, the pronouncements of certain colonial ideologues aside, it is remarkable how little that dubious entity known as 'reverse racism' manifested itself in the anticolonial movements. In this matter it is easy to be deceived by language. There is, for example, a sense in which the Javanese word *londo* (derived from Hollander or Nederlander) meant not only 'Dutch' but 'whites.' But the derivation itself shows that, for Javanese peasants, who scarcely ever encountered any 'whites' but Dutch, the two meanings effectively overlapped. Similarly, in French colonial territories, '*les blancs*' meant rulers whose Frenchness was indistinguishable from their whiteness. In neither case, so far as I know, did *londo* or *blanc* either lose caste or breed derogatory secondary distinctions.[25]

On the contrary, the spirit of anticolonial nationalism is that of the heart-rending Constitution of Makario Sakay's short-lived Republic of Katagalugan (1902), which said, among other things:[26]

---

25. I have never heard of an abusive argot word in Indonesian or Javanese for either 'Dutch' or 'white.' Compare the Anglo-Saxon treasury: niggers, wops, kikes, gooks, slants, fuzzywuzzies, and a hundred more. It is possible that this innocence of racist argots is true primarily of colonized populations. Blacks in America – and surely elsewhere – have developed a varied counter-vocabulary (honkies, ofays, etc.).

26. As cited in Reynaldo Ileto's masterly *Pasyón and Revolution: Popular Movements in the Philippines, 1840–1910*, p. 218. Sakay's rebel republic lasted until 1907, when he was captured and executed by the Americans. Understanding the first sentence requires remembering that three centuries of Spanish rule and Chinese immigration had produced a sizeable mestizo population in the islands.

No Tagalog, born in this Tagalog archipelago, shall exalt any person above the rest because of his race or the colour of his skin; fair, dark, rich, poor, educated and ignorant – all are completely equal, and should be in one *loób* [inward spirit]. There may be differences in education, wealth, or appearance, but never in essential nature (*pagkatao*) and ability to serve a cause.

One can find without difficulty analogies on the other side of the globe. Spanish-speaking mestizo Mexicans trace their ancestries, not to Castilian conquistadors, but to half-obliterated Aztecs, Mayans, Toltecs and Zapotecs. Uruguayan revolutionary patriots, creoles themselves, took up the name of Tupac Amarú, the last great indigenous rebel against creole oppression, who died under unspeakable tortures in 1781.

It may appear paradoxical that the objects of all these attachments are 'imagined' – anonymous, faceless fellow-Tagalogs, exterminated tribes, Mother Russia, or the *tanah air*. But *amor patriae* does not differ in this respect from the other affections, in which there is always an element of fond imagining. (This is why looking at the photo-albums of strangers' weddings is like studying the archaeologist's groundplan of the Hanging Gardens of Babylon.) What the eye is to the lover – that particular, ordinary eye he or she is born with – language – whatever language history has made his or her mother-tongue – is to the patriot. Through that language, encountered at mother's knee and parted with only at the grave, pasts are restored, fellowships are imagined, and futures dreamed.

9

The Angel of History

We began this brief study with the recent wars between the Socialist Republic of Vietnam, Democratic Kampuchea, and the People's Republic of China; so it is only fitting to return finally to that point of departure. Does anything of what has meantime been said help to deepen our understanding of their outbreak?

In *The Break-up of Britain*, Tom Nairn has some valuable words on the relationship between the British political system and those of the rest of the modern world.[1]

> Alone, [the British system] represented a 'slow, conventional growth, not like the others, the product of deliberate *invention*, resulting from a theory.' Arriving later, those others 'attempted to sum up at a stroke the fruits of the experience of the state which had evolved its constitutionalism through several centuries' . . . Because it was first, the English – later British – experience remained distinct. Because they came second, into a world where the English Revolution had already succeeded and expanded, later bourgeois societies could not repeat this early development. Their *study and imitation engendered something substantially different*: the truly modern doctrine of the

---

1. At pp. 17–18. Emphases added. The inner quotation is taken from Charles Frederick Strong's *Modern Political Constitutions*, p. 28.

abstract or 'impersonal' state which, because of its abstract nature, could be imitated in subsequent history.

This may of course be seen as the ordinary logic of developmental processes. It was an early specimen of what was later dignified with such titles as 'the law of uneven and combined development.' Actual repetition and imitation are scarcely ever possible, whether politically, economically, socially, or technologically, because the universe is already too much altered by the first cause one is copying.

What Nairn says of the modern state is no less true of the twin conceptions of which our three embattled socialist countries are contemporary realizations: revolution and nationalism. It is perhaps too easy to forget that this pair, like capitalism and Marxism, are *inventions*, on which patents are impossible to preserve. They are there, so to speak, for the pirating. Out of these piracies and *only* out of them, comes this well-known anomaly: societies such as those of Cuba, Albania, and China, which, insofar as they are revolutionary-socialist, conceive of themselves as 'ahead' of those of France, Switzerland, and the United States, but which, insofar as they are characterized by low productivity, miserable living standards, and backward technology, are no less certainly understood as 'behind.' (Thus Chou En-lai's melancholy dream of catching up with capitalist Britain by the year 2000.)

As noted earlier, Hobsbawm was right to observe that 'the French Revolution was not made or led by a formed party or movement in the modern sense, nor by men attempting to carry out a systematic programme.' But, thanks to print-capitalism, the French experience was not merely ineradicable from human memory, it was also learnable-from. Out of almost a century of modular theorizing and practical experimentation came the Bolsheviks, who made the first successful 'planned' revolution (even if the success would not have been possible without Hindenburg's earlier triumphs at Tannenberg and the Masurian Lakes) and attempted to carry out a systematic programme (even if in practice improvisation was the order of the day). It also seems clear that *without* such plans and programmes a revolution in a realm barely entering the era of industrial capitalism was out of the question. The Bolshevik revolutionary model has been decisive for all twentieth-

century revolutions because it made them imaginable in societies still
more backward than All the Russias. (It opened the possibility of, so to
speak, cutting history off at the pass.) The skilful early experimentations
of Mao Tse-tung confirmed the utility of the model outside Europe.
One can thus see a sort of culmination of the modular process in the case
of Cambodia, where in 1962 less than 2.5 per cent of the two-and-a-
half-million-strong adult work-force was 'working class,' and less than
0.5 per cent 'capitalists.'[2]

In much the same way, since the end of the eighteenth century
nationalism has undergone a process of modulation and adaptation,
according to different eras, political regimes, economies and social
structures. The 'imagined community' has, as a result, spread out to
every conceivable contemporary society. If it is permissible to use
modern Cambodia to illustrate an extreme modular transfer of 'revolution,' it is perhaps equitable to use Vietnam to illustrate that of
nationalism, by a brief excursus on the nation's name.

On his coronation in 1802, Gia-long wished to call his realm 'Nam
Việt' and sent envoys to gain Peking's assent. The Manchu Son of
Heaven, however, insisted that it be 'Việt Nam.' The reason for this
inversion is as follows: 'Việt Nam' (or in Chinese Yüeh-nan) means,
roughly, 'to the south of Việt (Yüeh),' a realm conquered by the Han
seventeen centuries earlier and reputed to cover today's Chinese
provinces of Kwangtung and Kwangsi, as well as the Red River
valley. Gia-long's 'Nam Việt,' however, meant 'Southern Việt/
Yüeh,' in effect a claim *to* the old realm. In the words of Alexander
Woodside, 'the name "Vietnam" as a whole was hardly so well
esteemed by Vietnamese rulers a century ago, emanating as it had
from Peking, as it is in this century. An artificial appellation then, it
was used extensively neither by the Chinese nor by the Vietnamese.
The Chinese clung to the offensive T'ang word "Annam" . . . The

---

2. According to the calculations of Edwin Wells, on the basis of Table 9 in
Cambodge, Ministère du Plan et Institut National de la Statistique et des Recherches
Economiques, *Résultats finals du Recensement Général de la Population 1962*. Wells divides
the rest of the working population as follows: government officials and new petty
bourgeoisie, 8%; traditional petty bourgeoisie (traders, etc.), 7.5%; agricultural proletariat, 1.8%; peasants, 78.3%. There were less than 1,300 capitalists owning actual
manufacturing enterprises.

Vietnamese court, on the other hand, privately invented another name for its kingdom in 1838–39 and did not bother to inform the Chinese. Its new name, Dại Nam, the "Great South" or "Imperial South," appeared with regularity on court documents and official historical compilations. But it has not survived to the present.'[3] This new name is interesting in two respects. First, it contains no 'Viet'-namese element. Second, its territorial reference seems purely relational – 'south' (of the Middle Kingdom).[4]

That today's Vietnamese proudly defend a Viet Nam scornfully invented by a nineteenth-century Manchu dynast reminds us of Renan's dictum that nations must have 'oublié bien des choses,' but also, paradoxically, of the imaginative power of nationalism.

If one looks back at the Vietnam of the 1930s or the Cambodia of the 1960s, one finds, *mutatis mutandis*, many similarities: a huge, illiterate, exploited peasantry, a minuscule working class, a fragmentary bourgeoisie, and a tiny, divided intelligentsia.[5] No sober contemporary analyst, viewing these conditions objectively, would in either case have predicted the revolutions soon to follow, or their wrecked triumphs. (In fact, much the same could be said, and for much the same reasons, of the China of 1910.) What made them possible, in the end, was 'planning revolution' and 'imagining the nation.'[6]

---

3. *Vietnam and the Chinese Model*, pp. 120–21.

4. This is not altogether surprising. 'The Vietnamese bureaucrat looked Chinese; the Vietnamese peasant looked Southeast Asian. The bureaucrat had to write Chinese, wear Chinese-style gowns, live in a Chinese-style house, ride in a Chinese-style sedan chair, and even follow Chinese-style idiosyncracies of conspicuous consumption, like keeping a goldfish pond in his Southeast Asian garden.' Ibid., p. 199.

5. According to the 1937 census, 93–95% of the Vietnamese population was still living in rural areas. No more than 10% of the population was functionally literate in any script. No more than 20,000 persons had completed upper primary (grade 7–10) schooling between 1920 and 1938. And what Vietnamese Marxists called the 'indigenous bourgeoisie' – described by Marr as mainly absentee landlords, combined with some entrepreneurs and a few higher officials – totalled about 10,500 families, or about 0.5% of the population. *Vietnamese Tradition*, 25–26, 34, and 37. Compare the data in note 2 above.

6. And, as in the case of the Bolsheviks, fortunate catastrophes: for China, Japan's massive invasion in 1937; for Vietnam, the smashing of the Maginot Line and her own

The policies of the Pol Pot regime can only in a very limited sense be attributed to traditional Khmer culture or to its leaders' cruelty, paranoia, and megalomania. The Khmer have had their share of megalomaniac despots; some of these, however, were responsible for Angkor. Far more important are the models of what revolutions have, can, should, and should not do, drawn from France, the USSR, China, and Vietnam – and all the books written about them in French.[7]

Much the same is true of nationalism. Contemporary nationalism is the heir to two centuries of historic change. For all the reasons that I have attempted to sketch out, the legacies are truly Janus-headed. For the legators include not only San Martín and Garibaldi, but Uvarov and Macaulay. As we have seen, 'official nationalism' was from the start a conscious, self-protective *policy*, intimately linked to the preservation of imperial-dynastic interests. But once 'out there for all to see,' it was as copyable as Prussia's early-nineteenth-century military reforms, and by the same variety of political and social systems. The one persistent feature of this style of nationalism was, and is, that it is *official* – i.e. something emanating from the state, and serving the interests of the state first and foremost.

Thus the model of official nationalism assumes its relevance above all at the moment when revolutionaries successfully take control of the state, and are for the first time in a position to use the power of the state in pursuit of their visions. The relevance is all the greater insofar as even the most determinedly radical revolutionaries always, to some degree, inherit the state from the fallen regime. Some of

---

brief occupation by the Japanese; for Cambodia, the massive overflow of the American war on Vietnam into her eastern territories after March 1970. In each case the existing *ancien régime*, whether Kuomintang, French colonial, or feudal-monarchist, was fatally undermined by extraneous forces.

7. One might suggest 'yes' to the *levée en masse* and the Terror, 'no' to Thermidor and Bonapartism, for France; 'yes' to War Communism, collectivization, and the Moscow Trials, 'no' to N.E.P. and de-Stalinization, for the Soviet Union; 'yes' to peasant guerrilla communism, the Great Leap Forward, and the Cultural Revolution, 'no' to the Lushan Plenum, for China; 'yes' to the August Revolution and the formal liquidation of the Indochinese Communist Party in 1945, 'no' to damaging concessions to 'senior' communist parties as exemplified in the Geneva Accords, for Vietnam.

these legacies are symbolic, but not the less important for that. Despite Trotsky's unease, the capital of the USSR was moved back to the old Czarist capital of Moscow; and for over 65 years CPSU leaders have made policy in the Kremlin, ancient citadel of Czarist power – out of all possible sites in the socialist state's vast territories. Similarly, the PRC's capital is that of the Manchus (while Chiang Kai-shek had moved it to Nanking), and the CCP leaders congregate in the Forbidden City of the Sons of Heaven. In fact, there are very few, if any, socialist leaderships which have *not* clambered up into such worn, warm seats. At a less obvious level, successful revolutionaries also inherit the wiring of the old state: sometimes functionaries and informers, but always files, dossiers, archives, laws, financial records, censuses, maps, treaties, correspondence, memoranda, and so on. Like the complex electrical system in any large mansion when the owner has fled, the state awaits the new owner's hand at the switch to be very much its old brilliant self again.

One should therefore not be much surprised if revolutionary *leaderships*, consciously or unconsciously, come to play lord of the manor. We are not thinking here simply of Djugashvili's self-identification with Ivan Groznii, or Mao's expressed admiration for the tyrant Ch'in Shih Huang-ti, or Josip Broz's revival of Ruritanian pomp and ceremony.[8] 'Official nationalism' enters post-revolutionary leadership styles in a much more subtle way. By this I mean that such leaderships come easily to adopt the putative *nationalnost* of the older dynasts *and* the dynastic state. In a striking retroactive movement, dynasts who knew nothing of 'China,' 'Yugoslavia,' 'Vietnam' or 'Cambodia' become nationals (even if not always 'deserving' nationals). Out of this accommodation comes invariably that 'state' Machiavellism which is so striking a feature of post-revolutionary regimes in contrast to revolutionary nationalist movements. The more the ancient dynastic state is naturalized, the more its antique finery can be wrapped around revolutionary shoulders. The image of Sūryavarman II's Angkor Wat, emblazoned on the flag of Marxist Democratic Kampuchea (as on those of Lon Nol's puppet

---

8. See the extraordinary account, by no means wholly polemical, in Milovan Djilas, *Tito: the Story from Inside*, chapter 4, especially pp. 133 ff.

republic and of Sihanouk's monarchical Cambodge), is a rebus not of piety but of power.[9]

I emphasize *leaderships*, because it is leaderships, not people, who inherit old switchboards and palaces. No one imagines, I presume, that the broad masses of the Chinese people give a fig for what happens along the colonial border between Cambodia and Vietnam. Nor is it at all likely that Khmer and Vietnamese peasants wanted wars between their peoples, or were consulted in the matter. In a very real sense these were 'chancellory wars' in which popular nationalism was mobilized largely after the fact and always in a language of self-defence. (Hence the particularly low enthusiasm in China, where this language was least plausible, even under the neon-lit blazon of 'Soviet hegemonism.')[10]

In all of this, China, Vietnam, and Cambodia are not in the least unique.[11] This is why there are small grounds for hope that the precedents they have set for inter-socialist wars will not be followed, or that the imagined community of the socialist nation will soon be remaindered. But nothing can be usefully done to limit or prevent such wars unless we abandon fictions like 'Marxists as such are not nationalists,' or 'nationalism is the pathology of modern developmental history,' and, instead, do our slow best to learn the real, and imagined, experience of the past.

Of the Angel of History, Walter Benjamin wrote that:[12]

---

9. Obviously, the tendencies outlined above are by no means characteristic only of revolutionary Marxist regimes. The focus here is on such regimes both because of the historic Marxist commitment to proletarian internationalism and the destruction of feudal and capitalist states, and because of the new Indochina wars. For a decipherment of the archaizing iconography of the right-wing Suharto regime in Indonesia, see my *Language and Power: Exploring Political Cultures in Indonesia*, chapter 5.

10. The difference between the inventions of 'official nationalism' and those of other types is usually that between lies and myths.

11. On the other hand, it is possible that at the end of this century historians may attribute 'official nationalist' excesses committed by post-revolutionary socialist regimes in no small part to the disjuncture between socialist model and agrarian reality.

12. *Illuminations*, p. 259. The angel's eye is that of *Weekend*'s back-turned moving camera, before which wreck after wreck looms up momentarily on an endless highway before vanishing over the horizon.

His face is turned towards the past. Where we perceive a chain of events, he sees one single catastrophe which keeps piling wreckage upon wreckage and hurls it in front of his feet. The angel would like to stay, awaken the dead, and make whole what has been smashed. But a storm is blowing from Paradise; it has got caught in his wings with such violence that the angel can no longer close them. This storm irresistibly propels him into the future to which his back is turned, while the pile of debris before him grows skyward. This storm is what we call progress.

But the Angel is immortal, and our faces are turned towards the obscurity ahead.

10

Census, Map, Museum

In the original edition of *Imagined Communities* I wrote that 'so often in the "nation-building" policies of the new states one sees both a genuine, popular nationalist enthusiasm, and a systematic, even Machiavellian, instilling of nationalist ideology through the mass media, the educational system, administrative regulations, and so forth.'[1] My short-sighted assumption then was that official nationalism in the colonized worlds of Asia and Africa was modelled directly on that of the dynastic states of nineteenth-century Europe. Subsequent reflection has persuaded me that this view was hasty and superficial, and that the immediate genealogy should be traced to the imaginings of the colonial state. At first sight, this conclusion may seem surprising, since colonial states were typically *anti*-nationalist, and often violently so. But if one looks beneath colonial ideologies and policies to the grammar in which, from the mid nineteenth century, they were deployed, the lineage becomes decidedly more clear.

Few things bring this grammar into more visible relief than three institutions of power which, although invented before the mid nineteenth century, changed their form and function as the colonized zones entered the age of mechanical reproduction. These three institutions were the census, the map, and the museum: together, they profoundly

---

1. See above, pp. 113–14.

shaped the way in which the colonial state imagined its dominion – the nature of the human beings it ruled, the geography of its domain, and the legitimacy of its ancestry. To explore the character of this nexus I shall, in this chapter, confine my attention to Southeast Asia, since my conclusions are tentative, and my claims to serious specialization limited to that region. Southeast Asia does, however, offer those with comparative historical interests special advantages, since it includes territories colonized by almost all the 'white' imperial powers – Britain, France, Spain, Portugal, The Netherlands, and the United States – as well as uncolonized Siam. Readers with greater knowledge of other parts of Asia and Africa than mine will be better positioned to judge if my argument is sustainable on a wider historical and geographical stage.

THE CENSUS

In two valuable recent papers the sociologist Charles Hirschman has begun the study of the *mentalités* of the British colonial census-makers for the Straits Settlements and peninsular Malaya, and their successors working for the independent conglomerate state of Malaysia.[2] Hirschman's facsimiles of the 'identity categories' of successive censuses from the late nineteenth century up to the recent present show an extraordinarily rapid, superficially arbitrary, series of changes, in which categories are continuously agglomerated, disaggregated, recombined, intermixed, and reordered (but the politically powerful identity categories always lead the list). From these censuses he draws two principal conclusions. The first is that, as the colonial period wore on, the census categories became more visibly and exclusively racial.[3] Religious identity, on the other hand, gradually

---

2. Charles Hirschman, 'The Meaning and Measurement of Ethnicity in Malaysia: An Analysis of Census Classifications,' *J. of Asian Studies*, 46:3 (August 1987), pp. 552–82; and 'The Making of Race in Colonial Malaya: Political Economy and Racial Ideology' *Sociological Forum*, 1:2 (Spring 1986), pp. 330–62.

3. An astonishing variety of 'Europeans' were enumerated right through the colonial era. But whereas in 1881 they were still grouped primarily under the headings 'resident,' 'floating,' and 'prisoners,' by 1911 they were fraternizing as members of a

disappeared as a primary census classification. 'Hindoos' – ranked alongside 'Klings,' and 'Bengalees' – vanished after the first census of 1871. 'Parsees' lasted until the census of 1901, where they still appeared – packed in with 'Bengalis,' 'Burmese,' and 'Tamils' – under the broad category 'Tamils and Other Natives of India.' His second conclusion is that, on the whole, the large racial categories were retained and even concentrated after independence, but now redesignated and reranked as 'Malaysian,' 'Chinese,' 'Indian,' and 'Other.' Yet anomalies continued up into the 1980s. In the 1980 census 'Sikh' still appeared nervously as a pseudoethnic subcategory – alongside 'Malayali' and 'Telegu,' 'Pakistani' and 'Bangladeshi,' 'Sri Lankan Tamil,' and 'Other Sri Lankan,' – under the general heading 'Indian.'

But Hirschman's wonderful facsimiles encourage one to go beyond his immediate analytical concerns. Take, for example, the 1911 Federated Malay States Census, which lists under 'Malay Population by Race' the following: 'Malay,' 'Javanese,' 'Sakai,' 'Banjarese,' 'Boyanese,' 'Mendeling' (sic), 'Krinchi' (sic), 'Jambi,' 'Achinese,' 'Bugis,' and 'Other.' Of these 'groups' all but (most) 'Malay' and 'Sakai' originated from the islands of Sumatra, Java, Southern Borneo, and the Celebes, all parts of the huge neighbouring colony of the Netherlands East Indies. But these extra-FMS origins receive no recognition from the census-makers who, in constructing their 'Malays,' keep their eyes modestly lowered to their own colonial borders. (Needless to say, across the waters, Dutch census-makers were constructing a different imagining of 'Malays,' as a minor ethnicity alongside, not above, 'Achinese,' 'Javanese,' and the like.) 'Jambi' and 'Krinchi' refer to places, rather than to anything remotely identifiable as ethnolinguistic. It is extremely unlikely that, in 1911, more than a tiny fraction of those categorized and subcategorized would have recognized themselves under such labels. These 'identities,' imagined by the (confusedly) classifying mind of the colonial state, still awaited a reification which imperial administrative penetration would soon make possible. One notices, in addition, the

---

(white) race'. It is agreeable that up to the end, the census-makers were visibly uneasy about where to place those they marked as 'Jews.'

census-makers' passion for completeness and unambiguity. Hence their intolerance of multiple, politically 'transvestite,' blurred, or changing identifications. Hence the weird subcategory, under each racial group, of 'Others' – who, nonetheless, are absolutely not to be confused with *other* 'Others.' The fiction of the census is that everyone is in it, and that everyone has one – and only one – extremely clear place. No fractions.

This mode of imagining by the colonial state had origins much older than the censuses of the 1870s, so that, in order fully to understand why the late-nineteenth-century censuses are yet profoundly novel, it is useful to look back to the earliest days of European penetration of Southeast Asia. Two examples, drawn from the Philippine and Indonesian archipelagoes, are instructive. In an important recent book, William Henry Scott has attempted meticulously to reconstruct the class structure of the pre-Hispanic Philippines, on the basis of the earliest Spanish records.[4] As a professional historian Scott is perfectly aware that the Philippines owes its name to Felipe II of 'Spain,' and that, but for mischance or luck, the archipelago might have fallen into Dutch or English hands, become politically segmented, or been recombined with further conquests.[5] It is tempting therefore to attribute his curious choice of topic to his long residence in the Philippines and his strong sympathy with a Filipino nationalism that has been, for a century now, on the trail of an aboriginal Eden. But the chances are good that the deeper basis for the shaping of his imagination was the sources on which he was

---

4. William Henry Scott, *Cracks in the Parchment Curtain*, chapter 7, 'Filipino Class Structure in the Sixteenth Century.'

5. In the first half of the seventeenth century, Spanish settlements in the archipelago came under repeated attack from the forces of the Vereenigde Oost-Indische Compagnie, the greatest 'transnational' corporation of the era. For their survival, the pious Catholic settlers owed a great debt to the arch-heretical Protector, who kept Amsterdam's back to the wall for much of his rule. Had the VOC been successful, Manila, rather than Batavia [Jakarta], might have become the centre of the 'Dutch' imperium in Southeast Asia. In 1762, London seized Manila from Spain, and held it for almost two years. It is entertaining to note that Madrid only got it back in exchange for, of all places, Florida, and the other 'Spanish' possessions east of the Mississippi. Had the negotiations proceeded differently, the archipelago could have been politically linked with Malaya and Singapore during the nineteenth century.

compelled to rely. For the fact is that wherever in the islands the earliest clerics and conquistadors ventured they espied, on shore, *principales, hidalgos, pecheros,* and *esclavos* (princes, noblemen, commoners and slaves) – quasi-estates adapted from the social classifications of late mediaeval Iberia. The documents they left behind offer plenty of incidental evidence that the *'hidalgos'* were mostly unaware of one another's existence in the huge, scattered, and sparsely populated archipelago, and, where aware, usually saw one another not as *hidalgos*, but as enemies or potential slaves. But the power of the grid is so great that such evidence is marginalized in Scott's imagination, and therefore it is hard for him to see that the 'class structure' of the precolonial period is a 'census' imagining created from the poops of Spanish galleons. Wherever *they* went, *hidalgos* and *esclavos* loomed up, who could only be aggregated as such, that is 'structurally,' by an incipient colonial state.

For Indonesia we have, thanks to the research of Mason Hoadley, a detailed account of an important judicial case decided in the coastal port of Cirebon, Java, at the end of the seventeenth century.[6] By luck, the Dutch (VOC) and local Cirebonese records are still available. If the Cirebonese account only had survived, we would know the accused murderer as a high official of the Cirebonese court, and only by his title Ki Aria Marta Ningrat, not a personal name. The VOC records, however, angrily identify him as a *Chinees* – indeed that is the single most important piece of information about him that they convey. It is clear then that the Cirebonese court classified people by rank and status, while the Company did so by something like 'race.' There is no reason whatever to think that the accused murderer – whose high status attests to his and his ancestors' long integration into Cirebonese society, no matter what their origins – thought of himself as 'a' *Chinees*. How then did the VOC arrive at this classification? From what poops was it possible to imagine *Chinees*? Surely only those ferociously mercantile poops which, under centralized command, roved ceaselessly from port to port between the Gulf of Mergui and the mouth of the Yangtze-kiang. Oblivious

6. Mason C. Hoadley, 'State vs. Ki Aria Marta Ningrat (1696) and Tian Siangko (1720–21)' (unpublished ms., 1982).

of the heterogeneous populations of the Middle Kingdom; of the mutual incomprehensibility of many of their spoken languages; and of the peculiar social and geographic origins of their diaspora across coastal Southeast Asia, the Company imagined, with its trans-oceanic eye, an endless series of *Chinezen*, as the conquistadors had seen an endless series of *hidalgos*. And on the basis of this inventive census it began to insist that those under its control whom it categorized as *Chinezen* dress, reside, marry, be buried, and bequeath property according to that census. It is striking that the much less far-faring and commercially minded Iberians in the Philippines imagined a quite different census category: what they called *sangley*. *Sangley* was an incorporation into Spanish of the Hokkien *sengli* – meaning 'trader.'[7] One can imagine Spanish proto-census men asking the traders drawn to Manila by the galleon trade: 'Who are you?', and being sensibly told: 'We are traders.'[8] Not sailing the seven Asian seas, for two centuries the Iberians remained in a comfortably provincial conceptual fog. Only very slowly did the *sangley* turn into 'Chinese' – until the word disappeared in the early nineteenth century to make way for a VOC-style *chino*.

The real innovation of the census-takers of the 1870s was, therefore, not in the *construction* of ethnic-racial classifications, but rather in their systematic *quantification*. Precolonial rulers in the Malayo-Javanese world had attempted enumerations of the populations under their control, but these took the form of tax-rolls and levy-lists. Their purposes were concrete and specific: to keep track of those on whom taxes and military conscription could effectively be imposed – for these rulers were interested solely in economic surplus and armable manpower. Early European regimes in the region did not, in this respect, differ markedly from their predecessors. But after 1850 colonial authorities were using increasingly sophisticated administrative means to enumerate populations, including the women and children (whom the ancient rulers had always ignored), according to

---

7. See, e.g., Edgar Wickberg, *The Chinese in Philippine Life, 1850–1898*, chapters 1 and 2.

8. The galleon trade – for which Manila was, for over two centuries, the *entrepôt* – exchanged Chinese silks and porcelain for Mexican silver.

a maze of grids which had no immediate financial or military purpose. In the old days, those subjects liable for taxes and con- scription were usually well aware of their numerability; ruler and ruled understood each other very well, if antagonistically, on the matter. But by 1870, a non-taxpaying, unlevyable 'Cochin-Chinese' woman could live out her life, happily or unhappily, in the Straits Settlements, without the slightest awareness that this was how she was being mapped from on high. Here the peculiarity of the new census becomes apparent. It tried carefully to count the objects of its feverish imagining. Given the exclusive nature of the classificatory system, and the logic of quantification itself, a 'Cochin-Chinese' had to be understood as one digit in an aggregable series of replicable 'Cochin-Chinese' – within, of course, the state's domain. The new demographic topography put down deep social and institutional roots as the colonial state multiplied its size and functions. Guided by its imagined map it organized the new educational, juridical, public-health, police, and immigration bureaucracies it was building on the principle of ethno-racial hierarchies which were, however, always understood in terms of parallel series. The flow of subject populations through the mesh of differential schools, courts, clinics, police stations and immigration offices created 'traffic-habits' which in time gave real social life to the state's earlier fantasies.

Needless to say, it was not always plain sailing, and the state frequently bumped into discomforting realities. Far and away the most important of these was religious affiliation, which served as the basis of very old, very stable imagined communities not in the least aligned with the secular state's authoritarian grid-map. To different degrees, in different Southeast Asian colonies, the rulers were com- pelled to make messy accommodations, especially to Islam and Buddhism. In particular, religious shrines, schools, and courts – access to which was determined by individual popular self-choice, not the census – continued to flourish. The state could rarely do more than try to regulate, constrict, count, standardize, and hierarchically sub- ordiante these institutions to its own.[9] It was precisely because

_____

9. See chapter 7, above (p. 125) for mention of French colonialism's struggle to sever Buddhism in Cambodia from its old links with Siam.

temples, mosques, schools and courts were topographically anomalous that they were understood as zones of freedom and – in time – fortresses from which religious, later nationalist, anticolonials could go forth to battle. At the same time, there were frequent endeavours to force a better alignment of census with religious communities by – so far as was possible – politically and juridically ethnicizing the latter. In the Federated States of colonial Malaya, this task was relatively easy. Those whom the regime regarded as being in the series 'Malay' were hustled off to the courts of 'their' castrated Sultans, which were in substantial part administered according to Islamic law.[10] 'Islamic' was thus treated as really just another name for 'Malay.' (Only after independence in 1957 were efforts made by certain political groups to reverse this logic by reading 'Malay' as really another name for 'Islamic'). In the vast, heterogeneous Netherlands Indies, where by the end of the colonial era an array of quarrelling missionary organizations had made substantial conversions in widely scattered zones, a parallel drive faced much more substantial obstacles. Yet even there, the 1920s and 1930s saw the growth of 'ethnic' Christianities (the Batak Church, the Karo Church, later the Dayak Church, and so on) which developed in part because the state allocated proselytizing zones to different missionary groups according to its own census-topography. With Islam Batavia had no comparable success. It did not dare to prohibit the pilgrimage to Mecca, though it tried to inhibit the growth of the pilgrims' numbers, policed their travels, and spied on them from an outpost at Jiddah set up just for this purpose. None of these measures sufficed to prevent the intensification of Indies Muslim contacts with the vast world of Islam outside, and especially the new currents of thought emanating from Cairo.[11]

THE MAP

In the meantime, however, Cairo and Mecca were beginning to be visualized in a strange new way, no longer simply as sites in a sacred

10. See William Roff, *The Origins of Malay Nationalism*, pp. 72–4.
11. See Harry J. Benda, *The Crescent and the Rising Sun*, chapters 1–2.

Muslim geography, but also as dots on paper sheets which included dots for Paris, Moscow, Manila and Caracas; and the plane relationship between these indifferently profane and sacred dots was determined by nothing beyond the mathematically calculated flight of the crow. The Mercatorian map, brought in by the European colonizers, was beginning, via print, to shape the imagination of Southeast Asians.

In a recent, brilliant thesis the Thai historian Thongchai Winichakul has traced the complex processes by which a bordered 'Siam' came into being between 1850 and 1910.[12] His account is instructive precisely because Siam was not colonized, though what, in the end, came to be its borders were colonially determined. In the Thai case, therefore, one can see unusually clearly the emergence of a new state-mind within a 'traditional' structure of political power.

Up until the accession, in 1851, of the intelligent Rama IV (the Mongkut of *The King and I*), only two types of map existed in Siam, and both were hand-made: the age of mechanical reproduction had not yet there dawned. One was what could be called a 'cosmograph,' a formal, symbolic representation of the Three Worlds of traditional Buddhist cosmology. The cosmograph was not organized horizontally, like our own maps; rather a series of supraterrestrial heavens and subterrestrial hells wedged in the visible world along a single vertical axis. It was useless for any journey save that in search of merit and salvation. The second type, wholly profane, consisted of diagrammatic guides for military campaigns and coastal shipping. Organized roughly by the quadrant, their main features were written-in notes on marching and sailing times, required because the mapmakers had no technical conception of scale. Covering only terrestrial, profane space, they were usually drawn in a queer oblique perspective or mixture of perspectives, as if the drawers' eyes, accustomed from daily life to see the landscape horizontally, at eye-level, nonetheless were influenced subliminally by the verticality of the cosmograph. Thongchai points out that these guide-maps, always local, were

---

12. Thongchai Winichakul, 'Siam Mapped: A History of the Geo-Body of Siam' (Ph.D. Thesis, University of Sydney, 1988).

never situated in a larger, stable geographic context, and that the bird's-eye view convention of modern maps was wholly foreign to them.

Neither type of map marked borders. Their makers would have found incomprehensible the following elegant formulation of Richard Muir:[13]

> Located at the interfaces between adjacent state territories, inter-national boundaries have a special significance in determining the limits of sovereign authority and defining the spatial form of the contained political regions. . . . Boundaries . . occur where the vertical interfaces between state sovereignties intersect the surface of the earth. . . . As vertical interfaces, boundaries have no horizontal extent. . . .

Boundary-stones and similar markers did exist, and indeed multiplied along the western fringes of the realm as the British pressed in from Lower Burma. But these stones were set up discontinuously at strategic mountain passes and fords, and were often substantial distances from corresponding stones set up by the adversary. They were understood horizontally, at eye level, as extension points of royal power; not 'from the air.' Only in the 1870s did Thai leaders begin thinking of boundaries as segments of a continuous map-line corresponding to nothing visible on the ground, but demarcating an exclusive sovereignty wedged between other sovereignties. In 1874 appeared the first geographical textbook, by the American missionary J.W. Van Dyke – an early product of the print-capitalism that was by then sweeping into Siam. In 1882, Rama V established a special mapping school in Bangkok. In 1892, Minister of Education Prince Damrong Rajanuphab, inaugurating a modern-style school system for the country, made geography a compulsory subject at the junior secondary level. In 1900, or thereabouts, was published *Phumisat Sayam* [Geography of Siam] by W.G. Johnson, the model for all printed geographies of the country from that time onwards.[14]

---

13. Richard Muir, *Modern Political Geography*, p. 119.
14. Thongchai, 'Siam Mapped,' pp. 105–10, 286.

Thongchai notes that the vectoral convergence of print-capitalism with the new conception of spatial reality presented by these maps had an immediate impact on the vocabulary of Thai politics. Between 1900 and 1915, the traditional words *krung* and *muang* largely disappeared, because they imaged dominion in terms of sacred capitals and visible, discontinuous population centres.[15] In their place came *prathet*, 'country,' which imaged it in the invisible terms of bounded territorial space.[16]

Like censuses, European-style maps worked on the basis of a totalizing classification, and led their bureaucratic producers and consumers towards policies with revolutionary consequences. Ever since John Harrison's 1761 invention of the chronometer, which made possible the precise calculation of longitudes, the entire planet's curved surface had been subjected to a geometrical grid which squared off empty seas and unexplored regions in measured boxes.[17] The task of, as it were, 'filling in' the boxes was to be accomplished by explorers, surveyors, and military forces. In Southeast Asia, the second half of the nineteenth century was the golden age of military surveyors – colonial and, a little later, Thai. They were on the march to put space under the same surveillance which the census-makers were trying to impose on persons. Triangulation by triangulation, war by war, treaty by treaty, the alignment of map and power proceeded. In the apt words of Thongchai:[18]

In terms of most communication theories and common sense, a map is a scientific abstraction of reality. A map merely represents something which already exists objectively 'there.' In the history I have described, this relationship was reversed. A map anticipated spatial reality, not vice versa. In other words, a map was a model for, rather than a model of, what it purported to represent. . . . It had become a

---

15. For a full discussion of old conceptions of power in Java (which, with minor differences, corresponded to that existing in Old Siam), see my *Language and Power*, chapter 1.

16. Thongchai, 'Siam Mapped,' p. 110.

17. David S. Landes, *Revolution in Time: Clocks and the Making of the Modern World*, chapter 9.

18. 'Siam Mapped,' p. 310.

real instrument to concretize projections on the earth's surface. A map was now necessary for the new administrative mechanisms and for the troops to back up their claims. . . . The discourse of mapping was the paradigm which both administrative and military operations worked within and served.

By the turn of the century, with Prince Damrong's reforms at the Ministry of the Interior (a fine mapping name), the administration of the realm was finally put on a wholly territorial–cartographic basis, following earlier practice in the neighbouring colonies.

It would be unwise to overlook the crucial intersection between map and census. For the new map served firmly to break off the infinite series of 'Hakkas,' 'Non-Tamil Sri Lankans,' and 'Javanese' that the formal apparatus of the census conjured up, by delimiting territorially where, for political purposes, they ended. Conversely, by a sort of demographic triangulation, the census filled in politically the formal topography of the map.

Out of these changes emerged two final avatars of the map (both instituted by the late colonial state) which directly prefigure the official nationalisms of twentieth century Southeast Asia. Fully aware of their interloper status in the distant tropics, but arriving from a civilization in which the legal inheritance and the legal transferability of geographic space had long been established,[19] the Europeans frequently attempted to legitimize the spread of their power by quasi-legal methods. Among the more popular of these was their 'inheritance' of the putative sovereignties of native rulers whom the Europeans had eliminated or subjected. Either way, the usurpers were in the business, especially vis-à-vis other Europeans, of re-constructing the property-history of their new possessions. Hence the appearance, late in the nineteenth century especially, of 'historical maps,' designed to demonstrate, in the new cartographic discourse,

---

19. I do not mean merely the inheritance and sale of private property in land in the usual sense. More important was the European practice of political transfers of lands, with their populations, via dynastic marriages. Princesses, on marriage, brought their husbands duchies and petty principalities, and these transfers were formally negotiated and 'signed.' The tag *Bella gerant alii, tu, felix Austria, nube!* would have been inconceivable for any state in precolonial Asia.

the antiquity of specific, tightly bounded territorial units. Through chronologically arranged sequences of such maps, a sort of political–biographical narrative of the realm came into being, sometimes with vast historical depth.[20] In turn, this narrative was adopted, if often adapted, by the nation-states which, in the twentieth century, became the colonial states' legatees.[21]

The second avatar was the map-as-logo. Its origins were reasonably innocent – the practice of the imperial states of colouring their colonies on maps with an imperial dye. In London's imperial maps, British colonies were usually pink-red, French purple-blue, Dutch yellow-brown, and so on. Dyed this way, each colony appeared like a detachable piece of a jigsaw puzzle. As this 'jigsaw' effect became normal, each 'piece' could be wholly detached from its geographic context. In its final form all explanatory glosses could be summarily removed: lines of longitude and latitude, place names, signs for rivers, seas, and mountains, *neighbours*. Pure sign, no longer compass to the world. In this shape, the map entered an infinitely reproducible series, available for transfer to posters, official seals, letterheads, magazine and textbook covers, tablecloths, and hotel walls. Instantly recognizable, everywhere visible, the logo-map penetrated deep into the popular imagination, forming a powerful emblem for the anticolonial nation-alisms being born.[22]

---

20. See Thongchai, 'Siam Mapped,' p. 387, on Thai ruling class absorption of this style of imagining. 'According to these historical maps, moreover, the geobody is not a modern particularity but is pushed back more than a thousand years. Historical maps thus help reject any suggestion that nationhood emerged only in the recent past, and the perspective that the present Siam was a result of ruptures is precluded. So is any idea that intercourse between Siam and the European powers was the parent of Siam.'

21. This adoption was by no means a Machiavellian ruse. The early nationalists in all the Southeast Asian colonies had their consciousnesses profoundly shaped by the 'format' of the colonial state and its institutions. See chapter 7 above.

22. In the writings of Nick Joaquín, the contemporary Philippines, preeminent man of letters – and an indubitable patriot – one can see how powerfully the emblem works on the most sophisticated intelligence. Of General Antonio Luna, tragic hero of the anti-American struggle of 1898–99, Joaquín writes that he hurried to 'perform the role that had been instinctive in the Creole for three centuries: the defense of *the form* of the Philippines from a foreign disrupter.' *A Question of Heroes*, p. 164 (italics added). Elsewhere he observes, astonishingly, that Spain's 'Filipino allies, converts, mercenaries

Modern Indonesia offers us a fine, painful example of this process. In 1828 the first fever-ridden Dutch settlement was made on the island of New Guinea. Although the settlement had to be abandoned in 1836, the Dutch Crown proclaimed sovereignty over that part of the island lying west of 141 degrees longitude (an invisible line which corresponded to nothing on the ground, but boxed in Conrad's diminishing white spaces), with the exception of some coastal stretches regarded as under the sovereignty of the Sultan of Tidore. Only in 1901 did The Hague buy out the Sultan, and incorporate West New Guinea into the Netherlands Indies – just in time for logoization. Large parts of the region remained Conrad-white until after World War II; the handful of Dutchmen there were mostly missionaries, mineral-prospectors – and wardens of special prison-camps for die-hard radical Indonesian nationalists. The swamps north of Merauke, at the extreme southeastern edge of Dutch New Guinea, were selected as the site of these facilities precisely because the region was regarded as utterly remote from the rest of the colony, and the 'stone-age' local population as wholly uncontaminated by nationalist thinking.[23]

The internment, and often interment, there of nationalist martyrs gave West New Guinea a central place in the folklore of the anticolonial struggle, and made it a sacred site in the national imagining: Indonesia Free, from Sabang (at the northwestern tip of Sumatra) to – where else but? – Merauke. It made no difference at all that, aside from the few hundred internees, no nationalists ever saw New Guinea with their own eyes until the 1960s. But Dutch colonial logo-maps sped across in the colony, showing a West New Guinea *with nothing to its East*, unconsciously reinforced the developing imagined ties. When, in the aftermath of the bitter anticolonial wars of 1945–49, the Dutch were forced to cede sovereignty of the archipelago to a United States of Indonesia, they attempted (for reasons that need not detain us here) to separate West New Guinea

sent against the Filipino rebel may have kept the archipelago Spanish and Christian, but they also kept it from falling apart;' and that they 'were fighting (whatever the Spaniards may have intended) to keep the Filipino one.' Ibid., p. 58.

23. See Robin Osborne, *Indonesia's Secret War, The Guerrilla Struggle in Irian Jaya*, pp. 8–9.

once again, keep it temporarily under colonial rule, and prepare it for independent nationhood. Not until 1963 was this enterprise abandoned, as a result of heavy American diplomatic pressure and Indonesian military raids. Only then did President Sukarno visit for the first time, at the age of sixty-two, a region about which he had tirelessly orated for four decades. The subsequent painful relations between the populations of West New Guinea and the emissaries of the independent Indonesian state can be attributed to the fact that Indonesians more or less sincerely regard these populations as 'brothers and sisters,' while the populations themselves, for the most part, see things very differently.[24]

This difference owes much to census and map. New Guinea's remoteness and rugged terrain created over the millennia an extraordinary linguistic fragmentation. When the Dutch left the region in 1963 they estimated that within the 700,000 population there existed well over 200 mostly mutually unintelligible languages.[25] Many of the remoter 'tribal' groups were not even aware of one another's existence. But, especially after 1950, Dutch missionaries and Dutch officials for the first time made serious efforts to 'unify' them by taking censuses, expanding communications networks, establishing schools, and erecting supra-'tribal' governmental structures. This effort was launched by a colonial state which, as we noted earlier, was unique in that it had governed the Indies, not primarily via a European language, but through 'administrative Malay.'[26] Hence West New Guinea was 'brought up' in the same language in which Indonesia had earlier been raised (and which became the national language in due course). The irony is that *bahasa Indonesia* thus

---

24. Since 1963 there have been many bloody episodes in West New Guinea (now called Irian Jaya – Great Irian), partly as a result of the militarization of the Indonesian state since 1965, partly because of the intermittently effective guerrilla activities of the so-called OPM (Organization for a Free Papua). But these brutalities pale by comparison with Jakarta's savagery in ex-Portuguese East Timor, where in the first three years after the 1976 invasion an estimated one-third of the population of 600,000 died from war, famine, disease and 'resettlement'. I do not think it a mistake to suggest that the difference derives in part from East Timor's absence from the logos of the Netherlands East Indies and, until 1976, of Indonesia's.

25. Osborne, *Indonesia's Secret War*, p. 2.

26. See above, p. 110.

became the lingua franca of a burgeoning West New Guinean, West Papuan nationalism.[27]

But what brought the often quarrelling young West Papuan nationalists together, especially after 1963, was the map. Though the Indonesian state changed the region's name from West Nieuw Guinea, first to Irian Barat (West Irian) and then to Irian Jaya, it read its local reality from the colonial-era bird's-eye atlas. A scattering of anthropologists, missionaries and local officials might know and think about the Ndanis, the Asmats, and the Baudis. But the state itself, and through it the Indonesian population as a whole, saw only a phantom 'Irianese' (*orang Irian*) named *after the map*; because phantom, to be imagined in quasi-logo form: 'negroid' features, penis-sheaths, and so on. In a way that reminds us how Indonesia came first to be imagined within the racist structures of the early-twentieth-century Netherlands East Indies, an embryo 'Irianese' national community, bounded by Meridian 141 and the neighbouring provinces of North and South Moluccas, emerged. At the time when its most prominent and attractive spokesman, Arnold Ap, was murdered by the state in 1984, he was curator of a state-built museum devoted to 'Irianese' (provincial) culture.

THE MUSEUM

The link between Ap's occupation and assassination is not at all accidental. For museums, and the museumizing imagination, are both profoundly political. That his museum was instituted by a distant Jakarta shows us how the new nation-state of Indonesia learned from its immediate ancestor, the colonial Netherlands East Indies. The present proliferation of museums around Southeast Asia suggests a general process of political inheriting at work. Any understanding of this process requires a consideration of the novel nineteenth-century colonial archaeology that made such museums possible.

---

27. The best sign for this is that the anti-Indonesian nationalist guerrilla organization's name, Organisasi Papua Merdeka (OPM), is composed of Indonesian words.

Up until the early nineteenth century the colonial rulers in Southeast Asia exhibited very little interest in the antique monuments of the civilizations they had subjected. Thomas Stamford Raffles, ominous emissary from William Jones's Calcutta, was the first prominent colonial official not merely to amass a large personal collection of local *objets d'art*, but systematically to study their history.[28] Thereafter, with increasing speed, the grandeurs of the Borobudur, of Angkor, of Pagan, and of other ancient sites were successively disinterred, unjungled, measured, photographed, reconstructed, fenced off, analysed, and displayed.[29] Colonial Archaeological Services became powerful and prestigious institutions, calling on the services of some exceptionally capable scholar-officials.[30]

---

28. In 1811, the East India Company's forces seized all the Dutch possessions in the Indies (Napoléon had absorbed the Netherlands into France the previous year). Raffles ruled in Java till 1815. His monumental *History of Java* appeared in 1817, two years prior to his founding of Singapore.

29. The museumizing of the Borobudur, the largest Buddhist stupa in the world, exemplifies this process. In 1814, the Raffles regime 'discovered' it, and had it unjungled. In 1845, the self-promoting German artist-adventurer Schaefer persuaded the Dutch authorities in Batavia to pay him to make the first daguerrotypes. In 1851, Batavia sent a team of state employees, led by civil engineer F.C. Wilsen, to make a systematic survey of the bas-reliefs and to produce a complete, 'scientific' set of lithographs. In 1874, Dr. C. Leemans, Director of the Museum of Antiquities in Leiden, published, at the behest of the Minister of Colonies, the first major scholarly monograph; he relied heavily on Wilsen's lithographs, never having visited the site himself. In the 1880s, the professional photographer Cephas produced a thorough modern-style photographic survey. In 1901, the colonial regime established an Oudheidkundige Commissie (Commission on Antiquities). Between 1907 and 1911, the Commission oversaw the complete restoration of the stupa, carried out at state expense by a team under the civil engineer Van Erp. Doubtless in recognition of this success, the Commission was promoted, in 1913, to an Oudheidkundigen Dienst (Antiquities Service), which kept the monument spick and span until the end of the colonial period. See C. Leemans, *Boro-Boudour*, pp. ii–lv; and N.J. Krom, *Inleiding tot de Hindoe-Javaansche Kunst*, I, chapter 1.

30. Viceroy Curzon (1899–1905), an antiquities buff who, writes Groslier, 'energized' the Archaeological Survey of India, put things very nicely: 'It is . . . equally our duty to dig and discover, to classify, reproduce and describe, to copy and decipher, and to cherish and conserve.' (Foucault could not have said it better). In 1899, the Archaeological Department of Burma – then part of British India – was founded, and soon began the restoration of Pagan. The previous year, the École Française d'Extrême-Orient was established in Saigon, followed almost at once by a

To explore fully why this happened, when it happened, would take us too far afield. It may be enough here to suggest that the change was associated with the eclipse of the commercial–colonial regimes of the two great East India Companies, and the rise of the true modern colony, directly attached to the metropole.[31] The prestige of the colonial state was accordingly now intimately linked to that of its homeland superior. It is noticeable how heavily concentrated archaeological efforts were on the restoration of imposing monuments (and how these monuments began to be plotted on maps for public distribution and edification: a kind of necrological census was under way). No doubt this emphasis reflected general Orientalist fashions. But the substantial funds invested allow us to suspect that the state had its own, non-scientific reasons. Three immediately suggest themselves, of which the last is surely the most important.

In the first place, the timing of the archaeological push coincided with the first political struggle over the state's educational policies.[32]

Directorate of Museums and Historical Monuments of Indochina. Immediately after the French seizure of Siemreap and Battambang from Siam in 1907, an Angkor Conservancy was established to Curzonize Southeast Asia's most awe-inspiring ancient monuments. See Bernard Philippe Groslier, *Indochina*, pp. 155–7, 174–7. As noted above, the Dutch colonial Antiquities Commission was founded in 1901. The coincidence in dates – 1899, 1898, 1901 – shows not only the keenness with which the rival colonial powers observed one another, but sea-changes in imperialism under way by the turn of the century. As was to be expected, independent Siam ambled along more slowly. Its Archaeological Service was only set up in 1924, its National Museum in 1926. See Charles Higham, *The Archaeology of Mainland Southeast Asia*, p. 25.

31. The VOC was liquidated, in bankruptcy, in 1799. The colony of the Netherlands Indies, however, dates from 1815, when the independence of The Netherlands was restored by the Holy Alliance, and Willem I of Orange put on a Dutch throne first invented in 1806 by Napoléon and his kindly brother Louis. The British East India Company survived till the great Indian Mutiny of 1857.

32. The Oudheidkundige Commissie was established by the same government that (in 1901) inaugurated the new 'Ethical Policy' for the Indies, a policy that for the first time aimed to establish a Western-style system of education for substantial numbers of the colonized. Governor-General Paul Doumer (1897–1902) created both the Directorate of Museums and Historical Monuments of Indochina and the colony's modern educational apparatus. In Burma, the huge expansion of higher education – which between 1900 and 1940 increased the number of secondary-school students eightfold, from 27,401 to 233,543, and of college students twentyfold, from 115 to 2,365 – began just as the Archaeological Department of Burma swung into action. See Robert H. Taylor, *The State in Burma*, p. 114.

'Progressives' – colonials as well as natives – were urging major investments in modern schooling. Against them were arrayed conservatives who feared the long-term consequences of such schooling, and preferred the natives to stay native. In this light, archaeological restorations – soon followed by state-sponsored printed editions of traditional literary texts – can be seen as a sort of conservative educational program, which also served as a pretext for resisting the pressure of the progressives. Second, the formal ideological programme of the reconstructions always placed the builders of the monuments and the colonial natives in a certain hierarchy. In some cases, as in the Dutch East Indies up until the 1930s, the idea was entertained that the builders were actually not of the same 'race' as the natives (they were 'really' Indian immigrants).[33] In other cases, as in Burma, what was imagined was a secular decadence, such that contemporary natives were no longer capable of their putative ancestors' achievements. Seen in this light, the reconstructed monuments, juxtaposed with the surrounding rural poverty, said to the natives: Our very presence shows that you have always been, or have long become, incapable of either greatness or self-rule.

The third reason takes us deeper, and closer to the map. We have seen earlier, in our discussion of the 'historical map,' how colonial regimes began attaching themself to antiquity as much as conquest, originally for quite straightforward Machiavellian–legalistic reasons. As time passed, however, there was less and less openly brutal talk about right of conquest, and more and more effort to create alternative legitimacies. More and more Europeans were being born in Southeast Asia, and being tempted to make it their home. Monumental archaeology, increasingly linked to tourism, allowed the state to appear as the guardian of a generalized, but also local, Tradition. The old sacred sites were to be incorporated into the map of the colony, and their ancient prestige (which, if this had

---

33. Influenced in part by this kind of thinking, conservative Thai intellectuals, archaeologists, and officials persist to this day in attributing Angkor to the mysterious Khom, who vanished without a trace, and certainly have no connection with today's despised Cambodians.

disappeared, as it often had, the state would attempt to revive) draped around the mappers. This paradoxical situation is nicely illustrated by the fact that the reconstructed monuments often had smartly laid-out lawns around them, and always explanatory tablets, complete with datings, planted here and there. Moreover, they were to be kept empty of people, except for perambulatory tourists (no religious ceremonies or pilgrimages, so far as possible). Museumized this way, they were repositioned as regalia for a *secular* colonial state.

But, as noted above, a characteristic feature of the instrumentalities of this profane state was infinite reproducibility, a reproducibility made technically possible by print and photography, but politico-culturally by the disbelief of the rulers themselves in the real sacredness of local sites. A sort of progression is detectable every-where: (1) massive, technically sophisticated archaeological reports, complete with dozens of photographs, recording the process of reconstruction of particular, distinct ruins; (2) Lavishly illustrated books for public consumption, including exemplary plates of all the major sites reconstructed *within the colony* (so much the better if, as in the Netherlands Indies, Hindu-Buddhist shrines could be juxtaposed to restored Islamic mosques).[34] Thanks to print-capitalism, a sort of pictorial census of the state's patrimony becomes available, even if at high cost, to the state's subjects; (3) A general logoization, made possible by the profaning processes outlined above. Postage stamps, with their characteristic series – tropical birds, fruits, fauna, why not monuments as well? – are exemplary of this stage. But postcards and schoolroom textbooks follow the same logic. From there it is only a step into the market: Hotel Pagan, Borobudur Fried Chicken, and so on.

While this kind of archaeology, maturing in the age of mechanical

<hr />

34. A fine late-blooming example is *Ancient Indonesian Art*, by the Dutch scholar, A.J. Bernet Kempers, self-described as 'former Director of Archaeology in Indonesia [sic].' On pages 24–5 one finds maps showing the location of the ancient sites. The first is especially instructive, since its rectangular shape (framed on the east by the 141st Meridian) willy-nilly includes Philippine Mindanao as well as British-Malaysian north Borneo, peninsular Malaya, and Singapore. All are blank of sites, indeed of any naming whatsoever, except for a single, inexplicable 'Kedah.' The switch from Hindu-Buddhism to Islam occurs after Plate 340.

reproduction, was profoundly political, it was political at such a deep level that almost everyone, including the personnel of the colonial state (who, by the 1930s, were in most of Southeast Asia 90 per cent native) was unconscious of the fact. It had all become normal and everyday. It was precisely the infinite quotidian reproducibility of its regalia that revealed the real power of the state.

It is probably not too surprising that post-independence states, which exhibited marked continuities with their colonial predecessors, inherited this form of political museumizing. For example, on 9 November 1968, as part of the celebrations commemorating the 15th anniversary of Cambodia's independence, Norodom Sihanouk had a large wood and papier-mâché replica of the great Bayon temple of Angkor displayed in the national sports stadium in Phnom Penh.[35] The replica was exceptionally coarse and crude, but it served its purpose – instant recognizability via a history of colonial-era logoization. 'Ah, our Bayon' – but with the memory of French colonial restorers wholly banished. French-reconstructed Angkor Wat, again in 'jigsaw' form, became, as noted in Chapter 9, the central symbol of the successive flags of Sihanouk's royalist, Lon Nol's militarist, and Pol Pot's Jacobin regimes.

More striking still is evidence of inheritance at a more popular level. One revealing example is a series of paintings of episodes in the national history commissioned by Indonesia's Ministry of Education in the 1950s. The paintings were to be mass-produced and distributed throughout the primary-school system; young Indonesians were to have on the walls of their classrooms – everywhere – visual representations of their country's past. Most of the backgrounds were done in the predictable sentimental-naturalist style of early-twentieth-century commercial art, and the human figures taken either from colonial-era museum dioramas or from the popular *wayang orang* pseudohistorical folk-drama. The most interesting of the series, however, offered children a representation of the Borobudur. In reality, this colossal monument, with its 504 Buddha images, 1,460 pictorial and 1,212 decorative stone panels, is a fantastic storehouse of ancient Javanese sculpture. But the well-regarded artist imagines the

---

35. See *Kambuja*, 45 (15 December 1968), for some curious photographs.

marvel in its ninth century A.D. heyday with instructive perversity. The Borobudur is painted completely white, with not a trace of sculpture visible. Surrounded by well-trimmed lawns and tidy tree-lined avenues, *not a single human being is in sight*.[36] One might argue that this emptiness reflects the unease of a contemporary Muslim painter in the face of an ancient Buddhist reality. But I suspect that what we are really seeing is an unselfconscious lineal descendant of colonial archaeology: the Borobudur as state regalia, and as 'of course, that's it' logo. A Borobudur all the more powerful as a sign for national identity because of everyone's awareness of its location in an infinite series of identical Borobudurs.

Interlinked with one another, then, the census, the map and the museum illuminate the late colonial state's style of thinking about its domain. The 'warp' of this thinking was a totalizing classificatory grid, which could be applied with endless flexibility to anything under the state's real or contemplated control: peoples, regions, religions, languages, products, monuments, and so forth. The effect of the grid was always to be able to say of anything that it was this, not that; it belonged here, not there. It was bounded, determinate, and therefore – in principle – countable. (The comic classificatory and subclassificatory census boxes entitled 'Other' concealed all real-life anomalies by a splendid bureaucratic *trompe l'oeil*). The 'weft' was what one could call serialization: the assumption that the world was made up of replicable plurals. The particular always stood as a provisional representative of a series, and was to be handled in this light. This is why the colonial state imagined a Chinese series before any Chinese, and a nationalist series before the appearance of any nationalists.

No one has found a better metaphor for this frame of mind than the great Indonesian novelist Pramoedya Ananta Toer, who entitled the final volume of his tetralogy on the colonial period *Rumah Kaca* – the Glass House. It is an image, as powerful as Bentham's Panopticon, of total surveyability. For the colonial state did not merely aspire to create,

---

36. The discussion here draws on material analysed more fully in *Language and Power*, chapter 5.

under its control, a human landscape of perfect visibility; the condition of this 'visibility' was that everyone, everything, had (as it were) a serial number.[37] This style of imagining did not come out of thin air. It was the product of the technologies of navigation, astronomy, horology, surveying, photography and print, to say nothing of the deep driving power of capitalism.

Map and census thus shaped the grammar which would in due course make possible 'Burma' and 'Burmese,' 'Indonesia' and 'Indonesians.' But the concretization of these possibilities – concretizations which have a powerful life today, long after the colonial state has disappeared – owed much to the colonial state's peculiar imagining of history and power. Archaeology was an unimaginable enterprise in precolonial Southeast Asia; it was adopted in uncolonized Siam late in the game, and after the colonial state's manner. It created the series 'ancient monuments,' segmented within the classificatory, geographic-demographic box 'Netherlands Indies,' and 'British Burma.' Conceived within this profane series, each ruin became available for surveillance and infinite replication. As the colonial state's archaeological service made it technically possible to assemble the series in mapped and photographed form, the state itself could regard the series, up historical time, as an album of its ancestors. The key thing was never the specific Borobudur, nor the specific Pagan, in which the state had no substantial interest and with which it had only archaeological connections. The replicable *series*, however, created a historical depth of field which was easily inherited by the state's postcolonial successor. The final logical outcome was the logo – of 'Pagan' or 'The Philippines,' it made little difference – which by its emptiness, contextlessness, visual memorableness, and infinite reproducibility in every direction brought census and map, warp and woof, into an inerasable embrace.

---

37. An exemplary policy-outcome of Glass House imaginings – an outcome of which ex-political prisoner Pramoedya is painfully aware – is the classificatory ID card that all adult Indonesians must now carry at all times. This ID is isomorphic with the census – it represents a sort of political census, with special punchings for those in the sub-series 'subversives' and 'traitors.' It is notable that this style of census was only perfected after the achievement of national independence.

Memory and Forgetting

SPACE NEW AND OLD

New York, Nueva Leon, Nouvelle Orléans, Nova Lisboa, Nieuw Amsterdam. Already in the sixteenth century Europeans had begun the strange habit of naming remote places, first in the Americas and Africa, later in Asia, Australia, and Oceania, as 'new' versions of (thereby) 'old' toponyms in their lands of origin. Moreover, they retained the tradition even when such places passed to different imperial masters, so the Nouvelle Orléans calmly became New Orleans, and Nieuw Zeeland New Zealand.

It was not that, in general, the naming of political or religious sites as 'new' was in itself so new. In Southeast Asia, for example, one finds towns of reasonable antiquity whose names also include a term for novelty: Chiangmai (New City), Kota Bahru (New Town), Pekanbaru (New Market). But in these names 'new' invariably has the meaning of 'successor' to, or 'inheritor' of, something vanished. 'New' and 'old' are aligned diachronically, and the former appears always to invoke an ambiguous blessing from the dead. What is startling in the American namings of the sixteenth to eighteenth centuries is that 'new' and 'old' were understood synchronically, coexisting within homogeneous, empty time. Vizcaya is there *alongside* Nueva Vizcaya, New London *alongside* London: an idiom of sibling competition rather than of inheritance.

This new synchronic novelty could arise historically only when substantial groups of people were in a position to think of themselves as living lives *parallel* to those of other substantial groups of people – if never meeting, yet certainly proceeding along the same trajectory. Between 1500 and 1800 an accumulation of technological innovations in the fields of shipbuilding, navigation, horology and cartography, mediated through print-capitalism, was making this type of imagining possible.[1] It became conceivable to dwell on the Peruvian altiplano, on the pampas of Argentina, or by the harbours of 'New' England, and yet feel connected to certain regions or communities, thousands of miles away, in England or the Iberian peninsula. One could be fully aware of sharing a language and a religious faith (to varying degrees), customs and traditions, without any great expectation of ever meeting one's partners.[2]

For this sense of parallelism or simultaneity not merely to arise, but also to have vast political consequences, it was necessary that the distance between the parallel groups be large, and that the newer of them be substantial in size and permanently settled, as well as firmly subordinated to the older. These conditions were met in the Americas as they had never been before. In the first place, the vast expanse of the Atlantic Ocean and the utterly different geographical conditions existing on each side of it, made impossible the sort of gradual absorption of populations into larger politico-cultural units that transformed Las Españas into España and submerged Scotland into the United Kingdom. Secondly, as noted in Chapter 4, European migration to the Americas took place on an astonishing scale.

---

1. The accumulation reached a frantic zenith in the 'international' (i.e., European) search for an accurate measure of longitude, amusingly recounted in Landes, *Revolution in Time*, chapter 9. In 1776, as the Thirteen Colonies declared their independence, the *Gentleman's Magazine* included this brief obituary for John Harrison: 'He was a most ingenious mechanic, and received the 20,000 pounds reward [from Westminster] for the discovery of the longitude [sic].'

2. The late spreading of this consciousness to Asia is deftly alluded to in the opening pages of Pramoedya Ananta Toer's great historical novel *Bumi Manusia* [Earth of Mankind]. The young nationalist hero muses that he was born on the same date as the future Queen Wilhelmina – 31 August 1880. 'But while my island was wrapped in the darkness of night, her country was bathed in sun; and if her country was embraced by night's blackness, my island glittered in the equatorial noon.' p. 4.

By the end of the eighteenth century there were no less than 3,200,000 'whites' (including no more than 150,000 *peninsulares*) within the 16,900,000 population of the Western empire of the Spanish Bourbons.[3] The sheer size of this immigrant community, no less than its overwhelming military, economic and technological power vis-à-vis the indigenous populations, ensured that it maintained its own cultural coherence and local political ascendancy.[4] Thirdly, the imperial metropole disposed of formidable bureaucratic and ideological apparatuses, which permitted them for many centuries to impose their will on the creoles. (When one thinks of the sheer logistical problems involved, the ability of London and Madrid to carry on long counter-revolutionary wars against rebel American colonists is quite impressive.)

The novelty of all these conditions is suggested by the contrast they afford with the great (and roughly contemporaneous) Chinese and Arab migrations into Southeast Asia and East Africa. These migrations were rarely 'planned' by any metropole, and even more rarely produced stable relations of subordination. In the Chinese case, the only dim parallel is the extraordinary series of voyages far across the Indian ocean which were led, early in the fifteenth century, by the brilliant eunuch admiral Cheng-ho. These daring enterprises, carried out at the orders of the Yung-lo Emperor, were intended to enforce a court monopoly of external trade with

---

3. Needless to say, 'whiteness' was a legal category which had a distinctly tangential relationship to complex social realities. As the Liberator himself put it, '*We* are the vile offspring of the predatory Spaniards who came to America to bleed her white and to breed with their victims. Later the illegitimate offspring of these unions joined with the offspring of slaves transported from Africa.' Italics added. Lynch, *The Spanish-American Revolutions*, p. 249. One should beware of assuming anything 'eternally European' in this *criollismo*. Remembering all those devoutly Buddhist-Singhalese Da Souzas, those piously Catholic-Florinese Da Silvas, and those cynically Catholic-Manileño Sorianos who play unproblematic social, economic, and political roles in contemporary Ceylon, Indonesia, and the Philippines, helps one to recognize that, under the right circumstances, Europeans could be gently absorbed into non-European cultures.

4. Compare the fate of the huge African immigrant population. The brutal mechanisms of slavery ensured not merely its political-cultural fragmentation, but also very rapidly removed the possibility of imagining black communities in Venezuela and West Africa moving in parallel trajectory.

Southeast Asia and the regions further west, against the depredations of private Chinese merchants.[5] By mid-century the failure of the policy was clear; whereupon the Ming abandoned overseas adventures and did everything they could to prevent emigration from the Middle Kingdom. The fall of southern China to the Manchus in 1645 produced a substantial wave of refugees into Southeast Asia for whom any political ties with the new dynasty were unthinkable. Subsequent Ch'ing policy did not differ substantially from that of the later Ming. In 1712, for example, an edict of the K'ang-hsi Emperor prohibited all trade with Southeast Asia and declared that his government would 'request foreign governments to have those Chinese who have been abroad repatriated so that they may be executed.'[6] The last great wave of overseas migration took place in the nineteenth century as the dynasty disintegrated and a huge demand for unskilled Chinese labour opened up in colonial Southeast Asia and Siam. Since virtually all migrants were politically cut off from Peking, and were also illiterate people speaking mutually unintelligible languages, they were either more or less absorbed into local cultures or were decisively subordinated to the advancing Europeans.[7]

As for the Arabs, most of their migrations originated from the Hadramaut, never a real metropole in the era of the Ottoman and Mughal empires. Enterprising individuals might find ways to establish local principalities, such as the merchant who founded the kingdom of Pontianak in western Borneo in 1772; but he married locally, soon lost his 'Arabness' if not his Islam, and remained subordinated to the rising Dutch and English empires in Southeast Asia, not to any power in the Near East. In 1832 Sayyid Sa'id, lord of Muscat, established a powerful base on the East African coast and settled on the island of Zanzibar, which he made the centre of a flourishing clove-growing economy. But the British used military means to

---

5. See O.W. Wolters, *The Fall of Srivijaya in Malay History*, Appendix C.

6. Cited in G. William Skinner, *Chinese Society in Thailand*, pp. 15–16.

7. Overseas Chinese communities loomed large enough to stimulate deep European paranoia up to the mid eighteenth century, when vicious anti-Chinese pogroms by Westerners finally ceased. Thereafter, this unlovely tradition was passed on to indigenous populations.

compel him to sever his ties with Muscat.[8] Thus neither Arabs nor Chinese, though they ventured overseas in very large numbers during more or less the same centuries as the Western Europeans, successfully established coherent, wealthy, selfconsciously creole communities subordinated to a great metropolitan core. Hence, the world never saw the rise of New Basras or New Wuhans.

The doubleness of the Americas and the reasons for it, sketched out above, help to explain why nationalism emerged first in the New World, not the Old.[9] They also illuminate two peculiar features of the revolutionary wars that raged in the New World between 1776 and 1825. On the one hand, none of the creole revolutionaries dreamed of keeping the empire intact but rearranging its internal distribution of power, *reversing* the previous relationship of subjection by transferring the metropole from a European to an American site.[10] In other words, the aim was not to have New London succeed, overthrow, or destroy Old London, but rather to safeguard their continuing parallelism. (How new this style of thought was can be inferred from the history of earlier empires in decline, where there was often a dream of *replacing* the old centre.) On the other hand, although these wars caused a great deal of suffering and were marked by much barbarity, in an odd way the stakes were rather low. Neither in North nor in South America did the creoles have to fear physical extermination or reduction to servitude, as did so many other peoples who got in the way of the juggernaut of European imperialism. They were after all 'whites,' Christians, and Spanish- or English-speakers; they were also the intermediaries necessary to the metropoles if the economic wealth of the Western empires was to continue under Europe's control. Hence, they were the one significant extra-

---

8. See Marshall G. Hodgson, *The Venture of Islam*; Vol. 3, pp. 233–5.

9. It is an astonishing sign of the depth of Eurocentrism that so many European scholars persist, in the face of all the evidence, in regarding nationalism as a European invention.

10. But note the ironic case of Brazil. In 1808, King João VI fled to Rio de Janeiro to escape Napoléon's armies. Though Wellington had expelled the French by 1811, the emigrant monarch, fearing republican unrest at home, stayed on in South America until 1822, so that between 1808 and 1822 Rio was the centre of a world empire stretching to Angola, Mozambique, Macao, and East Timor. But this empire was ruled by a European, not an American.

European group, subjected to Europe, that at the same time had no need to be desperately afraid of Europe. The revolutionary wars, bitter as they were, were still reassuring in that they were wars between kinsmen.[11] This family link ensured that, after a certain period of acrimony had passed, close cultural, and sometimes political and economic, ties could be reknit between the former metropoles and the new nations.

TIME NEW AND OLD

If for the creoles of the New World the strange toponyms discussed above represented figuratively their emerging capacity to imagine themselves as communities *parallel and comparable to* those in Europe, extraordinary events in the last quarter of the eighteenth century gave this novelty, quite suddenly, a completely new meaning. The first of these events was certainly the Declaration of (the Thirteen Colonies') Independence in 1776, and the successful military defence of that declaration in the years following. This independence, and the fact that it was a *republican* independence, was felt to be something absolutely unprecedented, yet at the same time, once in existence, absolutely reasonable. Hence, when history made it possible, in 1811, for Venezuelan revolutionaries to draw up a constitution for the First Venezuelan Republic, they saw nothing slavish in borrowing verbatim from the Constitution of the United States of America.[12] For what the men in Philadelphia had written was in the Venezuelans' eyes not something North American, but rather something of universal truth and value. Shortly thereafter, in 1789, the explosion in the New World was *paralleled* in the Old by the volcanic outbreak of the French Revolution.[13]

---

11. Doubtless this was what permitted the Liberator to exclaim at one point that a Negro, i.e. slave, revolt would be 'a thousand times worse than a Spanish invasion.' (See above, p. 49). A slave jacquerie, if successful, might mean the physical extermination of the creoles.

12. See Masur, *Bolívar*, p. 131.

13. The French Revolution was in turn *paralleled* in the New World by the outbreak of Toussaint L'Ouverture's insurrection in 1791, which by 1806 had resulted

It is difficult today to recreate in the imagination a condition of life in which the nation was felt to be something utterly new. But so it was in that epoch. The Declaration of Independence of 1776 makes absolutely no reference to Christopher Columbus, Roanoke, or the Pilgrim Fathers, nor are the grounds put forward to justify independence in any way 'historical,' in the sense of highlighting the antiquity of the American people. Indeed, marvellously, the American nation is not even mentioned. A profound feeling that a radical break with the past was occurring – a 'blasting open of the continuum of history'? – spread rapidly. Nothing exemplifies this intuition better than the decision, taken by the Convention *Nationale* on 5 October 1793, to scrap the centuries-old Christian calendar and to inaugurate a new world-era with the Year One, starting from the abolition of the *ancien régime* and the proclamation of the Republic on 22 September 1792.[14] (No subsequent revolution has had quite this sublime confidence of novelty, not least because the French Revolution has always been seen as an ancestor.)

Out of this profound sense of newness came also *nuestra santa revolución*, the beautiful neologism created by José María Morelos y Pavón (proclaimer in 1813 of the Republic of Mexico), not long before his execution by the Spaniards.[15] Out of it too came San Martín's 1821 decree that '*in the future* the aborigines shall not be called Indians or natives; they are children and citizens of Peru and they shall be known as Peruvians.'[16] This sentence does for 'Indians' and/or 'natives' what the Convention in Paris had done for the Christian calendar – it abolished the old time-dishonoured naming and inaugurated a completely new epoch. 'Peruvians' and 'Year One' thus mark rhetorically a profound rupture with the existing world.

---

in Haiti's former slaves creating the second independent republic of the Western hemisphere.

14. The young Wordsworth was in France in 1791–1792, and later, in *The Prelude*, wrote these famous reminiscent lines:

> Bliss was it in that *dawn* to be alive,
> But to be young was very heaven!

Italics added.

15. Lynch, *The Spanish-American Revolutions*, pp. 314–15.

16. As cited above in chapter 4.

Yet things could not long remain this way – for precisely the same reasons that had precipitated the sense of rupture in the first place. In the last quarter of the eighteenth century, Britain alone was manufacturing between 150,000 and 200,000 watches a year, many of them for export. Total European manufacture is likely to have then been close to 500,000 items annually.[17] Serially published newspapers were by then a familiar part of urban civilization. So was the novel, with its spectacular possibilities for the representation of simultaneous actions in homogeneous empty time.[18] The cosmic clocking which had made intelligible our synchronic transoceanic pairings was increasingly felt to entail a wholly intramundane, *serial* view of social causality; and this sense of the world was now speedily deepening its grip on Western imaginations. It is thus understandable that less than two decades after the Proclamation of Year One came the establishment of the first academic chairs in History – in 1810 at the University of Berlin, and in 1812 at Napoléon's Sorbonne. By the second quarter of the nineteenth century History had become formally constituted as a 'discipline,' with its own elaborate array of professional journals.[19] Very quickly the Year One made way for 1792 A.D., and the revolutionary ruptures of 1776 and 1789 came to be figured as embedded in the historical series and *thus as historical precedents and models.*[20]

Hence, for the members of what we might call 'second-generation' nationalist movements, those which developed in Europe

17. Landes, *Revolution in Time*, pp. 230–31, 442–43.

18. See above, Chapter 2.

19. See Hayden White, *Metahistory: The Historical Imagination in Nineteenth-Century Europe*, pp. 135–43, for a sophisticated discussion of this transformation.

20. But it was an A.D. with a difference. Before the rupture it still retained, however fragilely in enlightened quarters, a theological aura glowing from within its medieval Latin. Anno Domini recalled that irruption of eternity into mundane time which took place in Bethlehem. After the rupture, reduced monogrammatically to A.D., it joined an (English) vernacular B.C., Before Christ, that encompassed a serial cosmological history (to which the new science of geology was making signal contributions). We may judge how deep an abyss yawned between Anno Domini and A.D./B.C. by noting that neither the Buddhist nor the Islamic world, even today, imagines any epoch marked as 'Before the Gautama Buddha' or 'Before the Hegira.' Both make uneasy do with the alien monogram B.C.

between about 1815 to 1850, and also for the generation that inherited the independent national states of the Americas, it was no longer possible to 'recapture/The first fine careless rapture' of their revolutionary predecessors. For different reasons and with different consequences, the two groups thus began the process of reading nationalism *genealogically* – as the expression of an historical tradition of serial continuity.

In Europe, the new nationalisms almost immediately began to imagine themselves as 'awakening from sleep,' a trope wholly foreign to the Americas. Already in 1803 (as we have seen in Chapter 5) the young Greek nationalist Adamantios Koraes was telling a sympathetic Parisian audience: '*For the first time* the [Greek] nation surveys the hideous spectacle of its ignorance and *trembles* in measuring with the eye the distance separating it from its ancestors' glory.' Here is perfectly exemplified the transition from New Time to Old. 'For the first time' still echoes the ruptures of 1776 and 1789, but Koraes's sweet eyes are turned, not ahead to San Martín's future, but back, in trembling, to ancestral glories. It would not take long for this exhilarating doubleness to fade, replaced by a modular, 'continuous' awakening from a chronologically gauged, A.D.-style slumber: a guaranteed return to an aboriginal essence.

Undoubtedly, many different elements contributed to the astonishing popularity of this trope.[21] For present purposes, I would mention only two. In the first place, the trope took into account the sense of parallelism out of which the American nationalisms had been born and which the success of the American nationalist revolutions had greatly reinforced in Europe. It seemed to explain why nationalist movements had bizarrely cropped up in the civilized Old World so obviously *later than in the barbarous New*.[22] Read as late awakening, even if an awakening stimulated from afar, it opened up an immense antiquity

---

21. As late as 1951, the intelligent Indonesian socialist Lintong Mulia Sitorus could still write that: 'Till the end of the nineteenth century, the coloured peoples still slept soundly, while the whites were busily at work in every field.' *Sedjarah Pergerakan Kebangsaan Indonesia* [History of the Indonesian Nationalist Movement], p. 5.

22. One could perhaps say that these revolutions were, in European eyes, the first really important *political* events that had ever occurred across the Atlantic.

behind the epochal sleep. In the second place, the trope provided a crucial metaphorical link between the new European nationalisms and language. As observed earlier, the major states of nineteenth-century Europe were vast polyglot polities, of which the boundaries almost never coincided with language-communities. Most of their literate members had inherited from mediaeval times the habit of thinking of certain languages – if no longer Latin, then French, English, Spanish or German – as languages of civilization. Rich eighteenth-century Dutch burghers were proud to speak only French at home; German was the language of cultivation in much of the western Czarist empire, no less than in 'Czech' Bohemia. Until late in the eighteenth century no one thought of these languages as belonging to any territorially defined group. But soon thereafter, for reasons sketched out in Chapter 3, 'uncivilized' vernaculars began to function politically in the same way as the Atlantic Ocean had earlier done: i.e. to 'separate' subjected national communities off from ancient dynastic realms. And since in the vanguard of most European popular nationalist movements were literate people often *unaccustomed* to using these vernaculars, this anomaly needed explanation. None seemed better than 'sleep,' for it permitted those intelligentsias and bourgeoisies who were becoming conscious of themselves as Czechs, Hungarians, or Finns to figure their study of Czech, Magyar, or Finnish languages, folklores, and musics as 'rediscovering' something deep-down always known. (Furthermore, once one starts thinking about nationality in terms of continuity, few things seem as historically deep-rooted as languages, for which no dated origins can ever be given.)[23]

In the Americas the problem was differently posed. On the one hand, national independence had almost everywhere been internationally acknowledged by the 1830s. It had thus become an inheritance, and, *as an inheritance*, it was compelled to enter a genealogical series. Yet the developing European instrumentalities were not readily available. Language had never been an issue in the

---

23. Still, historical depth is not infinite. At some point English vanishes into Norman French and Anglo-Saxon; French into Latin and 'German' Frankish; and so on. We shall see below how additional depth of field came to be achieved.

American nationalist movements. As we have seen, it was precisely the sharing with the metropole of a common language (and common religion and common culture) that had made the first national imaginings possible. To be sure, there are some interesting cases where one detects a sort of 'European' thinking early at work. For example, Noah Webster's 1828 (i.e., 'second-generation') *American Dictionary of the English Language* was intended to give an official imprimatur to an American language whose lineage was distinct from that of English. In Paraguay, the eighteenth-century Jesuit tradition of using Guaraní made it possible for a radically non-Spanish 'native' language to become a *national* language, under the long, xenophobic dictatorship of José Gaspar Rodríguez de Francia (1814–1840). But, on the whole, any attempt to give historical depth to nationality via linguistic means faced insuperable obstacles. Virtually all the creoles were institutionally committed (via schools, print media, administrative habits, and so on) to European rather than indigenous American tongues. Any excessive emphasis on linguistic lineages threatened to blur precisely that 'memory of independence' which it was essential to retain.

The solution, eventually applicable in both New and Old Worlds, was found in History, or rather History emplotted in particular ways. We have observed the speed with which Chairs in History succeeded the Year One. As Hayden White remarks, it is no less striking that the five presiding geniuses of European historiography were all born within the quarter century following the Convention's rupturing of time: Ranke in 1795, Michelet in 1798, Tocqueville in 1805, and Marx and Burckhardt in 1818.[24] Of the five, it is perhaps natural that Michelet, self-appointed historian of the Revolution, most clearly exemplifies the national imagining being born, for he was the first selfconsciously to write *on behalf* of the dead.[25] The following passage is characteristic:

---

24. *Metahistory*, p. 140. Hegel, born in 1770, was already in his late teens when the Revolution broke out, but his *Vorlesungen über die Philosophie der Weltgeschichte* were only published in 1837, six years after his death.

25. White, *Metahistory*, p. 159.

Oui, chaque mort laisse un petit bien, sa mémoire, et demande qu'on la soigne. Pour celui qui n'a pas d'amis, il faut que le magistrat y supplée. Car la loi, la justice, est plus sûre que toutes nos tendresses oublieuses, nos larmes si vite séchées. Cette magistrature, c'est l'Histoire. Et les morts sont, pour dire comme le Droit romain, ces *miserabiles personae* dont le magistrat doit se préoccuper. Jamais dans ma carrière je n'ai pas perdu de vue ce devoir de l'historien. J'ai donné à beaucoup de morts trop oubliés l'assistance dont moi-même j'aurai besoin. Je les ai exhumés pour une seconde vie . . . Ils vivent maintenant avec nous qui nous sentons leurs parents, leurs amis. Ainsi se fait une famille, une cité commune entre les vivants et les morts.[26]

Here and elsewhere Michelet made it clear that those whom he was exhuming were by no means a random assemblage of forgotten, anonymous dead. They were those whose sacrifices, throughout History, made possible the rupture of 1789 and the selfconscious appearance of the French nation, *even when these sacrifices were not understood as such by the victims*. In 1842, he noted of these dead: 'Il leur faut un Oedipe qui leur explique leur propre énigme dont ils n'ont pas eu le sens, qui leur apprenne ce que voulaient dire leurs paroles, leurs actes, qu'ils n'ont pas compris.'[27]

This formulation is probably unprecedented. Michelet not only claimed to speak on behalf of large numbers of anonymous dead people, but insisted, with poignant authority, that he could say what they 'really' meant and 'really' wanted, since they themselves 'did not understand.' From then on, the silence of the dead was no obstacle to the exhumation of their deepest desires.

In this vein, more and more 'second-generation' nationalists, in the Americas and elsewhere, learned to speak 'for' dead people with whom it was impossible or undesirable to establish a linguistic connection. This reversed ventriloquism helped to open the way for a selfconscious *indigenismo*, especially in the southern Americas. At

26. Jules Michelet, *Oeuvres Complètes*, XXI, p. 268, in the preface to volume 2 ('Jusqu'au 18e Brumaire') of his uncompleted *Histoire du XIXe Siècle*. I owe the reference to *Metahistory*, but the translation White uses is unsatisfactory.
27. Cited in Roland Barthes, ed., *Michelet par lui-même*, p. 92. The volume of the *Oeuvres Complètes* containing this quotation has not yet been published.

the edge: Mexicans speaking in Spanish 'for' pre-Columbian 'Indian' civilizations whose languages they do not understand.[28] How revolutionary this kind of exhumation was appears most clearly if we contrast it with the formulation of Fermín de Vargas, cited in chapter 2. For where Fermín still thought cheerfully of 'extinguishing' living Indians, many of his political grandchildren became obsessed with 'remembering,' indeed 'speaking for' them, perhaps precisely because they had, by then, so often been *extinguished*.

THE REASSURANCE OF FRATRICIDE

It is striking that in Michelet's 'second generation' formulations the focus of attention is always the exhumation of people and events which stand in danger of oblivion.[29] He sees no need to think about 'forgetting.' But when, in 1882 – more than a century after the Declaration of Independence in Philadelphia, and eight years after the death of Michelet himself – Renan published his *Qu'est-ce qu'une nation?*, it was precisely the need for forgetting that preoccupied him. Reconsider, for example, the formulation cited earlier in chapter 1:[30]

> Or, l'essence d'une nation est que tous les individus aient beaucoup de choses en commun et aussi que tous aient oublié bien des choses.
> . . . Tout citoyen français *doit avoir oublié* la Saint-Barthélemy, les massacres du Midi au XIIIe siècle.

---

28. Conversely, in all Mexico there is only one statue of Hernán Cortés. This monument, tucked discreetly away in a niche of Mexico City, was only put up at the end of the 1970s, by the odious regime of José López Portillo.

29. Doubtless because for much of his life he suffered under restored or ersatz legitimacies. His commitment to 1789 and to France is movingly shown by his refusal to swear an oath of loyalty to Louis Napoléon. Abruptly dismissed from his post as National Archivist, he lived in near-poverty till his death in 1874 – long enough, however, to witness the mountebank's fall and the restoration of republican institutions.

30. Renan was born in 1823, a quarter of a century after Michelet, and passed much of his youth under the cynically official-nationalist regime of Michelet's persecutor.

At first sight these two sentences may seem straightforward.[31] Yet a few moments reflection reveals how bizarre they actually are. One notices, for example, that Renan saw no reason to explain for his readers what either 'la Saint-Barthélemy' or 'les massacres du Midi au XIIIe siècle' meant. Yet who but 'Frenchmen,' as it were, would have at once understood that 'la Saint-Barthélemy' referred to the ferocious anti-Huguenot pogrom launched on 24 August 1572 by the Valois dynast Charles IX and his Florentine mother; or that 'les massacres du Midi' alluded to the extermination of the Albigensians across the broad zone between the Pyrenees and the Southern Alps, instigated by Innocent III, one of the guiltier in a long line of guilty popes? Nor did Renan find anything queer about assuming 'memories' in his readers' minds even though the events themselves occurred 300 and 600 years previously. One is also struck by the peremptory syntax of *doit avoir oublié* (not *doit oublier*) – 'obliged already to have forgotten' – which suggests, in the ominous tone of revenue-codes and military conscription laws, that 'already having forgotten' ancient tragedies is a prime contemporary civic duty. In effect, Renan's readers were being told to 'have already forgotten' what Renan's own words assumed that they naturally remembered!

How are we to make sense of this paradox? We may start by observing that the singular *French* noun 'la Saint-Barthélemy' occludes killers and killed – i.e., those Catholics and Protestants who played one local part in the vast unholy Holy War that raged across central and northern Europe in the sixteenth century, and who certainly did not think of themselves cosily together as 'Frenchmen.' Similarly, 'thirteenth-century massacres of the Midi' blurs unnamed victims and assassins behind the pure Frenchness of 'Midi.' No need to remind his readers that most of the murdered Albigensians spoke Provençal or Catalan, and that their murderers came from many parts of Western Europe. The effect of this tropology is to figure episodes in the colossal religious conflicts of mediaeval and early modern Europe as reassuringly fratricidal wars between – who else? – *fellow Frenchmen.* Since we can be confident that, left to themselves, the overwhelming majority of Renan's French contemporaries would never have heard

---

31. I understood them so in 1983, alas.

of 'la Saint-Barthélemy' or 'les massacres du Midi,' we become aware of a systematic historiographical campaign, deployed by the state mainly through the state's school system, to 'remind' every young Frenchwoman and Frenchman of a series of antique slaughters which are now inscribed as 'family history.' Having to 'have already forgotten' tragedies of which one needs unceasingly to be 'reminded' turns out to be a characteristic device in the later construction of national genealogies. (It is instructive that Renan does *not* say that each French citizen is obliged to 'have already forgotten' the Paris Commune. In 1882 its memory was still real rather than mythic, and sufficiently painful to make it difficult to read under the sign of 'reassuring fratricide.')

Needless to say, in all this there was, and is, nothing especially French. A vast pedagogical industry works ceaselessly to oblige young Americans to remember/forget the hostilities of 1861–65 as a great 'civil' war between 'brothers' rather than between – as they briefly were – two sovereign nation-states. (We can be sure, however, that if the Confederacy had succeeded in maintaining its independence, this 'civil war' would have been replaced in memory by something quite unbrotherly.) English history textbooks offer the diverting spectacle of a great Founding Father whom every schoolchild is taught to call William the Conqueror. The same child is not informed that William spoke no English, indeed could not have done so, since the English language did not exist in his epoch; nor is he or she told 'Conqueror of what?'. For the only intelligible modern answer would have to be 'Conqueror of the English,' which would turn the old Norman predator into a more successful precursor of Napoléon and Hitler. Hence 'the Conqueror' operates as the same kind of ellipsis as 'la Saint-Barthélemy,' to remind one of something which it is imme- diately obligatory to forget. Norman William and Saxon Harold thus meet on the battlefield of Hastings, if not as dancing partners, at least as brothers.

But it is surely too easy to attribute these reassuring ancient fratricides simply to the icy calculations of state functionaries. At another level they reflect a deep reshaping of the imagination of which the state was barely conscious, and over which it had, and still has, only exiguous control. In the 1930s people of many nationalities went to fight in the Iberian peninsula because they viewed it as the arena in which global historical forces and causes were at stake. When the long-lived Franco regime constructed the Valley of the Fallen, it restricted membership in the gloomy necropolis to those who, in its eyes, had died in the world-struggle against Bolshevism and atheism. But, at the state's margins, a 'memory' was already emerging of a 'Spanish' Civil War. Only after the crafty tyrant's death, and the subsequent, startlingly smooth transition to bourgeois democracy – in which it played a crucial role – did this 'memory' become official. In much the same way, the colossal class war that, from 1918 to 1920, raged between the Pamirs and the Vistula came to be remembered/ forgotten in Soviet film and fiction as 'our' civil war, while the Soviet state, on the whole, held to an orthodox Marxist reading of the struggle.

In this regard the creole nationalisms of the Americas are especially instructive. For on the one hand, the American states were for many decades weak, effectively decentralized, and rather modest in their educational ambitions. On the other hand, the American societies, in which 'white' settlers were counterposed to 'black' slaves and half-exterminated 'natives,' were internally riven to a degree quite un-matched in Europe. Yet the imagining of that fraternity, without which the reassurance of fratricide can not be born, shows up remarkably early, and not without a curious authentic popularity. In the United States of America this paradox is particularly well exemplified.

In 1840, in the midst of a brutal eight-year war against the Seminoles of Florida (and as Michelet was summoning his Oedipus), James Fenimore Cooper published *The Pathfinder*, the fourth of his five, hugely popular, Leatherstocking Tales. Central to this novel (and to all but the first of its companions) is what Leslie Fiedler called the 'austere, almost inarticulate, but unquestioned love' binding the 'white' woodsman Natty Bumppo and the noble Delaware chieftain Chingachgook ('Chicago'!).[32] Yet the Renanesque setting for their

---

32. See his *Love and Death in the American Novel*, p. 192. Fiedler read this relationship psychologically, and ahistorically, as an instance of American fiction's failure to deal with adult heterosexual love and its obsession with death, incest, and innocent homoeroticism. Rather than a national eroticism, it is, I suspect, an

bloodbrotherhood is not the murderous 1830s but the last forgotten/ remembered years of British imperial rule. Both men are figured as 'Americans,' fighting for survival – against the French, their 'native' allies (the 'devilish Mingos'), and treacherous agents of George III.

When, in 1851, Herman Melville depicted Ishmael and Queequeg cosily in bed together at the Spouter Inn ('there, then, in our hearts' honeymoon, lay I and Queequeg'), the noble Polynesian savage was sardonically Americanized as follows:[33]

. . . . certain it was that his head was phrenologically an excellent one. It may seem ridiculous, but it reminded me of George Washington's head, as seen in popular busts of him. It had the same long regularly graded retreating slope above the brows, which were likewise very projecting, like two long promontories thickly wooded on top. Queequeg was George Washington cannibalistically developed.

It remained for Mark Twain to create in 1881, well after the 'Civil War' and Lincoln's Emancipation Proclamation, the first indelible image of black and white as American 'brothers': Jim and Huck companionably adrift on the wide Mississippi.[34] But the setting is a remembered/ forgotten antebellum in which the black is still a slave.

These striking nineteenth-century imaginings of fraternity, emerging 'naturally' in a society fractured by the most violent racial, class and regional antagonisms, show as clearly as anything else that nationalism in the age of Michelet and Renan represented a new form of consciousness – a consciousness that arose when it was no longer possible to experience the nation as new, at the wave-top moment of rupture.

---

eroticized nationalism that is at work. Male-male bondings in a Protestant society which from the start rigidly prohibited miscegenation are paralleled by male-female 'holy loves' in the nationalist fiction of Latin America, where Catholicism permitted the growth of a large mestizo population. (It is telling that English has had to borrow 'mestizo' from Spanish.)

33. Herman Melville, *Moby Dick*, p. 71. How the author must have savoured the malignant final phrase!

34. It is agreeable to note that the publication of *Huckleberry Finn* preceded by only a few months Renan's evocation of 'la Saint-Barthélemy.'

THE BIOGRAPHY OF NATIONS

All profound changes in consciousness, by their very nature, bring with them characteristic amnesias. Out of such oblivions, in specific historical circumstances, spring narratives. After experiencing the physiological and emotional changes produced by puberty, it is impossible to 'remember' the consciousness of childhood. How many thousands of days passed between infancy and early adulthood vanish beyond direct recall! How strange it is to need another's help to learn that this naked baby in the yellowed photograph, sprawled happily on rug or cot, is you. The photograph, fine child of the age of mechanical reproduction, is only the most peremptory of a huge modern accumulation of documentary evidence (birth certificates, diaries, report cards, letters, medical records, and the like) which simultaneously records a certain apparent continuity and emphasizes its loss from memory. Out of this estrangement comes a conception of personhood, *identity* (yes, you and that naked baby are identical) which, because it can not be 'remembered,' must be narrated. Against biology's demonstration that every single cell in a human body is replaced over seven years, the narratives of autobiography and biography flood print-capitalism's markets year by year.

These narratives, like the novels and newspapers discussed in Chapter 2, are set in homogeneous, empty time. Hence their frame is historical and their setting sociological. This is why so many autobiographies begin with the circumstances of parents and grandparents, for which the autobiographer can have only circumstantial, textual evidence; and why the biographer is at pains to record the calendrical, A.D. dates of two biographical events which his or her subject can never remember: birth-day and death-day. Nothing affords a sharper reminder of this narrative's modernity than the opening of the Gospel according to St. Matthew. For the Evangelist gives us an austere list of thirty males successively begetting one another, from the Patriarch Abraham down to Jesus Christ. (Only once is a woman mentioned, not because she is a begetter, but because she is a non-Jewish Moabite). No dates are given for any of Jesus's forebears, let alone sociological, cultural, physiological or political information about them. This narrative style (which also reflects the rupture-in-Bethlehem become memory) was entirely reasonable to the sainted genealogist because he did not conceive of Christ as an historical 'personality,' but only as the true Son of God.

As with modern persons, so it is with nations. Awareness of being embedded in secular, serial time, with all its implications of continuity, yet of 'forgetting' the experience of this continuity – product of the ruptures of the late eighteenth century – engenders the need for a narrative of 'identity.' The task is set for Michelet's magistrate. Yet between narratives of person and nation there is a central difference of emplotment. In the secular story of the 'person' there is a beginning and an end. She emerges from parental genes and social circumstances onto a brief historical stage, there to play a role until her death. After that, nothing but the penumbra of lingering fame or influence. (Imagine how strange it would be, today, to end a life of Hitler by observing that on 30 April 1945 he proceeded straight to Hell). Nations, however, have no clearly identifiable births, and their deaths, if they ever happen, are never natural.[35] Because there is no Originator, the nation's biography can not be written evangelically, 'down time,' through a long pro-creative chain of begettings. The only alternative is to fashion it 'up time' – towards Peking Man, Java Man, King Arthur, wherever the lamp of archaeology casts its fitful gleam. This fashioning, however, is marked by deaths, which, in a curious inversion of conventional genealogy, start from an originary present. World War II begets World War I; out of Sedan comes Austerlitz; the ancestor of the Warsaw Uprising is the state of Israel.

Yet the deaths that structure the nation's biography are of a special kind. In all the 1,200 pages of his awesome *La Méditerranée et le Monde Méditerranéen à l'Époque de Philippe II* Fernand Braudel mentions Renan's 'la Saint-Barthélemy' only in passing, though it occurred exactly *nel mezzo del camino* of the Habsburg dynast's reign. 'Les événements,' writes the Master (vol. 2, p. 223) 'sont poussière; ils traversent l'histoire comme des lueurs brèves; à peine naissent-ils qu'ils retournent déjà à la nuit et souvent à l'oubli.' For Braudel, the deaths that matter are those myriad anonymous events, which,

---

35. For such apocalypses the neologism 'genocide' was quite recently coined.

aggregated and averaged into secular mortality rates, permit him to chart the slow-changing conditions of life for millions of anonymous human beings of whom the last question asked is their nationality.

From Braudel's remorselessly accumulating cemeteries, however, the nation's biography snatches, against the going mortality rate, exemplary suicides, poignant martyrdoms, assassinations, executions, wars, and holocausts. But, to serve the narrative purpose, these violent deaths must be remembered/forgotten as 'our own.'

Travel and Traffic: On the Geo-biography of *Imagined Communities**

Now that almost a quarter of a century has passed since the first publication of *Imagined Communities*, it seems possible to sketch out its subsequent travel-history in the light of some of the book's own central themes: print-capitalism, piracy in the positive, metaphorical sense, vernacularization, and nationalism's undivorcible marriage to internationalism.

More generally, studies on the transnational diffusion of books are still fairly rare, except in the field of literary history where Franco Moretti has set an extraordinary example. The material for some preliminary comparative reflections is to hand. By the end of 2007, the book (henceforward to be referred to as *IC*) will have been published in thirty-three countries and in twenty-nine languages.[1] This spread has much less to do with its qualities than with its original publication in London, in the English language, which now serves as a kind of global-hegemonic, post-clerical Latin. (Had *IC* originally appeared in Tirana, in Albanian, or in Ho Chi Minh City, in Vietnamese, or even in Melbourne, in Australian, it is unlikely to have travelled very far). On

* Writing this Afterword would not have been possible without the selfless help of, above all, my brother Perry, but in addition, Choi Sung-eun, Yana Genova, Pothiti Hantzaroula, Joel Kuortti, Antonis Liakos, Silva Meznaric, Göran Therborn, and Tony Wood, to all of whom I would like to express my deepest thanks.

1. Aside from the advantages of brevity, *IC* restfully occludes a pair of words from which the vampires of banality have by now sucked almost all the blood.

the other hand, this proliferation of translations suggests that the force of vernacularization, which, in alliance with print-capitalism, eventually destroyed the hegemony of Church Latin and was midwife to the birth of nationalism, remains strong half a millennium later.

What I propose to do is to recount what I have been able to discover, thanks to the generous help of many colleagues, comrades, and friends, about these translations: what publishers were involved, with what motivations and strategies, and in what political contexts, both domestic and international. At the end I will try to draw a few tentative conclusions.

But it is necessary to start by saying something about my own original, assuredly polemical, intentions, since these have affected, often in unanticipated ways, the reception of the book and its translations. First of all, for reasons too complicated to get into here, the UK was the one country in the world, during the 1960s and 1970s, where high-level work was undertaken, in separate channels, on the nature and origins of nationalism in a general sense, by four influential Jewish intellectuals – the conservative historian Elie Kedourie, the Enlightenment-liberal philosopher and sociologist Ernest Gellner, the then Marxist historian Eric Hobsbawm, and the traditionalist historian Anthony Smith. But there was no real public debate until 1977, when the Scottish nationalist-cum-Marxist Tom Nairn published his iconoclastic *The Breakup of Britain*.[2] The Scottish nationalist described the United Kingdom – to which Gellner, Hobsbawm, and Smith were strongly attached – as the decrepit relic of a pre-national, pre-republican age and thus doomed to share the fate of Austro-Hungary. The revisionist Marxist turned his guns on what he saw as classical Marxism's shallow or evasive treatment of the historical–political importance of nationalism in the widest sense. In the debate that followed my sympathies were very much with Nairn.

Hence one important polemical intent behind *IC* was to support

2. Kedourie came from Baghdad, Gellner from Prague, while Hobsbawm's mother came from Vienna. Perhaps because of his origins, Kedourie was interested in the Near East, and beyond. His book on nationalism in Asia and Africa came out in 1970. Gellner's first essay on questions of nationalism was partly a rejoinder to Kedourie. Hobsbawm's big book on nationalism did not come out until 1990, but he had attacked Nairn's theses in *New Left Review* in the autumn of 1977, and played a major role in making the magisterial comparative work of Miroslav Hroch on Central and East European nationalist movements known in the Anglo-Saxon world.

('critically,' of course) Nairn's position on both accounts. The traces are obvious enough in the quite disproportionate amount of space devoted to the UK, the British Empire, and even Scotland (perhaps because I had been living and working in the US since 1958): in a plethora of quotations from and allusions to 'English' literature likely to be opaque to many readers not educated in the UK; provincial provocations in a republican spirit (all UK rulers named as if they were next-door neighbours [Anne Stuart], while foreign rulers were titled in the traditional manner [Louis XIV]); and some regrettably disobliging references to Nairn's debate-opponent Eric Hobsbawm.

A second polemical intent was to widen the scope of Nairn's theoretical criticisms, which were aimed almost exclusively at classical Marxism. It seemed to me that Marxism's 'failure' to grapple with nationalism in any deep way was in no way idiosyncratic. Exactly the same criticism could, and should, be levelled at classical liberalism and, at the margins, classical conservatism. (This is why *IC* joked about the implausibility of a Tomb of the Unknown Marxist and of a cenotaph for fallen Liberals). There had to be a common cause of this general inadequacy, but Marxism (with a difference) seemed likely to be a better place to look for it than Liberalism. But framed this way, *IC* could interest critical Marxists as well as critical liberals, by suggesting to both that a great deal of really new thinking and research was needed. So I was not at all downhearted when a generally favourable reviewer still rather irritably described the book as being too Marxist for a liberal, and too liberal for a Marxist.

A third polemical intent was to de-Europeanize the theoretical study of nationalism. This impulse had nothing to do with Nairn, but derived from long immersion in the societies, cultures, and languages of the then utterly remote Indonesia and Thailand/Siam. Despite the wonderfully broad stretch of the polyglot work of Gellner, Hobsbawm, and Smith, from the standpoint of Jakarta and Bangkok, they seemed irremediably Euro-centric. Gellner had indeed done research in the Maghreb, but Edward Said was probably right in attacking him for ignorance of Arabic – though the general acrimony of their exchange was far from elevating.[3] The problem was how to sail between the Scylla of nineteenth-century

---

3. Kedourie surely was familiar with Arabic, but his work does not show it very prominently. His 1970 book is mainly an anthology of texts by nationalist intellectuals in Asia and Africa, with an extensive, acerbic introduction of his own.

European-derived romantic fantasies about umpteen thousand years of Chinese, Japanese, Vietnamese, etc. nationhood, and the Charybdis of Partha Chatterjee's splendidly indignant later indictment of all anticolonial nationalisms outside Europe as 'derivative discourses.' Facing this quandary, the multiple national states created in South and Central America over the period 1810–1838 came to my rescue (even if, in 1983, I could read neither Spanish nor Portuguese). The multiplicity was as crucial as the world-historical early dates. The US and Haitian 'revolutions' preceded the nationalist movements in Spanish America, and national Brazil emerged much later, but each of these had the apparent advantage of idiosyncrasy. (A few days ago, my local newspaper in Bangkok sarcastically referred to the USA as the Land of the Free[ly Self-Centred]). But Spanish America was eminently comparable and, just as important, fought over many bloody years for multiple republican independences, while sharing language and religion with imperial Spain – long before Magyars, Czechs, Norwegians, Scots, and Italians got into the act.

Spanish America offered perfect arguments against both national incomparability and Eurocentrism. It allowed me to think about the early USA, in the Pan-American context, as just another creole-led revolutionary state, and furthermore in some respects more reactionary than its Southern sisters. (Unlike Washington, the Liberator put a step-by-step end to slavery, and unlike Jefferson, San Martín did not speak of the original inhabitants of his country as savages, but invited them to become Peruvians). My impression is that this de-Europeanization did not in fact leave much impression in Europe itself, but may have made *IC* more attractive to readers in the Global South.

A final polemical target was the United States. It was not simply a matter of hostility to bloody American imperialist interventions in Latin America, Asia and Africa. Nor was it primarily a reaction to the weird fact that when *Imagined Communities* was about to be published there were virtually no courses taught on nationalism in American universities – let alone on American nationalism, which was taken as a late nineteenth-century 'Manifest Destiny' aberration. Rather it was the remarkable solipsism, still highly visible today even in the liberal *New York Times*, and the 'big country' bias plain to readers of the *New York Review of Books*. (Later on, I found the same provincialism in the other 'big countries' – India, China, Russia, Indonesia, and Brazil). Karl Deutsch's cynical aphorism 'Power is not having to listen,' rang in my ears. Hence *IC*'s polemical strategy of foregrounding 'small countries' – Hungary, Thailand, Switzerland, Vietnam, Scotland, and the Philippines.

For the reasons indicated above, as well as others, the original version, published simultaneously in London and New York, had completely different receptions in the two countries. In those distant days, the UK still had a 'quality press,' and *IC* was almost immediately reviewed by Edmund Leach, Conor Cruise O'Brien, Neal Ascherson, and the Jamaican Marxist Winston James. In the US, which has never had a 'quality press,' it was scarcely noticed. The academic journals were no different. It was only in the early 1990s, after the collapse of the Soviet Union, the violent breakup of Yugoslavia, and the rapid rise of identity politics on the domestic front, that this situation changed.

The first foreign version of *IC* appeared in Tokyo, in 1987, as *Sozo no kyodotai*. The translation was the work of two gifted former students of mine, Takashi and Saya Shirashi, who believed it could help in the enduring paedagogical struggle against Japanese insularity, and the conservative doxa that the country's history and culture made comparisons with other countries impossible or irrelevant. The translation was itself novel, in that it kept to the polemical thrust of the London version rather than to its letter. Many of the original's references to, or quotations from, English literature, were ingeniously replaced by Japanese 'counterparts.' For example, the lengthy quotation from *Urne-Buriall* gave way to one from *The Tale of Heike*. As for the Tokyo publisher, Libroport, which was a bit left of centre, Takashi recently wrote to me: 'The company's owner, Tsutsumi, was the son of a tycoon, who rebelled against his father, and chose a career as a poet and writer, only to find himself inheriting part of his father's business when the father died. So he told his editors to publish good books without worrying about profit . . . This is why the firm went bankrupt in the 1990s.' But it survived long enough to see *Imagined Communities* become a standard textbook for advanced courses on nationalism in most of Japan's better universities.

During the four years remaining before a revised and substantially enlarged edition of *IC* was issued by Verso, translations appeared in German, Portuguese, and Serbo-Croat. The excellent German version (*Die Erfindung der Nation*) was published in 1988 in Frankfurt, with a striking cover featuring the Black Forest's colossal, kitschy Hermannsdenkmal, a nineteenth-century monument celebrating Arminius, 'Germanic' military tormentor of Roman emperors Augustus and Tiberius. The independent publisher, Campus Verlag, founded in 1975, had quickly developed a fine reputation for its serious books on history and politics. It is likely that one reason that a German translation appeared so early is that the 'quality' *Frankfurter Zeitung* kept a close watch on the book reviews in the 'quality press' of the UK.[4] As for the 1989 Portuguese translation (*Naçao y consiência nacional*), it was published not in Lisbon, but in São Paulo, by Ática. This institution has an unusually interesting history. According to its current website, it had its origins in 1956, when the Curso de Madureza [Adult Education] Santa Inês was established at the initiative of a group of progressive intellectuals and scholars, among them Anderson Fernandes Dias, Vasco Fernandes Dias Filho and Antonio Narvaes Filho. This was a time of great optimism and creativity in Brazilian political and cultural life – the era of bossa nova, the Cinema Novo, and the first Bienniale in Brasilia. By 1962, massive increases in enrolments at the Curso and the wide intellectual influence of its professors led to the creation of the Sociedade Editora do Santa Inês. Two years later, close to the time of the military coup against President Goulart, it was decided, at the initiative of Anderson Fernandes Dias, to create a professionally managed, critical publishing house, named after Attica, the cradle of ancient Greek civilization. In 1965, Ática published its first books, and somehow managed to survive two decades of repressive military dictatorship. In 1999, it was bought jointly by the twin-souled Brazilian conglomerate Editora Abril and the French conglomerate Vivendi; five years later, after a lengthy struggle, Abril – original importer of Disney comics, now publisher of Brazil's versions of *Time* and *Playboy* – became the majority shareholder. But Ática still seems to have a certain autonomy.

In the summer of 1989 I was invited by Ivo Banac of Yale University to serve as a 'comparativist' commentator for a conference in Dubrovnik on the subject of nationalism in the Balkans and Eastern Europe. There I

---

4. In 1998, Campusverlag issued a new edition, which replaced the Hermanns-denkmal with a lurid print of a popular riot: houses in flames, panicked people, incendiaries. In 2005, the publisher decided to reissue the book in its 'Classics' series, with a suitably severe, featureless cover. This edition has a lengthy Nachwort by Thomas Mergel, part of which is devoted to reflections on the reception of *IC*, and includes some alarming material on its afterlife in cyberspace.

met, and had animated discussions with, Silva Meznaric, who subsequently was primarily responsible for the Serbo-Croat translation of 1990 (*Nacija: Zamišljena zajednica*), for which she wrote a special introduction. Educated at the Law School of Zagreb University, and at the University of Chicago, she obtained her doctorate in sociology in 1984 at the University of Ljubljana; she had also been a Woodrow Wilson Center fellow that same year, where she may have come across *IC* for the first time. She recently wrote to me that she then believed that a translation of the book would be helpful in fighting the rising tide of Croatian and Serbian jingoism and mythomania – and thus in keeping Yugoslavia together. Alas, this hope disappeared in the spring of the following year. The publisher Školska knjiga was then a large state-owned publisher of textbooks. After the collapse of Yugoslavia, it was privatized and quite recently, *horribile dictu*, it bought the largest Serbian textbook publisher.[5]

Although the enlarged edition of *IC* was published in 1991, the following year the Korean publisher Naman put out a pirated translation (*Sang Sang Ui Kongdong Che*) based on the original 1983 text. Naman was established in 1979 by Cho Sangho, who, if not an activist himself, came from the 'dissident' province of Kwangju, which has produced many Leftist intellectuals. During the 1980s and early 1990s, Naman prospered as a publisher of the more 'popular' left-leaning social-science texts; thereafter, following market trends, it shifted to neoliberal and conservative books. *IC* seems to have survived the new tide, since the company issued in 2002 (i.e. ten years later) an unpirated version, based on the enlarged edition of 1991. (Characteristically, perhaps, the cover for this version is a colourful photograph of a mass of flag-waving young people, probably supporters of the astonishingly successful Korean football team in the World Cup competition held in June 2002). For many serious writers and publishers, Naman has a reputation for mass production and rapid output, sometimes-poor editing and clumsy translation jobs. It is also notorious for not paying many of its authors.[6]

---

5. Meznaric went on to found and manage, between 1992 and 1996, the Humanitarian Expert Group Project on Forced Migration; today she is on the faculty of the University of Ljubljana and serves as Senior Counselor to Zagreb's Institute for Migration and Ethnicity Research.

6. My thanks to Choi Sung-eun for the above information. Her father had the unlucky experience of having two of his books put out by Naman.

That the now-conservative Naman produced its new version can probably be explained by awareness of the commercial success of the Shiraishis' Japanese translation. By chance, during a brief visit to Seoul in 2005, I met the charming and modest Professor Yun Hyung-sook who was the translator. She apologized profusely for the quality of the pirated edition, saying she had had to work against brutal deadlines.

If the pattern of translations up to 1992 seems geographically random – Tokyo, Frankfurt, São Paulo, Zagreb, and Seoul – this is not at all the case for the rest of the decade. Of the fifteen translations involved, eleven were produced in Europe between 1995 and 1999. But first came Ciudad México (*Comunidades imaginadas*) and Istanbul (*Hayali Cemaatler*), in 1993.

The Fondo de Cultura Económica was established in 1934 by the economist and diplomat Daniel Cosío Villegas, initially to provide Spanish-language texts for the recently founded National School of Economics, but soon broadening out to cover history, culture, literature, and so on. State-run from the outset, it remained a part of the official cultural bureaucracy (in the 1990s it was headed by ex-president Miguel de la Madrid). After World War II, it expanded its 'empire' to Argentina (1945), Chile (1954), Mother Spain (1963), and later to Brazil, Colombia, the US (San Diego), Guatemala, Peru, and Venezuela. Its production was also vast in the 1990s: 2,300 new titles and 5,000 reprints. It seems likely that the stimulus for this translation came from among the large number of Mexican scholars and intellectuals who studied or taught at American universities, in which *IC* was by this time widely used as a sort of textbook in departments of history, anthropology, sociology, and comparative literature. In 1986, I was invited to a huge conference on Mexican nationalism in Zamora, and was startled that the only other obviously foreign attendee was David Brading, the magisterial historian of Mexico and Peru, and, later, Spanish America in general. Although very embarrassed to be the only participant who could speak no Spanish, I was taken under the kindly wing of Enrique Krauze, the young, virtually bilingual, right-hand man of Octavio Paz, who had long been the dominant intellectual influence at the Fondo.

Nothing could be more different than Istanbul's Metis Yayinlari. What would become Metis was originally set up in 1983 by Müge

Gürsoy Sökmen, Verso's 'agent' in Turkey, together with a few Leftist friends. In order to avoid the risk of having the whole staff arrested, Metis was registered legally under the name of a single individual, who would serve any prison time meted out by the regime. From this uncertain start, the company became very successful in the more open 1990s, publishing Turkish and translated fiction (from Tolkien to Perec), philosophy (Adorno, Benjamin, Lukács), political and feminist theory (Badiou, Arrighi, MacKinnon), current affairs (Oliver Roy), and most recently texts on the anti-globalization and anti-Iraq war movements. The success of Metis seems to have derived from three independent factors; the country's young, increasingly well-educated population, many of them supporters of Ankara's drive for EC membership; the company's long-standing friendly relations with the Islamicists; and the cultural policies of the major banks, who judge the performance of publishers whom they support by the reviews their books receive rather than by their profit margins, and are content if the cost of running the companies is less than what advertising would demand.[7] Perhaps it is worth adding that during the later 1990s I would occasionally run into students from the ex-Soviet Turkic-speaking republics, who reported that they read *IC* first in Metis's translation.

Then Europe proper. Sweden (1993); The Netherlands (1995); Norway, France and Italy (1996); Greece and Poland (1997); Bulgaria, Slovenia, Macedonia and Serbia (1998). The Swedish translation (*Den förestcällda gemen-skapen*) was published in Göteborg by Daidalos. Founded in 1982, Daidalos is a rather small, but well-respected, independent left publisher, emerging originally from the student movement; it is a serious house, which also publishes dissertations (with state funding). It has a strong philosophical profile – from the classics to Arendt, Gadamer, Habermas, Heidegger, Rawls, and Taylor. On history and social analysis it has published Marx, Bauman, Bourdieu, Castells, and Giddens.[8]

The Dutch translation (*Verbeelde gemeenschappen*) is interesting for two quite different reasons. Until 1995, the covers of the translations were generally plain, not to say nondescript. (Only the Japanese translation

---

7. My thanks to Tony Wood for this history of Metis.
8. My thanks to Göran Therborn for this description.

used the colonial-era Indonesian trick-photograph that I imposed upon
Verso.) The solitary exception was Campusverlag's Hermannsdenkmal,
which was surely intended ironically. But from then on the trend was to
create 'nationalist' covers – the later Dutch cover, for example, being a
fine reproduction of a woodcut showing the interior of an early Dutch
printery. The second curiosity is the way the translation came into
being. At some point in the 1970s I began a regular correspondence
with Soerjono, a tough, witty, and eccentric old Indonesian Communist then resident in Moscow. He had been active during his country's
Revolution (1945–49), and after independence was achieved, worked
for the Party's newspaper, *Harian Rakjat* [People's Daily]. Perhaps
because of his strong individualism, perhaps on account of some sexual
peccadillo, he was gradually sidelined. But he was lucky enough to be
on a visit to China when the 'attempted coup' of October 1, 1965
occurred, after which the Party was destroyed, with hundreds of
thousands of its members either massacred or imprisoned for many
years without trial. Disliking what he saw of Mao's Cultural Revolution, and annoyed by the factional infighting among the Indonesian
communist exiles, he found a way to move to Moscow, where for years
he was employed as a translator. Eventually he fell foul of a clique of
exiles sponsored and managed by the KGB, had a massive stroke from
which he never fully recovered, and spent a long time in gloomy
veterans' hospitals outside Moscow. Eventually, he was rescued by a
small group of Dutch Leftists with connections in the Soviet capital, and
brought to Amsterdam. He lodged in an old people's home near the city
limits, where I visited him on a number of occasions. I met the
independent publisher Jan Mets, also a regular visitor, because of
our common friendship with the invalid, who toughed it out with
an unbroken spirit till he died. The decision to translate *IC* was not,
however, a sentimental gesture. Mets was quite aware of the book's
relative commercial success in London. The Dutch translation was my
first experience of direct involvement in the translation process. Because
I read Dutch pretty well, I had insisted that I inspect the translation
before it went to press. Grudgingly the publisher agreed, while warning
me that the translator's English was far better than my Dutch. On the
first page, I found that in the sentence 'But, having traced the nationalist
explosions that destroyed the vast polyglot and polyethnic realms which

were ruled from Vienna, London, Constantinople, Paris, and Madrid, I could not see that the train was laid at least far as Moscow' – 'train' (i.e. 'fuse') was unintelligibly translated as 'railway-line.' Some, if not all, of my corrections were eventually, unenthusiastically, accepted.

The Norwegian translation (*Forestilte fellesskap*) may have come out of my friendship with Professor Harald Bøckman, a distinguished Sinologist specializing on the CPR's minorities along the border with Southeast Asia, who spent a couple of years as a visiting fellow at Cornell University. He is a man with a great sense of humour, and an admirably calm, unsentimental attitude towards the Maoist regime and its successors. In any event, the book was published by Spartacus Vorlag, a small (20–30 titles a year) company founded in 1989, with which Bøckman had good personal relations. The cover design showed the new trend: a pretty and colourful representation of Norway's national holiday parade featuring cute small children in national costumes. When I asked Bøckman why a Norse edition was needed – in a country with a small population, most of whom would have no trouble reading the Swedish translation – he laughed and said: 'You know how we feel about the Swedes and Swedish. We'd rather read the English original than the Swedish version. But best of all would be one in our own national language.'

As for the Italian translation (*Comunità immaginate*), it is probable that it emerged from a chance meeting with Marco d'Eramo in Chicago, where I had been invited to give a series of lectures. A distinguished Roman intellectual and journalist with *Il Manifesto*, Italy's quality radical-left newspaper (the last in Europe?), he was on leave at the University of Chicago to write a history of the city, which Verso published in 2002. We became good friends in a very short time. Hence the Italian *IC* was published in Rome by Manifestolibri, founded by the Feltrinelli-associated newspaper in 1991. The company puts out only about 40 titles a year, but its emphasis on quality and support for talented young writers has ensured that its books are widely used for university teaching. The cheerful cover looks as if it was taken from a late Fellini film. It could be taken as 'nationalist,' but I prefer to think of it as ironical in the spirit of the Hermannsdenkmal cover.

The French translation (*L'imaginaire national*) was put out by La Découverte, directed by François Gèze, a medium-sized 'independent Left' publisher (80–100 titles annually) with a serious interest in translations. La Découverte came out of the famous Éditions François Maspero, established in 1959. When Maspero handed the reins over to Gèze in 1983, he asked that the enterprise's name be changed as well. In 1996, just as the French *IC* appeared, the company merged with Éditions Syros, founded in 1974 and an active player in the struggle for the political and social renovation of the French Left. The cover for the book is a severe picture of a fragment of a Parisian neo-classical building, looking very much as if it has just been cleaned by Malraux. Irony? Probably, but delicate French irony. For the first and only time, I was involved directly, and wholly pleasurably, with the translation as it proceeded. Pierre-Emmanuel Dauzat, one of France's best translators, not only produced a text that in many places is an improvement over the original English, but checked all the French references, and brought several errors to my attention. Thanks to him, I made an interesting discovery. When I expressed my reservations about the title, *L'imaginaire nationale*, he replied that the French language has no equivalent to the English 'community,' with its overtones of social warmth and solidarity. 'Communauté' (as in Communauté Européenne) has an unavoidably cold, bureaucratic feel to it. (Marco d'Eramo later laughingly wrote to me that the Italian 'comunità' commonly means a drug-addicts' halfway house.)

Translations into Polish (*Wspólotny wyobrażone*) and Greek appeared in 1997. The Polish version was published in Kraków (not Warsaw) by the Spoleczny Instytut Wydawniczy Znak. About this Institute I have learned little beyond the fact that it is a well-regarded publisher both of scholarly studies and of fiction.

The Greek version (*Phantasiakés Koinótites*) is, however, another matter. The publishing house Nepheli was set up a few years after the fall of the Papadopoulos-Ioannides military regime, i.e. after 1974, by the late Yannis Douvitsas, an intellectual of the liberal Left. A small but distinguished publisher, it has specialized mainly in fiction and carefully done translations of works in the humanities and social sciences. Besides books, it also publishes three journals, *Poiesis* (Poetry), *Cogito* (Philosophy) and *Historein* (*History, A Review of the Past and Other Stories!* – printed in English). The guiding spirit of *Historein* has been Professor Antonis Liakos of the University of Athens, who was trained in Salonika, then in Rome (where he did research on Italian reunification) and finally in Birmingham circa 1989, where he joined the

Historical Materialism Group. By this time, the study of nationalism was on the Group's agenda because of the successes of Thatcherism. Nepheli also published Carlo Ginzburg, Natalie Zemon Davis, and others. The main target of these books has been students and young scholars in the humanities and social sciences. But *Historein*, as its sardonic subtitle suggests, had a clear political objective as well, to 'trouble the well-established ideology of the 3,000 years of the Greek nation.'[9]

According to the translator, Pothiti Hantzaroula,[10] the idea of translating *IC* came at the time of the nationalist marches in the early 1990s, which claimed the name of Macedonia for Greece. The publication was meant to establish a dissenting voice and an alternative way of thinking about the way in which the nation was made. While the book catered to the general public, it was mainly aimed at students in universities where the history curriculum was still strongly influenced by nineteenth-century romanticism.[11]

It is instructive that what *Historein* had in its sights was not the traditional Greek Right, but the main parties of the Left, which from at least the early 1990s increasingly advertised themselves as defenders of the '3,000-year old' Greek nation, and even of Orthodoxy. Professor Liakos notes that in the specific case of *IC*, *Historein* was accused of promoting, publishing, and teaching a book full of inaccurate information on Greek history, and of idealist tendencies, not giving enough room to the economic transformations that have produced the modern nation.[12]

One might say that with this Greek translation one 'era' closed and a new one opened. In the mid-1990s George Soros brought together a panel of scholars and librarians, and asked them to draw up a list of the 100 most significant (fairly recent) books in the humanities and social sciences.[13] (Fortunately or unfortunately, *IC* was among the final

---

9. My thanks to Antonis Liakos for this background.

10. Liakos described her to me as a 'fine scholar, having written a not yet published book, in English, on The Making of Subordination, Domestic Servants in Greece, 1900–1950.'

11. My thanks to Pothiti Hantzaroula for this account.

12. Paraphrased from a letter recently received from Liakos.

13. I have only a partial list of these titles. What is interesting is that books by Americans are not at all dominant. German authors are the most numerous, followed by French and Americans, then a handful of UK-ers, and here and there an Italian, a Slovenian, a Belgian, and so on.

selections.) His plan was to offer partial subsidization of translations of these works to publishers in the former Communist states of Eastern Europe, and the republics that came into existence with the collapse of the Soviet Union. Out of this massively funded transnational effort came the *IC* translations into Slovenian (*Zamišljene skupnosti*), Macedonian (*Zamisleni zayednisti*), Serbian (*Natsia: zamislenja zayednitsa*), and Bulgarian (*Vobrazenije obshchnosti*) in 1998, Romanian (*Comunități imaginate*), Russian (*Voobrazhayemie soobshchestva*), and Ukrainian (*Uyavleni spilnoti*) in 2001, and Lithuanian (*Isivaizduojamos bendruomenés*) in 2002.

The stretch of this endeavour is such that it warrants a break with the strictly chronological ordering so far employed.

As luck would have it, the translations project officer for Soros' Open Society Institute has been Yana Genova, who herself translated *IC* into Bulgarian, Recently, she was kind enough to relate to me that:

The OSI's Translation Project . . . started around 1994 with the aim to make available in the local languages of Eastern Europe at least the minimum of basic texts in the social sciences needed to renew higher education and to sustain informed public discussion of social and political issues. The first grant competitions were held in 1995 in Romania and Bulgaria, quickly followed by other countries in the years that followed. OSI has spent approximately $5,000,000 for nearly 2,000 editions. The list of recommended titles . . . was intended as a point of reference to publishers, but they could also offer other titles in the humanities . . . Grants covered from 30 per cent to 80 per cent of the total publishing costs depending on the country. The impact of the project has varied from country to country as the number of titles published varies a lot and it was not very well managed everywhere. But I can say with full confidence that the project has had an enormous effect on the way that the humanities and social sciences have been, and are now being taught in the region. For example, translations supported by the project form 40 per cent of all titles on the reading lists of eleven disciplines in major universities in Bulgaria and the Ukraine . . . All the publishers [of your book] were established in the early 1990s as small (2–10 employees), independent companies. They publish academic books and survive mostly on grants by private donors such as Soros, foreign government agencies such as the French Cultural Institute and – more recently – EU cultural programs.

On most of these editions I have obtained little information beyond what Yana Genova has generously furnished. The Slovenian publisher was Studia Humanitatis, the Macedonian Kultura, the Serbian Biblioteka Episteme Plato, the Bulgarian Kritika i Humanizm, the Romanian Integral, the Russian Kanon-Press, the Ukrainian Kritika, and the Lithuanian Baltos Lankos. About these publishers I have only a little information. Kritika i Humanizm was established in Sofia in 1991 as an independent company, which has become the only Bulgarian publisher specializing in the humanities and social sciences. Its main target is the publication of many translations (primarily of French authors, it would seem) in order to support a 'pluralist climate in these sciences.' Since the Serbian version is clearly an extension, in Cyrillic script, of the 1990 Serbo-Croat translation published in Zagreb, there may be some financial or other connection between the two publishers. The Russian translation has a curious history. A very bad, and probably pirated, version was actually issued by Kanon in 1998, as part of a series called Conditio Humana set up by the Centre for Fundamental Sociology in Moscow, which also published texts by Montesquieu, Burke, Marx, Weber, Bergson, and Schmitt. It was then completely and professionally retranslated, and legally published in 2001 by Kanon 'with the support of the Open Society Institute within the framework of the "Pushkin Library" megaproject.' It is worth adding that the covers of all these 'Soros' translations are plain and simple, without any concessions to commercial marketing or blatant nationalist imagery.

At the same time, in Western Europe, the early twenty-first century produced some interesting variations. In 2001, a Danish translation (*Forestillede fællesskaber*) appeared at the hand of the Roskilde Universitetsforlag, with an engagingly enigmatic, 'post-modern' cover. This was the first translation of *IC* published by a university press. When I asked the translator, the energetic young professor Lars Jensen, why a Danish version was needed, given the existence of both Norwegian and Swedish versions, he replied more or less as Harald Bøckman had done earlier. In effect, 'Yes, we can read these translations, but we should have our national own.' In 2003, Miroslav Hroch included Czech translations of *IC*'s first two chapters in his textbook compendium *Pohledy na narod a nacionalismus* [Views of Nation and Nationalism], published in Prague by the 'sociological' house of Plon. In 2005, a Catalan version appeared (*Comunitats imaginades*), published by Editorial Afers in collaboration with the University of Valencia. The same year, in Lisbon, Edições 70 published an excellent translation, sixteen years after the first, not very good, Portuguese version produced in São Paulo. But Brazil's mindless tariff policy on 'foreign' books makes this new edition available to Brazilians only at an enormously inflated price. Most recently, in 2007, Joel Kuortti's Finnish translation, *Kuvitellut Yhteisöt*, was issued by the independent intellectual publishing house Vastapaino.

It remains only to discuss briefly the story of seven translations published east of Europe after 1998. In 1999, editions appeared in Taipei, Tel Aviv and Cairo. The translator of the Taipei version (*Hsiang-hsiang ti kung-tung ti*) was Wu Rwei-ren, a young hero of the struggle against the Kuomintang dictatorship, a strong, but open-minded Taiwanese nationalist, and the author of a brilliant, iconoclastic University of Chicago dissertation on the complex origins and development of Taiwanese nationalism. The translator followed in the footsteps of the Shiraishis in transforming the original 'UK polemic' into something relevant for young Taiwanese today, by adding numerous explanatory footnotes and a lengthy academic introduction. The publisher, China Times, is the largest commercial publisher in Taiwan, but alas, as we shall see, without a shred of Rwei-ren's integrity and political commitment.

The Hebrew translation (*Qehiliot madumaynot*) came out under the auspices of the Open University of Israel, and was intended as a critical intervention against prevailing Zionist-Likudist orthodoxy. It included an introduction by Azmi Bishara, the foremost Palestinian Israeli politician, and a scholar of Marx and Hegel who completed his PhD at the University of Jena when the DDR state still existed. Curiously enough, the cover design looks like a scene in snowy Vermont at Christmas time. The Arabic version (*Al Jama'at Al Khayaliah*), however, had a completely different origin and intent. In 1995, perhaps in response to UN reports that the 'Arab World' produced far fewer translations of foreign language works than any other major region on the planet, the Majlis al-'Ala lil-Thaqafah (Supreme Council of Culture), an adjunct of Egypt's Ministry of Education, launched a massive Translation Project under the direction of Dr Gaber Asfour. Over the following decade the Project published no less than one thousand translations (usually in runs of 1,000 copies), including works by, or on, Neruda, Rousseau, Trotsky, Pessoa, Kafka, Eliot, Hegel, Sartre, Woolf, Foucault, Cavafy, Chomsky, and Freud. Most of the early titles were pirated, including *IC* (No. 81). The books are sold at low, subsidized prices, and are distributed almost entirely in Egypt. The Project has been successful enough that it is likely soon to become a permanent subsection of the Supreme Council of Culture.

After the fall of the interminable Suharto regime in Indonesia (May 1998), censorship was largely abolished. Dozens of good and bad publishing houses mushroomed into existence, many devoted to the republication of books long banned or deliberately allowed to go out of print. Soon after I was allowed back into Indonesia for the first time in twenty-seven years, I discovered that a pirated translation of *IC* had been rushed out by Pustaka Pelajar, a notoriously unscrupulous publisher in Jogjakarta preying on the curiosity, and ignorance, of students in this university city. I was able to force the withdrawal of the book, not for monetary reasons, but because of the truly terrible quality of the translation. With the help of various former students of mine, and a subsidy from the Ford Foundation office in Jakarta, a substantially new edition (*Komunitas-Komunitas Terbayang*) was finally published in 2001. Taking a cue from Wu Rwei-ren, I added many supplementary footnotes in colloquial Indonesian to help students understand the book's many allusions and references that English readers took entirely in their stride. The publisher this time was INSIST, a progressive NGO specializing on freedom of information – today, alas, moribund on account of internal factional conflicts.

It is indicative that when I offered to do the same thing for the cheap English-language edition put out in the Philippines in 2003 by Anvil, Manila's best popular imprint, the offer was indignantly rejected. Of course, the Filipino students, schooled in English, would get all the references!

Finally two very idiosyncratic versions, one published in Shanghai in 2003, and the other due out in Bangkok in late 2006. The publisher in the CPR was The Shanghai People's Publishing House, a huge state-owned conglomerate. It turned out that this edition of *IC* was the result of a secret deal with Taipei's China Times, which not only colluded with what was essentially negative piracy, but also permitted its Shanghai confederate to censor Wu Rwei-ren's text as it saw fit. One notable result was the deletion of the entirety of Chapter 9, which included some ironical remarks about the Great Helmsman and the Party's recent investment in a Machiavellian 'official nationalism.' 'You should take it as a compliment,' said a Chinese friend with a mischievous smile, 'they almost never delete whole chapters of a book they intend to publish. Look at Hillary Clinton's book, for example – the deletions are only sentences here and there!' Rwei-ren's introduction too was deleted without his knowledge or consent, even though it was a careful and scholarly account of my personal background, the political and intellectual context in which *IC* was written, its main features compared with the books of Gellner and Smith, and the criticisms of Sinologist Prasenjit Duara and of Partha Chatterjee. Perhaps its conclusion, an invocation of Taiwan as 'the beautiful but vulgar, passionate but anti-intellectual' island whose future remains so uncertain, doomed it with Peking's censors.[14]

The Thai version now close to completion in manuscript form has been prepared by a team of progressive, critical professors, several among them former students of mine. Going over the draft chapters I was very surprised by one thing. The aura of the Thai monarchy is such that I expected the translators to use the special 'feudal' vocabulary required when describing any activity by Thai kings present and past. What I did not expect was that the same special vocabulary was applied to all foreign monarchs as well, including such unlovely figures as London's William the Conqueror, Paris's François I, Vienna's Franz II, Berlin's Wilhelm II, and so on. When I objected that the entire spirit of *IC* is republican, and almost all monarchs are handled with irony or hostility, the objection was quickly brushed aside. 'You don't understand our traditions and our situation.' With a mixture of laughter and apprehension I look forward to what may be taken as *IC*'s first 'royalist' translation!

On the basis of this rather fragmentary evidence, what kinds of preliminary conclusions seem warranted?

---

14. My thanks to Wang Chao-hua for this account of the introduction.

Geographical distribution. With the exception of the OSI's coordinated translation programmes for Eastern Europe and the former Soviet Union, launched in the second half of the 1990s, there is little evidence for a graded time-hierarchy originating in 'The West,' and ending, later on, in the *ci-devant* Third World. In the first decade after *IC*'s original publication, one finds two Western European versions (German and Swedish), one Eastern European (Yugoslav), two Latin American (Brazilian and Mexican), two Asian (Japanese and Korean), and one Near Eastern (Turkish). The big surge in European language translations only began in the second half of the 1990s. So far as I can tell, all the translations have been based on the original English, not on previous translations in the languages of regional or colonial hegemons, showing English's extraordinary global ascendancy.

At the same time, there are conspicuous absences, if one thinks of languages with large numbers of speakers and, to a varying, lesser extent, readers. The most obvious example is the 'Subcontinent,' which contains millions of people reading in Urdu, Hindi, Bengali, Tamil, and so on. The reason for this lacuna must be the British colonial heritage, which, perhaps surprisingly, helped make English even today the dominant language of 'national level' education and intellectual discourse. The second is Africa (if one cares to locate Egypt in the Near East). No translations exist into, say, Swahili, Amharic, Wolof, or Hausa. One might try to explain this by adducing the status of the former colonial languages (French, English, and Portuguese) as languages of state and higher education in much of Africa. But this dominance requires its own explanation in the troubled economic, social, and political conditions of the continent after the achievement of national independences. The absence of a Vietnamese edition may be a temporary matter, as the rapidly developing country emerges from the relative intellectual isolation imposed by three decades of terrible warfare. The strangest case is Mother Spain, which has yet to emulate Portugal's decision to catch up with its gigantic American colony after waiting fifteen years. On the other hand, Spain is the one country where a translation into a 'sub-national' language (Catalan) has occurred.

Publishers and readers. The incomplete data available to me reveal some very striking patterns. In the first place, only one publishing house

(Mexico's Fondo) has a history beginning before World War II, and the vast majority were founded during the past three decades or, perhaps better put, in the aftermath of the world-turbulent 'long 1960s.' In the second place, a clear majority of these publishing houses have been small to medium in size, and to various degrees independent in character. This independence has to be seen from three angles. Only in the cases of Mexico, Yugoslavia, Egypt, and the CPR (all authoritarian one-party states at the time of *IC*'s local publication) have the publishers been state institutions. On the other hand, only in the case of Taiwan does one see a very large private commercial publisher involved, and there are no cases of intervention by giant transnational conglomerates. Perhaps more surprisingly, given the nature of *IC*'s readership (on which more below), is the relative absence of university presses: those that are visible are only the Open University of Israel, Roskilde University, the University of Valencia, and perhaps Kraków's Znak. In the third place, the political orientations of the publishers, where identifiable, stretch primarily from liberal (in the political sense) to varying types of independent Left. One could say that, given Verso's political stance and my own political sympathies, this pattern is not surprising.

In its original form, as indicated earlier, *IC* was aimed at a general, well-educated public, primarily in the UK, and secondarily in the United States. It was not written out of, or on behalf of, my own academic discipline ('political science,' shall one say) or any other. I also tried hard to make sure it was free of academic jargon. The last thing that would then have occurred to me was that it would become a university-level textbook. But, on the whole, this has been its fate, in English and in translation. Yet this destiny should not be understood in too Anglo-Saxon a manner. In many parts of the world, students and their teachers have a much more significant political and social role than do their counterparts in the UK and the US, and it is characteristically oppositionist to some degree. But this role is of quite recent (early twentieth-century) origin – one reason why 'students' loom up only sporadically in *IC* itself.

In attempting to grasp why *IC* ended up being so widely, and fairly rapidly, translated in 'textbook' form, the likeliest answers are as follows.

In the first place, its polemical thrusts turned out to have an unexpectedly wide appeal. In the 1980s it was the only comparative study of nationalism's history intended to combat Eurocentrism, and making use of non-European language sources. It was also the only one with a marked prejudice in favour of 'small countries' (in terms of geography, population, or world-political influence). In many parts of the world, faculty members and students, if they have political commitments at all, are Left, or liberal-left in their sympathies and are open to *IC*'s agenda. That the book, though written in English, was also partly aimed at British and American imperialism, may also have been a factor. In the second place, however, by proposing the concept of 'imagined community' *IC* juxtaposed paradoxically a kind of *gemeinschaft* attractive to all nationalists with something unsettling, neither 'imaginary' as in 'unicorn,' nor matter-of-factly 'real' as in 'TV set,' but rather something analogous to Madame Bovary and Queequeg, whose existence stemmed only from the moment Flaubert and Melville imagined them for us. This formulation opened the door wide for critical assessment of the kind of 'age-old' nationalism propagated in most contemporary states through the means of mass communications and state-controlled educational institutions. In the same paradoxical manner, *IC* was both visibly sympathetic to many forms of nationalism and yet deliberately interested less in the particular nationalist mythologies dear to nationalists' hearts, than in the general morphology of nationalist consciousness. Finally, the book attempted to combine a kind of historical materialism with what later on came to be called discourse analysis; Marxist modernism married to post-modernism *avant la lettre*. I think that this helps to explain the nationalist iconography on the covers of various translations of *IC* after 1995, which can usually be read as either naive or ironical (Norway versus Italy?).

A further paedagogical advantage in *IC* for teachers eager to develop students' civic consciousness in a progressive, critical manner, was simply the unusual style of the comparisons it drew: the US juxtaposed to Venezuela rather than Britain, Japan played off not against Confucian-Asian neighbours such as China, but to Tsarist Russia and Imperial Ukania, Indonesia rubbing noses with Switzerland rather than with Malaysia. Such comparisons were useful for teachers concerned to break down naive national exceptionalism, as well as mendacious 'cultural-regional' clichés such as the notorious 'Asian Values.'

Stimuli. In a substantial number of cases, the original stimulus for translation is not easy to trace. What is clear is that Verso made no special effort to encourage translations, and that those done by former students of mine (Japanese, Indonesian, and Thai) were done on their initiative, not mine.

This pattern seems, in a small way, to be an endorsement of *IC*'s metaphorical use of 'piracy,' emphasizing local initiative, rather than external coercion or slavish imitation, to describe the processes of nationalism's rapid diffusion in different forms around the planet. But in cases where a clear stimulus can be detected, the Open Society Institute's broad campaign to transform the political cultures of Eastern Europe and the states of the former Soviet Union in a liberal and pluralist direction, is easily the most conspicuous. Teachers and students who spent time in the United States or the United Kingdom, where *IC* had been normalized as a textbook from the early 1990s, surely played a role. Yet the most instructive cases are those where translators and publishers had motives beyond the immediately paedagogic. The Serbo-Croat version of 1990 came from the hope of Silva Meznaric and her associates that it might help the struggle to save 'Yugoslavia' from bloody self-destruction. Wu Rwei-ren's version was meant to bolster the nerve of Taiwanese nationalism by explaining comparatively its late emergence, and by undermining Peking's claim to the island on the basis, not only of Chinese nationalism, but also 'ancestral tradition' inherited from Manchu dynasts. The Greek translation, as we have seen, was part of an endeavour to check mindless local chauvinism over 'Macedonia,' and to criticize the parties of the Left for craven or unscrupulous adoption of essentially right-wing nationalist positions. Similarly, The Open University of Israel's Hebrew translation, with an introduction by a well-known Palestinian Israeli, was part of an attempt to resist the long slide towards apartheid in the Likud-ruled state. Doubtless the Catalan version was also intended to help Catalonia achieve the maximum autonomy possible in what was once nicely called Las Españas.

Transformation. Proverbially, a writer loses his/her book at the moment that it is published and enters the public sphere. But to feel the full melancholy force of the adage, there is nothing like facing a translation of a book into a language the author does not understand. He, or she, can have little idea of what has happened to it: misunderstandings, distortions, word-by-word literalisms, additions, deletions, or: creative adaptations, seductive rereadings, changed emphases, and more beautiful prose than in the original. Hence, initially, I was miffed that neither the German nor the Mexican translator communicated with me at all, and that the Dutch translation was sent to me only at the last minute. I believed that the book was still 'mine,' and forgot the sardonic maxim *traduttori traditori*: translation is necessarily a useful treason. I learned a lesson in the course of a long and warm correspondence with Pierre-Emmanuel Dauzat. Despite the fact that England and France are very close neighbours, the difficulties of rendering French into English and vice versa are notorious. The French version contained elegancies of which I had not dreamed with reorderings which allowed me to see what I 'really' meant, but could not properly express. The correspondence was an education in itself, symbolized by the discovery that the Latinism of 'community' thinly concealed a filiation with the Germanic *gemeinschaft*, and that *imaginé* cannot convey the sombre possibilities of 'imagined.' The final lesson came with the pilfered initial translation into Indonesian, the one language other than English in which I am completely at home. Quickly finding that there were many passages of which I could make neither head nor tail, I put in two or three months of intensive work 'correcting' it line by line. The outcome was a version that is, I think, much easier for Indonesian students to understand conceptually; but it remains rather lifeless, because I was insufficiently treacherous towards the original. English's elaborate and nuanced conjugational system for verbs, and its typical insistence on the active, 'imperial' voice, are foreign to elegant Indonesian, which prefers the passive voice, and is gifted with the untranslatable *ter-* verb-prefix, by which the agent versus object axis disappears in a connotational cloud whose silver lining is Chance. Fine Indonesian prose is still infused with an orality long vanished from formal English – which is why Anglicized Indonesian academic writing is, if possible, even more ugly than its UK or US counterparts. Hence, initially the pleasure of adding new explanatory footnotes in a quotidian idiom that engages, rather than annoying, befuddling, or terrorizing readers. Still, at the end I realized that I was impersonating an Indonesian, fighting off major 'piracy' with small-scale self-piracy, to no great avail. 'I shouldn't be doing this,' I said to myself, 'it's just political ventriloquism, and a non-commercial defence of the ludicrous American insistence on "intellectual" (!) property rights.' This is why, while inspecting the 'royalist' Thai translation of *IC*, I have decided to be a translational traitor. *IC* is not my book any more.

Bibliography

Alers, Henri J. *Om een rode of groene Merdeka. Tien jaren biennenlandse politiek. Indonesië, 1943–53.* Eindhoven: Vulkaan. 1956.

Ambler, John Steward. *The French Army in Politics, 1945–1962.* Columbus: Ohio State University Press. 1966.

Anderson, Benedict R. O'Gorman. *Language and Power: Exploring Political Cultures in Indonesia.* Ithaca: Cornell University Press. 1990.

————— 'Studies of the Thai State: The State of Thai Studies.' In Eliezer B. Ayal, ed. *The State of Thai Studies: Analyses of Knowledge, Approaches, and Prospects in Anthropology, Art History, Economics, History and Political Science.* Athens, Ohio: Ohio University, Center for International Studies, Southeast Asia Program. 1979. pp. 193–247.

Auerbach, Erich. *Mimesis. The Representation of Reality in Western Literature.* Trans. Willard Trask. Garden City, N.Y.: Doubleday Anchor. 1957.

Baltazar [Balagtas], Francisco, *Florante at Laura.* Manila: Florentino. 1973. Based on the original Ramirez and Giraudier imprint of 1861.

Barnett, Anthony. 'Inter-Communist Conflicts and Vietnam.' *Bulletin of Concerned Asian Scholars,* 11:4 (October–December 1979). pp. 2–9. (Reprinted from *Marxism Today,* August 1979).

Barthes, Roland. *Michelet par lui-même.* Bourges: Editions du Seuil. 1954.

Battye, Noel A. 'The Military, Government and Society in Siam, 1868–1910. Politics and Military Reform in the Reign of King Chulalongkorn.' PhD. thesis. Cornell University. 1974.

Bauer, Otto. *Die Nationalitätenfrage und die Sozialdemocratie* (1907), in his *Werkausgabe.* Vienna: Europaverlag. 1975. Vol. I, pp. 49–602.

Benda, Harry J. *The Crescent and the Rising Sun: Indonesian Islam under the Japanese Occupation.* The Hague and Bandung: van Hoeve. 1958.

Benda, Harry J., and John A. Larkin, eds. *The World of Southeast Asia: Selected Historical Readings.* New York: Harper and Row. 1967.

Benjamin, Walter. *Illuminations.* London: Fontana. 1973.

Bloch, Marc. *Feudal Society.* Trans. I.A. Manyon. Chicago: University of Chicago Press. 1961. 2 vols.

————— *Les Rois Thaumaturges.* Strasbourg: Librairie Istra. 1924.

Boxer, Charles R. *The Portuguese Seaborne Empire, 1415–1825.* New York: Knopf. 1969.

Braudel, Fernand. *La Méditerranée et le Monde Méditerranéen à l'Époque de Philippe II.* Paris: Armand Colin. 1966.

Browne, Thomas. *Hydriotaphia, Urne-Buriall, or A Discourse of the Sepulchrall Urnes lately found in Norfolk.* London: Noel Douglas Replicas. 1927.

Cambodge. Ministère du Plan et Institut National de la Statistique et des Recherches Économiques. *Résultats Finals du Recensement Général de la Population, 1962.* Phnom Penh. 1966.

Chambert-Loir, Henri. 'Mas Marco Kartodikromo (*c.* 1890–1932) ou L'Éducation Politique.' In Pierre-Bernard Lafont and Denys Lombard, eds. *Littératures contemporaines de l'asie du sud-est.* Paris: L'Asiathèque. 1974. pp. 203–214.

Cooper, James Fenimore. *The Pathfinder.* New York: Signet Classics. 1961.

Craig, Albert M. *Chōshū in the Meiji Restoration.* Cambridge, Mass.: Harvard University Press. 1967.

Craig, Gordon A. *The Politics of the Prussian Army, 1640–1945.* New York and Oxford: Oxford University Press. 1956.

Debray, Régis. 'Marxism and the National Question.' *New Left Review,* 105 (September–October 1977). pp. 25–41.

Defoe, Daniel. *Selected Poetry and Prose of Daniel Defoe,* ed. Michael F. Shugrue. New York: Holt, Rinehart and Winston. 1968.

Djilas, Milovan. *Tito, the Inside Story.* Trans. Vasilije Kojač and Richard Hayes. London: Weidenfeld and Nicolson. 1980.

Eisenstein, Elizabeth L. 'Some Conjectures about the Impact of Printing on Western Society and Thought: A Preliminary Report.' *Journal of Modern History,* 40:1 (March 1968). pp. 1–56.

Fall, Bernard B. *Hell is a Very Small Place. The Siege of Dien Bien Phu.* New York: Vintage. 1968.

Febvre, Lucien, and Henri-Jean Martin. *The Coming of the Book. The Impact of Printing, 1450–1800.* London: New Left Books. 1976. [Translation of *L'Apparition du Livre.* Paris: Albin Michel. 1958]

Fiedler, Leslie. *Love and Death in the American Novel.* New York: Stein and Day. 1966.

Fields, Rona M. *The Portuguese Revolution and the Armed Forces Movement.* New York, Washington and London: Praeger. 1975.

Franco, Jean. *An Introduction to Spanish-American Literature.* Cambridge: Cambridge University Press. 1969.

Gellner, Ernest. *Thought and Change.* London: Weidenfeld and Nicolson. 1964.

Gilmore, Robert L. *Caudillism and Militarism in Venezuela, 1810–1919.* Athens, Ohio: Ohio University Press. 1964.

Greene, Stephen. 'Thai Government and Administration in the Reign of Rama VI (1910–1925).' Ph.D. thesis. University of London. 1971.

Groslier, Bernard Philippe. *Indochina.* Cleveland and New York: The World Publishing Company. 1966.

Heder, Stephen P. 'The Kampuchean-Vietnamese Conflict.' In David W.P. Elliott, ed. *The Third Indochina Conflict.* Boulder: Westview Press. 1981. pp. 21–67. (Reprinted from Institute of Southeast Asian Studies, ed. *Southeast Asian Affairs.* [London: Heinemann Educational Books. 1979]).

Higham, Charles. *The Archaeology of Mainland Southeast Asia.* New York and Cambridge: Cambridge University Press. 1989.

Hirschman, Charles. 'The Making of Race in Colonial Malaya: Political Economy and Racial Ideology.' *Sociological Forum,* 1 : 2 (Spring 1986). pp. 330–62.

————— 'The Meaning and Measurement of Ethnicity in Malaysia: An Analysis of Census Classifications.' *Journal of Asian Studies,* 46 : 3 (August 1987). pp. 555–82.

Hobsbawm, Eric. 'Some Reflections on "The Break-up of Britain." ' *New Left Review,* 105 (September–October 1977). pp. 3–24.

————— *The Age of Revolution, 1789–1848.* New York: Mentor. 1964.

Hodgson, Marshall G. *The Venture of Islam.* Chicago: Chicago University Press. 1974. 3 vols.

Hoffman, John. 'A Foreign Investment: Indies Malay to 1901.' *Indonesia,* 27 (April 1979). pp. 65–92.

Hughes, Christopher. *Switzerland.* New York: Praeger. 1975.

Ieu Koeus. *Pheasa Khmer. La Langue Cambodgienne (Un Essai d'étude raisonné).* Phnom Penh: n.p. 1964.

Ignotus, Paul. *Hungary.* New York and Washington, D.C.: Praeger. 1972.

Ileto, Reynaldo Clemeña. *Pasyon and Revolution: Popular Movements in the Philippines, 1840–1910.* Manila: Ateneo Press. 1979.

Jászi, Oscar. *The Dissolution of the Habsburg Monarchy.* Chicago: University of Chicago Press. 1929.

Joaquín, Nick. *A Question of Heroes.* Manila: Ayala Museum. 1977.

Kahin, George McTurnan. *Nationalism and Revolution in Indonesia.* Ithaca: Cornell University Press. 1952.

Katzenstein, Peter J. *Disjoined Partners. Austria and Germany since 1815.* Berkeley and Los Angeles: University of California Press. 1976.

Kedourie, Elie, ed. and intro. *Nationalism in Asia and Africa.* New York: Meridian. 1970.

Kelly, Gail Paradise. 'Franco-Vietnamese Schools, 1918 to 1938.' Ph.D. thesis. University of Wisconsin. 1975.

Kemiläinen, Aira. *Nationalism: Problems Concerning the Word, the Concept and Classification.* Jyväskylä: Kustantajat. 1964.

Kempers, A.J. Bernet. *Ancient Indonesian Art.* Amsterdam: van der Peet. 1959.

Kirk-Greene, Anthony H.M. *Crisis and Conflict in Nigeria: A Documentary Source Book.* London: Oxford University Press. 1971.

Kohn, Hans. *The Age of Nationalism.* New York: Harper. 1962.

Krom, N.J. *Inleiding tot de Hindoe-Javaansche Kunst.* Second revised edition. The Hague: Nijhoff. 1923.

Kumar, Ann. 'Diponegoro (1778?–1855).' *Indonesia*, 13 (April 1972). pp. 69–118.

Landes, David S. *Revolution in Time: Clocks and the Making of the Modern World*. Cambridge, Mass.: Harvard University Press. 1983.

Leemans, C. *Boro-Boudour*. Leiden: Brill. 1874.

Luckham, Robin. *The Nigerian Military: A Sociological Analysis of Authority and Revolt, 1960–67*. Cambridge: Cambridge University Press. 1971.

Lumbera, Bienvenido L. *Tagalog Poetry 1570–1898. Tradition and Influences in its Development*. Quezon City: Ateneo de Manila Press. 1986.

Lyautey, Louis-Hubert-Gonzalve. *Lettres du Tonkin et de Madagascar (1894–1899)*. Paris: Librairie Armand Colin. 1946.

Lynch, John. *The Spanish-American Revolutions, 1808–1826*. New York: Norton. 1973.

Mabry, Bevars D. *The Development of Labor Institutions in Thailand*. Ithaca: Cornell University, Southeast Asia Program, Data Paper No. 112. 1979.

MacArthur, Douglas. *A Soldier Speaks. Public Papers and Speeches of General of the Army Douglas MacArthur*. New York: Praeger. 1965.

McLuhan, Marshall. *The Gutenberg Galaxy: The Making of Typographic Man*. Toronto: University of Toronto Press. 1962.

Maki, John M. *Japanese Militarism, Its Cause and Cure*. New York: Knopf. 1945.

Marr, David G. *Vietnamese Tradition on Trial, 1920–1945*. Berkeley and Los Angeles: University of California Press. 1981.

Maruyama Masao. *Thought and Behaviour in Modern Japanese Politics*. London and Oxford: Oxford University Press. 1963.

Marx, Karl, and Friedrich Engels. *The Communist Manifesto*. In *Selected Works*. Moscow: Foreign Languages Publishing House. 1958. vol. I.

Masur, Gerhard. *Simón Bolívar*. Albuquerque: University of New Mexico Press. 1948.

Melville, Herman. *Moby Dick*. London and Toronto: Cassell. 1930.

Michelet, Jules. 'Histoire du XIXe Siècle.' In *Oeuvres Complètes*, ed. Paul Viallaneix. Paris: Flammarion. 1982. Vol. XXI.

Montesquieu, Henri de. *Persian Letters*. Trans. C.J. Betts. Harmondsworth: Penguin. 1973.

Moore, Jr., Barrington. *Social Origins of Dictatorship and Democracy. Lord and Peasant in the Making of the Modern World*. Boston: Beacon Press. 1966.

Morgan, Edward S. 'The Heart of Jefferson.' *New York Review of Books*. August 17, 1978.

Morgenthau, Ruth Schachter. *Political Parties in French-Speaking West Africa*. Oxford: Clarendon Press. 1964.

Moumouni, Abdou. *L'Éducation en Afrique*. Paris: Maspéro. 1964.

Muir, Richard. *Modern Political Geography*. New York: Macmillan. 1975.

Musil, Robert. *The Man Without Qualities*. Trans. Eithne Wilkins and Ernst Kaiser. New York: Howard-McCann. 1953. vol. I.

Nairn, Tom. *The Break-up of Britain*. London: New Left Books. 1977.

———— 'The Modern Janus.' *New Left Review*, 94 (November–December 1975). pp. 3–29. Reprinted as Chapter 9 in *The Break-up of Britain*.

'Nijs, E. Breton de'. *Tempo Doeloe*. Amsterdam: Querido. 1973.

Norman, E. Herbert. *Soldier and Peasant in Japan. The Origins of Conscription*. New York: Institute of Pacific Relations. 1943.

Orwell, George. *The Orwell Reader*. New York: Harcourt-Brace-Jovanovich. 1956.

Osborne, Robin. *Indonesia's Secret War, The Guerrilla Struggle in Irian Jaya*. Sydney: Allen and Unwin. 1985.

Pal, Bipin Chandra. *Memories of My Life and Times*. Calcutta: Bipin Chandra Pal Institute. 1973.

'3349' [pseudonym for Phetsarath Ratanavongsa]. *Iron Man of Laos: Prince Phetsarath Ratanavongsa*. Trans. John B. Murdoch. Ed. David K. Wyatt. Ithaca: Cornell University, Southeast Asia Program Data Paper No. 110. 1978.

Polo, Marco. *The Travels of Marco Polo*. Trans. and ed. William Marsden. London and New York: Everyman's Library. 1946.

Pramoedya Ananta Toer. *Bumi Manusia*. Jakarta: Hasta Mitra. 1980.

———— *Rumah Kaca*. Jakarta: Hasta Mitra. 1988.

———— *Tjerita dari Blora*. Jakarta: Balai Pustaka. 1952.

Reid, Anthony J.S. *The Indonesian National Revolution, 1945–50*. Hawthorn, Victoria: Longman. 1974.

Renan, Ernest. 'Qu'est-ce qu'une nation?' In *Oeuvres Complètes*. Paris: Calmann-Lévy. 1947–61. vol. I. pp. 887–906.

Rizal, José. *Noli Me Tangere*. Manila: Instituto Nacional de Historia. 1978.

————— *The Lost Eden. Noli Me Tangere*. Trans. León Ma. Guerrero. Bloomington: Indiana University Press. 1961.

Roff, William R. *The Origins of Malay Nationalism*. New Haven and London: Yale University Press. 1967.

Said, Edward. *Orientalism*. New York: Pantheon, 1978.

Scherer, Savitri. 'Harmony and Dissonance. Early Nationalist Thought in Java.' M.A. thesis. Cornell University. 1975.

Schwartz, Stuart B. 'The Formation of a Colonial Identity in Brazil.' In Nicholas Canny and Anthony Pagden, eds. *Colonial Identity in the Atlantic World, 1500–1800*. Princeton: Princeton University Press, 1987. pp. 15–50.

Scott, William Henry. *Cracks in the Parchment Curtain*. Manila: New Day. 1982.

Seton-Watson, Hugh. *Nations and States. An Enquiry into the Origins of Nations and the Politics of Nationalism*. Boulder, Colo.: Westview Press. 1977.

Shiraishi, Takashi. *An Age in Motion: Popular Radicalism in Java, 1912–1926*. Ithaca: Cornell University Press. 1990.

Sitorus, Lintong Mulia. *Sedjarah Pergerakan Kebangsaan Indonesia*. Jakarta: Pustaka Rakjat. 1951.

Skinner, G. William. *Chinese Society in Thailand*. Ithaca: Cornell University Press. 1957.

Smith, Donald Eugene. *India as a Secular State*. Princeton: Princeton University Press. 1963.

Spear, Percival. *India, Pakistan and the West*, London, New York and Toronto: Oxford University Press. 1949.

Steinberg, S.H. *Five Hundred Years of Printing*. Rev. ed. Harmondsworth: Penguin, 1966.

Storry, Richard. *The Double Patriots. A Study of Japanese Nationalism*. London: Chatto and Windus. 1957.

Strong, Charles Frederick. *Modern Political Constitutions*. 8th Rev. ed. London: Sedgwick and Jackson. 1972.

Summers, Laura. 'In Matters of War and Socialism, Anthony Barnett would Shame and Honour Kampuchea Too Much.' *Bulletin of Concerned Asian Scholars*, 11: 4 (October–December 1979). pp. 10–18.

Taylor, Robert H. *The State in Burma*. London: C. Hurst & Co. 1987.

Tickell, Paul. *Three Early Indonesian Short Stories by Mas Marco Kartodikromo (c. 1890–1932)*. Melbourne: Monash University, Centre of Southeast Asian Studies, Working Paper No. 23. 1981.

Timpanaro, Sebastiano. *On Materialism*. London: New Left Books. 1975.

————— *The Freudian Slip*. London: New Left Books. 1976.

Thongchai Winichakul. 'Siam Mapped: A History of the Geo-Body of Siam.' Ph.D. thesis. University of Sydney. 1988.

Toye, Hugh. *Laos: Buffer State or Battleground*. London: Oxford University Press. 1968.

Turner, Victor. *Dramas, Fields and Metaphors. Symbolic Action in Human Society*. Ithaca: Cornell University Press. 1974.

————— *The Forest of Symbols. Aspects of Ndembu Ritual*. Ithaca: Cornell University Press. 1967.

Vagts, Alfred. *A History of Militarism, Civilian and Military*. Rev. ed. New York: The Free Press. 1959.

Vandenbosch, Amry. *The Dutch East Indies: Its Government, Problems, and Politics*. Berkeley and Los Angeles: University of California Press. 1944.

Vella, Walter F. *Chaiyo! King Vajiravudh and the Development of Thai Nationalism*. Honolulu: University of Hawaii Press. 1978.

Veyra, Jaime de. *El 'Último Adiós' de Rizal: estudio crítico-expositivo*. Manila: Bureau of Printing. 1946.

White, Hayden. *Metahistory: The Historical Imagination in Nineteenth-Century Europe*. Baltimore: The Johns Hopkins University Press. 1973.

Wickberg, Edgar. *The Chinese in Philippine Life, 1850–1898*. New Haven: Yale University Press. 1965.

Williams, Raymond. 'Timpanaro's Materialist Challenge.' *New Left Review*, 109 (May–June 1978). pp. 3–17.

Wills, Gary. *Inventing America: Jefferson's Declaration of Independence*. New York: Doubleday. 1978.

Wolfe, Charles. *The Poems of Charles Wolfe*. London: Bullen. 1903.

Wolters, O.W. *The Fall of Srivijaya in Malay History*. Ithaca: Cornell University Press. 1970.

Woodside, Alexander B. *Vietnam and the Chinese Model. A Comparative Study of Vietnamese and Chinese Government in the First Half of the Nineteenth Century*. Cambridge, Mass.: Harvard University Press. 1971.

Yabes, Leopoldo Y. 'The Modern Literature of the Philippines.' In Pierre-Bernard Lafont and Denys Lombard, eds. *Littératures contemporaines de l'asie du sud-est*. Paris: L'Asiathèque. 1974. pp. 287–302.

Zasloff, Joseph J. *The Pathet Lao: Leadership and Organization*. Lexington, Mass.: Lexington Books. 1973.

Index

INDEX

Bessenyei, György, 73
Bethlehem, 194
Biafra, 120
Binondo, 27–8
Bloch, Marc, 18, 23, 42, 89
Blois, 130
Blora, 147
Blücher, Gebhard Leberecht von, 95
Boadicea, 12
Bogotá, 62, 69, 147
Bohemia, 20, 33, 73, 79, 196
Bolívar, Simón, 49, 53, 57, 81, 189
Bolivia, 53
Bonaparte *see* Napoléon; Louis Napoléon
Bonifacio, Andrés, 143
Bordeaux, 123, 131
Borneo, 165, 182, 190
Borobudur, 179, 183–5
Boston, 64
Botha, Pieter, 150
Bourbon *see* Carlos III; Louis XIV; Louis XV;
  Louis XVI
Boven Digul, 31
Boxer, Charles R., 60
Brakespear, Nicholas (Adrian IV), 15
Braudel, Fernand, 205–6
Brazil, xiii, 14, 46–7, 51, 60, 134, 191
Bregenz, 20
Breuilly, John, xii
Brezhnev, Leonid Ilyich, 150
Brizen (Brienz), 20
Browne, Thomas, 147
Broz, Josip (Tito), 160
Budapest, 73
Buddha (Gautama), 194
Buenos Aires, 52, 62–3
Bukovina, 20
Bulgaria, 79
Bumppo, Natty, 202
Burckhardt, Jakob, 197
Burma, 93, 99, 119, 151, 172, 179–81, 185

Cairo, 170
Calais, 123
Calcutta, 179
California, 64
Calvin, John, 40
Cambodia (Cambodge, Kampuchea), 1, 125,
  128–31, 155, 157–61, 169, 183
Canada, 64, 93
Canberra, 94
Cape Coast, 124
Capetown, 93
Caracas, 49, 62, 147, 171
Carinthia, 20
Carlos III (Bourbon), 51
Carniola, 20
Cartagena, 52, 57
Carter, James Earl, 18
Cattaro (Kotor), 20

Celebes, 16
Cephas, Kasihan, 179
Ceylon, 189 *see also* Sri Lanka
Chambas, Mohamed, 124
Champollion, Jean François, 70
Charles I (Stuart), 21
Charles V (Habsburg), 147
Charles IX (Valois), 200
Chatterjee, Partha, xii
Cheng-ho, 189
Chiang Kai-shek, 160
Chiangmai, 187
Ch'in Shi Huang-ti, 160
Chile, 51, 57
China, 1–2, 41–2, 44, 69–70, 96, 100, 125–6,
  155–6, 158–61, 168
Chingachgook, 202
Chōshū, 94–5
Chou En-lai, 156, 172
Chulalongkorn (Rama V), 21, 99–100, 172
Cirebon, 167
Clausewitz, Karl von, 22, 87, 152
Cochin China, 125–6, 128–9, 131
Coimbra, 51
Colombia, 53
Colombo, 114
Columbus, Christopher, 193
Congo, Belgian, 110
Congo, French, 152
Conrad, Joseph, 55, 176
Constant, Benjamin, 136
Constantinople (Istanbul), xi, 75, 79
Cooper, James Fenimore, 202–3
Corneille, Pierre, 40
Cortés, Hernán, 199
Coruña, 146
Cotonou, 130
Cracow, 20
Croatia, 20
Cromwell, Oliver, 166
Cuba, 156
Curzon, George Nathaniel, 179
Czechoslovakia, 1

Dakar, 123–4, 130
Dalmatia, 20
Damrong Rajanuphab, 172, 174
Darwin, Charles Robert, 10
De Castries, Christian Marie Ferdinand de la
  Croix, 152
De Lattre de Tassigny, Jean, 152
De Staël-Holstein, Anne, 136
Debray, Régis, 10, 118, 149
Defoe, Daniel, 25
Denmark, 21
Descartes, René, 18
Deshima, 94
Dickens, Charles, 35
Diderot, Denis, 34
Diponegoro, 11